POTTERY &
PORCELAIN

THE OFFICIAL®
IDENTIFICATION
AND PRICE GUIDE TO
POTTERY &
PORCELAIN

Harvey Duke

SEVENTH EDITION

House of Collectibles • New York

Important Notice. All of the information, including valuations, in this book has been compiled from the most reliable sources, and every effort has been made to eliminate errors and questionable data. Nevertheless, the possibility of error, in a work of such immense scope, always exists. The publisher will not be held responsible for losses which may occur in the purchase, sale, or other transaction of items because of information contained herein. Readers who feel they have discovered errors are invited to *write* and inform us, so they may be corrected in subsequent editions. Those seeking further information on the topics covered in this book are advised to refer to the complete line of *Official Price Guides* published by the House of Collectibles.

Cover photo: Sebastian J. Lamicella and Jon Brothers provided the Fiesta pieces from their private collections.

Published by: The House of Collectibles
201 East 50th Street
New York, New York 10022

Distributed by Ballantine Books, a division of Random House, Inc., New York, and simultaneously in Canada by Random House of Canada Limited, Toronto.

Manufactured in the United States of America

ISBN: 0-876-37785-1

Seventh Edition: October 1989

10 9 8 7 6 5 4 3 2

To my "support group"
Gary, Gus, Jeff, Mickey and Gene, Mike, Norbert, and Pat

CONTENTS

CONSULTANTS

One of the pleasures of doing this book has been working with dealers, collectors, and writers whose enthusiasm and generosity of time and knowledge have been great. They form a community of people bound by the love of pottery.

If you have a question or information to relay, please write directly to the consultant. It will save time as I will only be forwarding your letter to them. Always include a legal-size self-addressed stamped envelope (abbreviated SASE). Please don't ask a lot of questions or "tell me everything you know about . . ." questions; their time is limited, and they do this as a courtesy.

You can write to me about Hall China and any of the potteries covered in this book that are not listed below. My address: c/o ELO Books, P.O. Box 627, Brooklyn, NY 11202.

As far as buying and selling goes, I have identified authors, consultants, and dealers by an (A), (C), or (D) after their name. Authors and consultants would be glad for the opportunity to buy any unusual pieces. But if you're looking to buy, or sell in quantity, contact the dealers.

Al Alberts (C)/*Kay Finch*
2645 California Street, #101, Mountain View, CA 94040

Phyllis Bess (A)/*Frankoma*
14535 East 13th Street, Tulsa, OK 74108

Elizabeth Boyce (D)/*Hall China*
38 Carlotia Drive, Jeffersonville, IN 47130

Jack Chipman (A/D)/*California Potteries*
P.O. Box 1429, Redondo Beach, CA 90278

Pat Dole (A)/*Purinton*
P.O. Box 4782, Birmingham, AL 35206

Lee Feenstra (D)/*Watt*
Box 419, Hull, IA 51239

Jeanne Fredericks (C)/*Florence*
12364 Downey Avenue, Downey, CA 90242

Gerry and Christie Geisler (D)/*Railroad China*
The Great Delaware & New England Antiques Trading Company
P.O. Box 1065, Chatham, NJ 07928

Gus Gustafson (D)/*Fiesta*
Butzville Center, P.O. Box 106, Butzville, NJ 07829

Burdell and Doris Hall (A)/*Morton/Cliftwood/Camark*
P.O. Box 1501, Fairfield Bay, AR 72088

Bob Hoover (C)/*Purinton*
Rd 4, Box 94, Blairsville, PA 15717

Richard Lewis (D)/*American Belleek*
23 Bank Street, Medford, NJ 08055

Marilee Meyer (D)/*Dedham*
Skinner, Inc, Bolton Gallery, Rte 117, Bolton, MA 01740

John Miller (D)/*Fiesta/Luray/Russel Wright*
Raccoon's Tail, 6 High Street, Mullica Hill, NJ 08062

Susan Moore (A)/*Southern Potteries*
3046 H Clairmont Road NE, Atlanta, GA 30329

Maxine Feek Nelson (A)/*Vernon Kilns*
873 Marigold Court, Carlsbad, CA 92008

Scott Nelson (A)/*Van Briggle*
P.O. Box 5327, Rockville, MD 20851

Ed Nenstiel (C)/*Luray*
4905 Bristow Drive, Annandale, VA 22003

David Newkirk (A)/*Redwing*
Rte 3, Box 146, Monticello, MN 55362

Sally Oge (C)/*Van Tellingen*
2344 104th Avenue, Otsego, MI 49078

Bob Perzel (D)/*Stangl*
Popkorn, P.O. Box 1057, Flemington, NJ 08822

Judy Posner (D)/*Cookie Jars*
Rd 1, Box 273, Effort, PA 18330

Robert Rush (C)/*Abingdon*
210 No. Main Street, Abingdon, IL 61410

Gunther Schmidt (C)/*Ceramic Art Studios*
1440 Boston Post Road, Larchmont, NY 10538

Glenn Seabolt (C)/*Watt*
130 Collingwood Drive, Bristol, TN 37620

Karen Silvermintz (D)/*Metlox*
1908 Antwerp Avenue, Plano, TX 75023

Mark Supnick (A)/*Little Red Riding Hood*/*Shawnee*
8524 NW 2nd Street, Coral Springs, FL 33071 305

Terry Telford (C)/*Franciscan*
192 Sixth Avenue, New York, NY 10013

Dave Walsh (C)/*Pfaltzgraff*
The Pfaltzgraff Co., 140 East Market, York, PA 17401

Elaine Westover (C)/*Abingdon*
Rte 1, Abingdon, IL 61410

Mike Zimpfer (D)/*Hull*
D & M Collectibles, 3714 Lexington Road,
Michigan City, IN 46360

PREFACE

American ceramic products run the gamut from doorknobs to sewer pipes, from bricks to insulators. And they're all collectible (well, I haven't met any sewer pipe collectors yet). But the most popular collectible is the pottery and porcelain that was made for table, kitchen, and decorative use.

It is my intention to cover these areas as effectively as possible, and to make this as much a reference book as a price guide by providing more in-depth coverage of the most popularly collected potteries than you will normally find in a price guide.

For example, with a number of the potteries, rather than give you prices across the board, we've told you what colors or decorations are more valuable and how to figure that value. We've categorized as to desirability almost a hundred Stangl plate decorations, and given you five price ranges for them. For the popular Vernon Kilns dinnerware, we've given you ways to figure the desirable decorations, in both the flatware and hollowware. We've done a plate chart for Dedham, and comparison lists for Van Briggle.

For some rare pieces, rather than leave them out and leave you wondering what happened to them, we've indicated that they are too rare to price or price is ND (Not Determined)—which should be exciting for those of you that own them. For hard-to-find pieces we've used a plus sign ($350+) which indicates that the piece is worth at least the sum indicated but that it's a seller's market and the sky's the limit. Finally, ranges have not been used in some instances because a consultant feels that levels have been established so that a single price tells the whole story.

I am already collecting information for my next edition which will include more potteries and more listings. If you are a collector or dealer, and would like to be involved, for either a pottery covered in this edition or one you think should be covered, please don't hesitate to write to me. I would be glad to hear from you.

Finally, the introductory material that follows will, I believe, provide answers to questions you have yet to ask.

ACKNOWLEDGMENTS

A book like this is not written in a vacuum. It is a collaboration, and there are many people who helped make it special.

My consultants (see list of names and addresses) worked very hard. I asked more of them than is usual in putting together a price guide and they were enthusiastic and generous.

My thanks to Bill Gates and the Ohio Historical Society for all their assistance and contributions; to Robert Fryman, curator of the Museum of Ceramics in East Liverpool, Ohio, my favorite pottery museum; and to the staff and resources of the New York Public Library.

At the potteries, my thanks to John Thompson, John Sayle, and Everson Hall of the Hall China Company, Ed Carson of the Homer Laughlin China Company, and Melinda Avery at the Metlox Potteries for all their kindnesses.

At Ballantine/House of Collectibles, special thanks to George Davidson, without whom this book wouldn't exist, and Dorothy Harris, who knows that being an editor is more than just books. Thanks to Kathy Morris as well, who has the courage of her convictions beyond her job description.

Special thanks also to Betty Carson (Betty's Collectibles, 11154 Mashoning, P.O. Box 187, No. Jackson, Ohio 44451), a dealer's dealer who is on the cutting edge of what is up-and-coming in pottery collecting, especially figurals, for helping get this book off the ground.

Thanks to Harry Heft and Wayne and Diane Weigand for their invaluable help with the Stangl Bird listing, Bill Stern and Stan Pawlowski for their work on the Vernon Kilns chapter, Renee and Derek Schultz for their cookie jars, and Irene Kendall for being so encouraging.

xv

Two people who were contributors as well as consultants should also be thanked: Dave Walsh, historian at Pfaltzgraff, and Jack Chipman, pre-eminent historian of California pottery. Both helped improve this book.

Special thanks to the Boyce women, Elizabeth and her daughter Susan, and Susan's husband Tom, for their resourcefulness, kindnesses, and encouragement, and Bob and Nancy Perzel, who were always there when I called on them for help.

Last and most important, I would like to thank some special friends: Pat Lyons, who saw me through the changes this book engendered and contributed in hidden ways, Mickey and Gene Meier, whom I've known almost since I began my pottery voyage, and Gus Gustafson, whom I can always depend upon for sage counsel and advice. Their love and presence have enhanced my collecting and my life in many ways, as well as this book. Thanks folks.

ART CREDITS

Jean A. Rettmer, 90-18 247th Street, Bellerose, NY 11426

PHOTO CREDITS

All of the photos in this book are by:

Vincent D'Alessio
Vincent D'Alessio Photography
230 West 55th Street
New York, NY 10019

Unless otherwise credited to:

Tony Oge
Oge Photography
2344 104th Avenue
Otsego, MI 49078

Larry Walton
Camera Mart
East Liverpool, OH 43920

David Pritchard
Grey Barn Photography
RD 1, Box 197
Belvidere, NJ 07823

PART I

INTRODUCTION

THE MARKETPLACE

The collector's market is an active, organic entity, with change being the rule. There are always potteries that are popular or up-and-coming, and there are those in which interest is stagnating. But they're not always the same potteries and a pottery can move from one category to another. A broad generalization, such as that interest in Weller has declined, ignores the fact that early Weller is still very desirable. Keeping in mind that this is being written in March of 1989, certain observations can be made.

AMERICAN BELLEEK

Ceramic Art Company/Lenox and Willets pieces are easier to find than Knowles, Taylor, Knowles and Ott & Brewer. The market is small but strong and prices are still slowly rising. The American Porcelain show at the Metropolitan Museum in New York in the spring of 1989 should focus new attention on this area.

ART POTTERY

Strong growth has been shown in this area as prices continue to rise. While new collectors continue to become attracted to the established favorites, the interesting movement here is the growing number of potteries that are not "household names" and yet have begun to attract collector attention over the past few years. Check the books on Art Pottery in the Bibliography to learn about these.

Specifically, Rookwood, Grueby, Roseville, and Dedham head the list of interest. There is still growth potential in Fulper, Cowan, Newcomb College, and Van Briggle. The Teco show at the Erie Art Museum in Erie, Pennsylvania, in July of 1989, could affect prices, and many collectors and dealers are holding on to George Ohr pieces in anticipation of the new book and the exhibit at the Metropolitan Museum in the fall of 1989.

DINNERWARE/KITCHENWARE

Prices have stabilized nationally for many of the popular potteries such as Hall, Homer Laughlin, Redwing, and Stangl. Blue Ridge prices have been fluctuating, with some rising and others falling. California dinnerware interest continues strong, but a good book could have a major impact.

NOVELTIES

Cookie jars are big news. While they have always been a popular collectible, they were given a boost by the presence of many cookie jars in the auction of the Andy Warhol estate. Prices jumped unreasonably high in some cases but settled back after a short while. More recently, *USA Today* ran an article about cookie jars in both the paper and on the TV show, and prices are rising again.

Florence prices have jumped higher than many dealers and collectors feel they are worth, but, as we have seen in the past with other potteries, that doesn't mean that prices will fall. California figurals are still sleepers in certain parts of the country.

* * * *

As always, supply and demand plays an important role. More and more people are collecting, and as supplies of the more traditionally collected pottery dry up, new companies will become popular.

BACKGROUND ON AMERICAN BELLEEK

by Richard Lewis

Consultant: American Belleek

Belleek china was undecorated, pale colored, highly translucent porcelain first developed in Ireland and later produced in America. It was commonly used by both amateur and professional china painters.

AMATEUR DECORATION

China painting was a popular pastime from 1880 to 1920, mostly for women. These "home china painters" decorated porcelain in their spare time for pleasure. They were individuals who had neither skill nor professional training. Usually the art work is sloppy, of poor quality, or well conceived but lacking technique. American and European porcelain companies sold a lot of undecorated white ware to this amateur china painting market. Amateur-decorated items are usually not collected for their artistic appeal, but as examples of this major use for American Belleek.

PROFESSIONAL DECORATION

There are two areas covered under professional decoration.

First, there are the home or studio decorators who either decorated porcelain for pleasure or as a means of earning extra money. Unlike other amateur decorators, these individuals customarily belonged to china painting clubs or were professionally trained. They had talent and developed skills which put their art work at the same level as that of professionals who earned a living by decorating porcelain. In fact, some of the more creative and artistic forms of decorated American Belleek come from this group who were decorating for their own creative outlet, and not for popular taste.

Second, there are the professional artists who earned their living by decorating porcelain. They either worked alone or for decorating studios such as Pickard, which purchased undecorated white ware from American and European porcelain companies. Sometimes department stores, gift shops, and jewelry stores employed their own decorators to create original designs.

FACTORY DECORATION

Every American Belleek company had its own staff of artists and produced its own line of decorated porcelain. These artists either painted standard factory patterns or created original works. Unfortunately, factory and professional decorators usually did not sign their work, making it difficult for collectors to determine whether or not a piece was decorated at the factory. Only knowledge of the artists and their style can give a clue.

The area of professional and factory decorating can sometimes cause additional confusion because some of the artists employed by one of the American Belleek factories also decorated china on their own time. This means that a collector may find a signature of an artist from one factory on another manufacturer's ware. For instance, there are several known examples of Willets Belleek decorated by Walter Marsh who worked for the Ceramic Art Company and Lenox. Marsh also ran his own decorating studio in Trenton, New Jersey.

BACKGROUND
ON ART POTTERY

Art pottery is ornamental ware that is either hand-decorated by an artist or glazed with a special controlled effect. There are some things about art pottery beginning collectors should keep in mind. Remember that these are generalizations; there is always an exception. When you know those, you are an advanced collector.

ARTIST

Certain artists, although the quality of their work can vary, are more desirable than others.

MANUFACTURER

Certain potteries are more desirable than others. Currently Rookwood and Grueby are among the most popular. But be aware that while Roseville is more popular than Weller, an early Weller piece has more value than a middle period Roseville. When evaluating one pottery against another, make sure you are speaking of comparable lines and periods.

SUBJECT MATTER

People, animals, and scenics are more desirable than florals. But, to give you an idea about exceptions, a beautiful, elaborate floral by a more desirable artist can bring a higher price than a poor scenic by a lesser artist.

SIZE

Larger pieces are more valuable than smaller pieces—the taller the vase the better. Pieces with fragile details that have survived intact—handles, delicate ewer lips—are more desirable. But size alone is not enough; it has to have good line. If it is clunky, that detracts from price.

CONDITION

Americans are used to having everything cleanly packaged—preferably in clear plastic and untouched by human hands. Therefore, damage will have a negative effect on price. But a small chip on the bottom of a vase that does not interfere with the beauty of the decoration is a world apart from the crack that runs through a decoration.

ESTHETICS

Finally, remember the old cliche, "Beauty is in the eye of the beholder." What is clunky to one person is well proportioned to another. What is a poor color scheme to one is a bold approach to color for another. Good luck.

BACKGROUND
ON DINNERWARE

Here are some useful things to know about industry practices that will help you understand what you are finding and avoid confusion.

SHAPES

Styles

There is often a strong similarity of style between potteries. In the late nineteenth century, every pottery had at least one plain round shape, one shape with an embossed rim, and an octagonal shape. The larger potteries, with stronger sales forces, could market more lines than their smaller competitors, but the shapes were still variations on these themes.

In the late twenties, many potteries began hiring designers to create original shapes, but they also kept an eye on their competitor's lines and often urged their designers to create something similar.

Composition of Dinnerware Sets

From the Victorian era to the early twentieth century, dinnerware lines had multiple pieces; one line might include ten different sized platters. It was not unusual to have 75 or more different items in one line.

In the thirties, the number of items in a set were drastically reduced, and certain pieces had multiple uses: the demitasse set, for example, could be used as a breakfast set or a children's set, and the pickle tray served as the underplate for the gravy.

A basic set consisted of a cup and saucer, dinner plate, luncheon plate, salad plate, bread and butter plate, fruit and cereal dish, soup bowl, round and oval vegetable bowls, covered casserole, gravy boat and underplate, teapot, sugar, and creamer.

Sets might also include: shakers, egg cups, square underplates for round casseroles, coffee pots (sometimes when a line has a coffee pot there is no teapot), gravy faststands, demitasse sets, batter sets, jugs, cream soups and saucers, large coffee cups, and saucers. The more popular and long lived a line, the more items were made for it.

Different practices at different potteries are interesting. For example, W. S. George seems to have only one shaker shape. It was plain enough to use with several different dinnerware shapes. Yet Homer Laughlin, which designed a shaker for most of their shapes, did not design one for Virginia Rose, one of their most popular shapes, until the fifties, 20 years after the line was first introduced. If you are collecting a Virginia Rose decal from the thirties, you need to know that the shaker was not brought out until the fifties. Otherwise, you'll search in vain for a shaker with your decal.

Pick-Up Pieces

Shape lines could be expanded in two ways. One was with interchangeable pieces, such as pie plates, cake plates, etc., that are not designed to go with one particular shape. Luray has a number of these pieces. Another way was to use pieces from other shapes even if there wasn't a particularly good match. Homer Laughlin's use of the plain rectangular Century butter with the embossed round Virginia Rose line is a good example of that. Either way, these are called pick-up pieces.

Measurements and Sizes

A word about 36s, which seems to confuse some collectors. This designation dates back to a time when china was packed in standard-size barrels with straw. A 36s bowl refers to a bowl of such a size that 36 of them will fit in a barrel. A 12s bowl means that 12 of them will fit in a barrel. Therefore, the higher the number, the smaller the piece. This designation was used primarily with bowls, pitchers, and other pieces of hollowware, and seems to have fallen out of general use by the mid-twentieth century.

Restyling

It was not unusual for a pottery to redesign an item, either because there were problems in manufacturing or to respond to changing public taste.

Reusing

It was easy and economical for a company to bring out a new shape using the flatware from a previous shape—plain flatware was definitely interchangeable. Although, in the case of Paden City's Shellcrest, they kept the hollowware from Elite and changed the flatware.

Shape Names

Different potteries sometimes used the same name for a shape or decoration. Cronin, French-Saxon, and Harker all had a Zephyr shape.

DECORATIONS

Decals

Decals were first used in the United States ca. 1890 but reached the peak of their popularity in the thirties. Most were printed by stone lithography, which was replaced by photolithography in the forties.

If you were to collect as many different examples of decal as you could find, you could have thousands in your collection and still have a long way to go. Tens of thousands were designed. The decal manufacturers employed designers, who would custom design a decal upon request, but many of their designs were done for the company to use as customers samples. Many of these were never put into production.

A number of potteries chose decals from these sample books. Often a pottery received exclusive rights to a decal, but sometimes they used a decal that was in the public domain. If they gave up exclusivity, it was not uncommon for other potteries to pick up that same decal afterward, which explains why you might find one pottery's shape with another's decal.

Certain subject matter was very common; every pottery had a Mexican or Southwestern decal, sometimes several Petitpoint decals, Cottage decals, and Bird decals, plus hundreds of floral decals, ranging from the realistic to the fantastic.

When you collect a particular decal, especially one of the less popular ones, you have no guarantee that every piece made in a particular shape will be found with that decal. If the shape was in production for many years, your decal might have been used early on and then retired before certain items were added to the shape. Or, the orders for your decal may never have included a cream soup, for example, or some other piece.

Finally, the most popular decals were given names by the potteries; most had only a number.

Underglaze vs. Overglaze

There is an easy way to differentiate between underglaze and overglaze. Run your finger over the surface of the ware, starting on an undecorated section and moving over a decorated section. If you feel a change in texture, it is overglaze; otherwise, it is underglaze.

Glazes

Some potteries had shapes which were decorated with both solid colors and with decals on an ivory body. Some lines, like Fiesta, had Ivory as one of its colors. Others did not. For those lines, a plain Ivory piece is probably an undecorated second.

Conversely, a piece in a shape that is usually decal-decorated might be found in a solid color. This is unusual, but makes for a happy find, certainly more desirable than an undecorated second.

Treatment

Treatment refers to the interplay between the various decorative elements. For example, the same decal might have different treatments— it might have a colored line or a gold stamping. One of the well-known examples of this is Homer Laughlin's Mexicana; it is usually found trimmed with a red line, but has also been found with blue, green or yellow lines. Be especially aware of this when buying or selling by mail.

Trade Show Samples

Prospective new decals were shown to buyers at two annual shows in January and July. The pieces that met with little interest were not put into production; there is no way to differentiate them from items that were produced.

Decorating Companies

There were (and still are) a number of companies that bought pottery from the factories and decorated it themselves. To plain, ivory-glazed pieces, they added decals. To decal-decorated pieces, they added elaborate gold rim and/or well decoration. Identify these pieces by (1) their sometimes garish over-decoration, and (2) the decorator's mark overprinting the manufacturer's mark, sometimes obliterating it. Some of these pieces will just have the decorating company's mark and some are unmarked.

Gypsy Ware

Gypsy ware comprises items made by pottery workers for their own use (also called "end-of-day pieces"), either at the factory or in back-yard kilns using odd pieces of pottery and decal. Some of this was sold along the roadside, hence the name. It was especially common during the Depression.

BACKGROUND ON MARKS

A mark could be stamped, impressed, incised, or a decal. Stamped marks (backstamps) were usually applied with a rubber stamp in ink, platinum, or gold. Impressed marks were either in the mold or a branding iron-type device was used. Incised marks were done by hand. Some marks, especially four-color ones, were decals.

A number of different elements can be part of a mark. Custom varied among manufacturers as to which elements were used, and often a pottery wasn't consistent even on its own wares. And since the stamping was done by hand, there is the human error factor. Here are the basic elements you will find.

Artist's Signature Most often found on art pottery; usually just initials, sometimes the name.

Body/Glaze Color The color of the glaze or body on dinnerware may be incorporated into the mark or the shape name. Look for words such as dawn, rose or blush to signify pink, creme or ivo- for ivory, and golden for yellow. Rarely, just the color name was marked.

Decorating Firm Name If you find a piece with more gold on it than good taste would dictate, it is likely from a decorating firm. Sometimes these appear stamped along with the manufacturer's name.

Gold Some pieces with gold decoration are so marked ("14-carat gold"). The amount of gold is negligible and the mark is more a sales device. What looks like silver decoration is really platinum; rarely will you find a piece marked as such.

Good Housekeeping Seal of Approval Yes, Virginia, there was such a thing, and it (or an equivalent institute's name) will be found on some pottery. With rare exception, it does not increase the value of a piece.

Graphic Element Some marks were designed by the shape designer, and could range from fancy type to a small drawing.

Hand Painted Hand painting runs the gamut from an elaborate painting to a few strokes to give expression to a face on a cookie jar. There was a vogue for hand painting starting in the late thirties, and these words in a mark could boost sales.

Made For . . . When a line was exclusive for a distributor or department store, their name was usually included in the mark.

Made in USA In 1898, Congress required all ware made for export to be so marked.

Manufacturer's Name Whether the full name or the initials, this is the element found most often. Surprisingly, it is not present in every mark. Sometimes a company marked only the shape name or the body color.

Numbers Can mean several things: (1) Impressed numbers usually reflect a pottery's system of shape numbering; (2) Stamped numbers could reflect a) the shape number, b) the month and date of manufacture or c) quality control information. Some dates are obvious, some are coded; (3) Some numbers which seem to have been written by hand in gold or ink reflect a glaze or decal.

Patent Pending/Patented Some shapes or processes (such as Cameoware) were patented.

Second Selection Ware that did not pass quality control was either (1) sent to a reclaim department, (2) given an inexpensive decal decoration, marked "Second Selection," and sold cheaply, (3) went to an outlet shop, or (4) was discarded.

Shape/Line Name Sometimes the shape name was just lettered below the manufacturer's name, sometimes a special stamp was designed.

Symbolism During the nineteenth century, many American potteries employed familiar British symbols, such as the lion and the unicorn, in combination with a coat of arms, shield, or heraldic escutcheon, to deceive consumers into believing their product was British. Only a few American firms were bold enough to challenge British domination of the market and employ straightforward names and American symbolism. The most famous of these was Homer Laughlin's stamp with the American eagle vanquishing the British lion.

Union Mark Found on some dinnerware. The Brotherhood of Operative Potters campaigned to have ware marked to indicate it was made in a union shop. Not all potteries complied.

HOW TO USE THIS BOOK

HOW THIS BOOK IS DIFFERENT

Most general price guides give you just that—prices, and not many. Thanks to our format, we can give you more. History, mark information, and, most important, many listings that are complete, not just a few pieces. We've included more photos and drawings for visual identification, and there's a comprehensive glossary, bibliography, traveler's directory, and club and newsletter listing to enhance your collecting.

PRICING

Mark Twain said, "I'd rather decline two beers than one German verb." I feel the same way about compiling a price list. A startling admission by the author of a price guide but it's the word "guide" that gives the clue.

There are a lot of factors in pricing that need reconciling. Geography is one of them. For example, there's more Stangl in the Northeast, and more knowledgeable collectors, therefore prices are higher than in the West. Conversely, prices for Bauer are higher in California than in the East. Public auctions can also affect prices, which are usually higher due to the nature of the competitive bidding. Also, some hungry collectors or dealers can artificially inflate prices in a small area.

Putting together a price guide to reflect all three factors is difficult. So, as we have said, this is a guide and not a bible. Our book intends to reflect prices, not set them, to reflect prices that are realistic, neither unnaturally high or low. It is always possible to find a dealer who has a low price on an item because he can't know everything, and to find auction prices well above market if a bidding war takes place. Because we don't believe these prices are realistic, they have not been factored into this book. For those lines that are established collectibles, with a national collectors base, our prices will be most accurate. For those lines that are still coming into their own, you will find prices that vary somewhat from these listings. Lines with a regional base will reflect prices in that region.

Prices are for mint condition. In general, discoloration, crazing, chipping, and repairs will fetch lower prices.

For covered pieces, the lid is usually worth 60% of the total price. And please check for marriages. Marriages are mismatched tops and bottoms. Sometimes, they're immediately apparent; other times, they're not. If you're buying via mail order, you can return it; if you buy a marriage at a flea market and find out when you get home, you're out of luck.

MEASUREMENT AND SIZES

You will find small variations in measurements between your pieces and the listings because there were variations in the pieces themselves. Pottery shrinks when fired. Shrinkage is not always uniform, although the potteries try to control it. Sometimes the body formula changes and that affects shrinkage. Also, when new production molds are made from the master mold, slight size changes can occur. Therefore, a 6″ plate can vary from an eighth to a quarter of an inch, and a 13″ platter can vary up to half an inch.

Where possible, I have given the pottery's own measurement. When I didn't have that information, the measurement comes from (1) my own collection, (2) someone else's collection, and (3) measurements taken at collector's shows and flea markets.

LISTINGS

There is some variation in terminology among potteries. What one calls a Batter Set, another calls a Waffle Set. Where I could, I have used consistent terminology, and I have also grouped similar items, so that looking up the same piece in different listings is easier. In some cases, a piece is so strongly identified with a particular name, I have left it rather than confuse anyone.

I have tried to standardize terminology in the following ways:

1. Egg cup always means double, unless listed as single.
2. Casseroles, drip jars, jugs (batter, syrup, and refrigerator), and sugars should be considered covered unless the word ''open'' is used.
3. Bookend, candleholder, and shaker prices are for a single, unless pair is indicated.
4. Small bowls are listed as dishes. I have not used ''baker'' and ''nappy'' although they are the correct industry terminology, as they might confuse; they indicate oval and round vegetable bowls.
5. In general, I have used ''jug'' for pitcher.
6. ''Leftover sets'' refers to the pieces, often round, that come in sets of three, with a lid for each piece, which can stack and nest. ''Refrigerator sets'' are leftovers that come in three- or four-piece sets, either round or square, that stack but cannot nest and have only one lid. A three-piece stack set means two containers and a lid, a four-piece stack set means three containers and a lid.

See the glossary for other definitions.

VERIFICATION

A lot of the information in this book is based on original research, taken primarily from trade journals and pottery catalogs. I am wary of sources such as department store ads, mail-order catalogs (Sears/ Montgomery Ward), and interviews with pottery workers. In the first two instances, the companies sometimes made up their own names. As to interviews, time dims memory and no one can be expected to remember everything. In several instances my information differs from what you may have read elsewhere, but I stand behind my research.

I have tried to use the pottery's names for shapes and decorations wherever possible. When I have had to make up my own, or used names made up by other authors or collectors, I have employed Hazel Marie Weatherman's device of putting them in quotation marks. Where a pottery has named a particular color, I have used capitals (Powder Blue), otherwise I have used lowercase letters (blue).

PART II

POTTERY AND PORCELAIN LISTINGS

ABINGDON POTTERIES, INC.

Abingdon, Illinois

In 1908, the Abingdon Sanitary Manufacturing Company began making bathroom fixtures. In 1934, they introduced a line of art pottery made in a vitreous body. This line was manufactured until 1950.

Marks

The shape number will usually be impressed in the bottom of a piece. The most commonly found stamp is "Abingdon, USA" in a rectangular box.

ART POTTERY

Over 1,000 shapes were made and, over the years, almost 150 colors were used, most of them high gloss. The most desirable colors are: Bronze Black/renamed Gunmetal Black (lustrous black with metallic sheen), Copper Brown (semi-matte, mottled metallic copper brown with iridescent sheen), Fire Red (brilliant glaze with crystalline sparkle), Riviera Blue (semi-gloss dark blue), Royal Red/renamed Dubonnet (semi-gloss purplish-red), and Sudan Red (matte reddish-tan).

Pricing

Use the upper end of the price range for the desirable colors listed above. /B indicates the item can be found in black; add 30%. /D indicates the item can be found decorated; add 15–20%.

Animals

Goose, 5″/B (571)	*$25–$30*
Goose, leaning, 5″ (98)	*$25–$30*
Goose, upright, 2½″ (99)	*$25–$30*
Gull, 5″/B (562)	*$40–$50*
Heron, 5½″/D (574)	*$25–$30*
Kangaroo, 7″/D (605)	*$50–$60*
Peacock, 8″ (416)	*$25–$30*
Pelican, 5″/D (572)	*$25–$30*
Penguin, 5½″/BD (573)	*$25–$30*
Pouter Pigeon, 4½″	*$25–$30*
Swan, 3¾″/D (661)	*$40–$50*
Swordfish, 4½″/D (657)	*$25–$30*

Bookends

There is a Colt bookend that is too rare to price.

Cactus, 6″ (370)	*$50–$75*
Cactus planter, 7″ (374)	*$50–$75*
Cossack/Russian, 6½″/B (321)	*$50–$75*
Dolphin, 5½″ (444)	*$15–$25*
Fern Leaf, 5½″ (428)	*$35–$50*
Horsehead, 7″/B (441)	*$35–$50*
Quill, 8¼″/B (595)	*$50–$75*
Scotty, 7½″/B (650)	*$50–$75*
Sea Gull, 6″ (305)	*$35–$50*

Cookie Jars

All cookie jars, except Baby, are decorated, which is reflected in the prices.

Baby, 11″ (561)	*$85–$100*
Choo Choo, 7½″ (651)	*$65–$75*
Clock, 9″ (653)	*$40–$50*

Daisy, 8″ (677)	*$25–$35*
Fat Boy, 8¼″ (495)	*$175–$225*
(Happy) Hippo, 8″/B (549)	
"Bar Jar"	*$150–$175*
Hand decorated	*$125–$150*
Solid colors	*$125–$150*
Hobby Horse, 10½″ (602)	*$150–$175*
Humpty-Dumpty, 10½″ (663)	*$100–$125*
Jack-in-the-Box, 11″ (611)	*$150–$175*
Little Bo Peep, 12″ (694)	*$195–$225*
Little Girl, 9½″ (693)	*$40–$50*
Little Miss Muffet, 11″ (662)	*$175–$225*
Little Ol' Lady, 7½″ (471)	
Hand decorated	*$75–$95*
Little Ol' Lady/Black Lady/Mammy	
Cold paint	*$125*
Solid color: black, blue, chartreuse, or pink	*$175–$225*
Underglaze decoration	*$250–$300*
Money Bag, 7″ (588)	*$25–$35*

Tepee cookie jar. *(Photo courtesy of Dave Pritchard)*

Mother Goose, 12″ (695)	$200+
Pineapple, 10½″ (664)	$65–$75
Pumpkin (Jack O'Lantern), 8″ (674)	$95–$125
Three Bears, 8¾″ (696)	$75–$95
Wigwam, 11″ (665)	$175–$225
Windmill, 10½″ (678)	$175–$225
Witch, 11½″ (692)	$250+

Figures

There are chess pieces (Bishop, Castle, King, Knight, Pawn, and Queen) that are too rare to price.

Blackamoor, 7½″/D (497)	$35–$45
Fruit Girl, 10″ (3904)	$75–$100
Kneeling Nude, 7″/B (3903)	$150–$175
Scarf Dancer, 13″ (3902)	$150–$175
Shepherdess & Faun, 11½″/B (3906)	$75–$100

Planters

Burro, 4½″ (673)	$25–$35
Donkey, 7½″ (669)	$25–$35
Dutch Shoe, 5″ long/D	$35–$50
Fawn, 5″ (672)	$25–$35
Gourd, 5½″ (667)	$25–$35
Pooch, 5½″ (670)	$25–$35
Puppy, 6¾″ long/D (652)	$25–$35
Ram, 4″ (671)	$25–$35

All prices given are for items in *mint* condition. In general, discoloration, crazing, chipping, and repairs will fetch lower prices.

String Holders

Chinese Face, 5½"/D (702)	*$100–$125*
Mouse, 8½"/D (712)	*$75–$100*

Vases

There is an Egret sand jar which is the floor vase with a dish fitted on top—same price as the floor vase. There is a small head vase that is too rare to price.

Cactus, 6½"/D (616)	*$15–$25*
Dutch Boy, 8" (469)	*$30–$40*
Dutch Girl, 8" (470)	*$30–$40*
Egret floor vase, 17½"/B (524)	*$90–$110*
Head, large (3801)	*$150–$175*
Medallion, 8" (464)	*$20–$30*
Reeded, 8" (472)	*$20–$30*
Sea Horse, 8"/D (596)	*$25–$30*
Trojan Head, 7½"/B (499)	*$50–$60*
Wheel Handle, 8" (466)	*$15–$25*

Wall Pockets

There is a small male mask and female mask that are too rare to price.

Acanthus bracket, 7" (589)	*$30–$45*
Acanthus bracket, 8¾" (649)	*$30–$45*
Acanthus wall vase, 8¾" (618)	*$30–$45*
Book, 6½"/D (676)	*$35–$50*
Butterfly, 8½"/D (601)	*$20–$30*
Calla, 9"/D (586)	*$20–$30*
Carriage Lamp, 10" (711)	*$35–$45*
Cherub, 7½" (587)	*$40–$50*
Daisy, 7¾" (379)	*$30–$35*
Dutch Boy planter, 10" (489)	*$70–$80*

Dutch Girl planter, 10″ (490)	*$70–$80*
Female mask, large, 7½″ (376F)	*$80–$85*
Ionic, 9″ (457)	*$35–$50*
Ivy basket, 7″/D (590)	*$60–$70*
Male mask, large, 7½″ (376M)	*$80–$85*
Match box, 5½″/D (675)	*$25–$35*
Morning Glory, 7½″ (377)	*$12–$18*
Morning Glory, double, 6½″ (375)	*$20–$28*
Shell, 7″ (508)	*$25–$35*
Trifern, 8″ wide (435)	*$50–$60*

AMERICAN BISQUE COMPANY
Williamstown, West Virginia

Founded in 1919, the American Bisque Company produced cookie jars, florist ware, and kitchenware in an earthenware body. Their figural cookie jars are their most collectible items. The firm closed in 1982.

Marks

Most cookie jars will be found either unmarked or with "USA" impressed.

Cookie Jars

After School	*$30–$40*
Amish Boy	*$75–$95*
Amish Girl	*$75–$95*
Animal Crackers	*$25–$35*
Apple	*$20–$25*
Baby Huey	*$300+*

ND = price is not determined; item too rare to price.
+ = worth at least sum indicated, but could be higher.

Ball of Yarn w/Kittens	*$45–$55*
Barrel	*$15–$25*
Beehive w/Cat	*$35–$45*
Bell, Liberty	*$35–$45*
Boots	*$45–$55*
Boy w/Blackboard	*$75–$85*
Boy w/Churn	*$95–$125*
Bum w/Blackboard	*$75–$85*
Candy Baby	*$35–$45*
Casper	*$300+*
Cat	*$45–$55*
Cheerleaders (Flasher/Corner)	*$75–$95*
Chef	*$45–$55*
Chick	*$50–$60*
Churn	*$15–$25*
Clock	*$30–$35*
Clown (Flasher)	*$45–$55*
Clown w/Blackboard	*$75–$85*
Clown, hands high	*$65–$75*
Clown, w/peaked hat	*$75–$85*
Coffee Pot, metal handle	*$25–$35*
Coffee Pot	*$25–$35*
Cow	*$35–$45*
Cow/Steer (4 in 1 turnabout)	*$95–$150*
Davy Crockett (Boy)	*$150–$175*
Davy Crockett (Man)	*$150–$175*
Dino (Flintstones)	*$250–$300*
Donkey w/White Wagon	*$45–$55*
Donkey w/Yellow Wagon	*$55–$65*
Drum Majorette	*$75–$85*
Dutch Boy (cold paint)	*$25–$35*
Dutch Boy (underglaze)	*$55–$65*
Dutch Girl (cold paint)	*$25–$35*
Dutch Girl (underglaze)	*$55–$65*
Elephant, w/Bib	*$55–$65*
Elephant w/Beanie	*$45–$55*

Cookie jars: Jack-in-the-Box, Spaceship, and Davy Crockett. *(Photo courtesy of Dave Pritchard.)*

Fred (Flintstones)	$250–$300
Girl w/Blackboard	$75–$85
Granny	$55–$65
Honey Bear (Flasher/Corner)	$65–$75
Horse, sitting	$125–$150
Hot Chocolate	$40–$50
Igloo	$45–$55
Indian Boy	$150–$175
Iron	$35–$45
Jack-in-the-Box	$45–$55
Lamb	$45–$55
Ludwig Von Drake	$250–$275
Merry-Go-Round	$45–$55
Olive Oyl	$300+
Owl	$35–$45
Peasant Girl	$75–$85
Pig (4 in 1 turnabout)	$95–$150
Pig, w/cold paint	$45–$55
Pig, Boy	$45–$55
Pig, Farmer	$45–$55

Pig, Lady	$45–$55
Pig, in Sack	$40–$50
Pig w/Patch	$45–$55
Popeye	$300+
Rabbit, farmer hat w/patch	$75–$85
Rabbit in Hat	$45–$55
Recipes	$25–$35
Ring for Cookies	$30–$35
Rooster	$35–$45
Rooster, crowing	$35–$45
Rubble House (Flintstones)	$250–$300
Saddle	$45–$55
Saddle w/Blackboard	$65–$75
Sandman (Flasher)	$55–$65
Snacks	$25–$35
Spaceship	$45–$55
Spaceship w/Spaceman	$75–$85
Stove	$15–$25
Sweet Pea	$300+
Teapot	$15–$25
Tortoise/Hare (Flasher)	$75–$95
Toy Soldier	$35–$45
Train	$65–$75
Train, elongated	$45–$55
Truck	$45–$50
Umbrella Kids	$95–$125
Wilma (Flintstones)	$250–$300
Yarn Doll	$45–$55
Yogi Bear	$195–$225

J. A. BAUER
POTTERY COMPANY
Los Angeles, California

J. A. Bauer, who had run a family pottery in Paducah, Kentucky, moved to California for his health, and established a new pottery in 1909. Red clay flower pots were the first major item produced but stoneware soon followed that included many utilitarian items made. Art pottery was added ca. 1915. The colored dinnerware was introduced in 1930, and art wares were added a little later in the decade. The firm closed in 1962.

There is some argument about who produced the first colored dinnerware, but there is no doubt about who popularized it—Bauer. In 1936, Homer Laughlin would introduce its own colored line, Fiesta, and dominate the market due to its superior sales force, but Bauer led the way. It made a number of colored dinnerware lines. Ring is the most popular among collectors. Oil jars create high interest also.

Marks

Most items have an impressed mark with either the name "Bauer" or with some combination of the words Bauer, Los Angeles, Pottery, and USA. Many items will be found unmarked or stamped "Made in USA."

La Linda (1939–1959)

Hard-to-find pieces are the plain ball jug, cookie jar, and oblong, plain (no band) butter dish.

Colors: Matte colors of green, blue, ivory, and dusty pink. Gloss colors of Burgundy, Chartreuse, Dark Brown, Gray, Green, Ivory, Light Brown, Olive Green, Pink, Turquoise, and Yellow.

Pricing

Burgundy and Dark Brown are at the high end of the range.

Ball jug	*$35–$45*
Butter dish, oblong plain	*$45–$60*

La Linda place setting: 9″ dinner, 7½″ salad, 6″ bread & butter; 6″ soup/cereal; cup & saucer; "old" salt and pepper; "old" creamer and sugar; 13″ chop plate. *(Photo courtesy of Jack Chipman)*

Chop plate, 13″	*$25–$30*
Cookie jar, plain	*$60–$75*
Creamer, old	*$7–$10*
Creamer, new	*$7–$10*
Cup	*$10–$15*
Custard	*$6–$8*
Dish, 5″	*$6–$8*
Dish, 6″	*$10–$15*
Gravy	*$15–$20*
Jumbo cup	*$25–$30*
Jumbo saucer	*$3–$4*
Plate, 6″	*$4–$6*
Plate, 7½″	*$7–$10*
Plate, 9″	*$10–$15*
Platter, oblong, 10″	*$12–$16*
Platter, oblong, 12″	*$15–$20*
Ramekin	*$6–$8*
Saucer	*$3–$4*
Shaker, short, old	*$4–$6*
Shaker, tall, new	*$4–$6*
Soup, 7″	*$15–$20*
Sugar, old	*$12–$16*
Sugar, new	*$12–$16*
Teapot, plain, 6 cup	*$30–$40*
Tumbler, 8 oz	*$12–$16*
Vegetable, oval, 8″	*$18–$24*
Vegetable, oval, 10″	*$25–$30*
Vegetable, rd, 9½″	*$25–$30*

Monterey (1936–1945)

Hard-to-find pieces in this line are the beverage server, cake plate, candlestick, midget set, sauce boat, 10½″ plate, and relish. Rare pieces are the console set and ashtray.

Colors: Burgundy, California Orange Red, Canary Yellow, Green, Ivory, Monterey Blue, Red Brown, Turquoise Blue, and White.

All prices given are for items in *mint* condition. In general, discoloration, crazing, chipping, and repairs will fetch lower prices.

Pricing

Burgundy and Orange Red are at the high end of the range. Add 25% for White if it is uncrazed.

Beverage server w/cover	*$60–$75*
Butter dish	*$40–$55*
Cake plate, pedestal	*$75–$100*
Candleholder	*$25–$30*
Chop plate, 13″	*$35–$45*
Coffee server	*$30–$40*
Console set, 3-piece	*$200–$250*
Creamer	*$10–$12*
Creamer, midget	*$15–$20*
Cup	*$18–$24*
Dish, 6″	*$10–$15*
Fruit, ftd, 8″	*$25–$30*
Fruit, ftd, 9″	*$30–$40*
Fruit, ftd, 12″	*$45–$60*
Gravy	*$30–$40*
Pitcher, 2 qt	*$30–$40*
Plate, 6″	*$8–$10*
Plate, 7½″	*$10–$12*
Plate, 9″	*$12–$16*
Plate, 10½″	*$25–$30*
Platter, oval, 12″	*$25–$30*
Platter, oval, 17″	*$30–$40*
Relish, 3-part, 10½″	*$40–$55*
Salad, 11½″	*$30–$40*
Sauce boat	*$35–$45*
Saucer	*$6–$8*
Shaker	*$6–$8*
Soup, 7″	*$15–$20*

Monterey: *clockwise from top:* 13″ chop plate; cup & saucer; gravy boat; shakers; oval vegetable; coffee server w/lid; 9″ dinner plates. *(Photo courtesy of Jack Chipman)*

Sugar	*$18–$24*
Sugar, midget	*$12–$16*
Teapot, old, 6 cup	*$45–$60*
Teapot, new, 6 cup	*$40–$55*
Tray, midget cream & sugar	*$30–$40*
Tumbler, 8 oz	*$15–$20*
Vegetable, oval, 10½″	*$30–$40*
Vegetable, rd, 9½″	*$25–$30*
Vegetable, oval, divided	*$35–$40*

Oil Jars

These jars seem to have been made in all colors.

Pricing

Add 50% for black.

12"	*$250–$300*
16"	*$400–$500*
22"	*$650–$750*
24"	*$750–$850*

Pastel Kitchenware

This is the shape with wide ribs. It was made in the same colors as La Linda.

Batter bowl, 1 qt	*$25–$30*
Batter bowl, 2 qt	*$30–$40*
Casserole, metal holder, 1 ½ pt	*$28–$35*
Casserole, metal holder, 1 qt	*$35–$45*
Mixing bowl, 1 pt	*$10–$12*
Mixing bowl, 1 ½ pt	*$12–$16*
Mixing bowl, 1 qt	*$15–$20*
Mixing bowl, 1 ½ qt	*$18–$24*
Mixing bowl, ½ gal	*$25–$30*
Pitcher, 1 ½ pt	*$18–$24*
Pitcher, 1 qt	*$25–$30*
Pitcher, ice lip, 2 qt	*$30–$40*
Teapot, Aladdin, 4 cup	*$35–$45*
Teapot, Aladdin, 8 cup	*$50–$65*

Ring (ca. 1931)

This is the line of dinnerware that prompted Homer Laughlin to create Fiesta. Rare pieces are the AD cup and saucer, ball jug, barrel-shaped items, and beer items, 5½" casserole, cigarette jar, coffee pot, egg cup, goblet, honey jar, jumbo cup, mustard, sugar shaker, the lids for the water bottle and beating bowl pitcher, and these bowls: pedestal, punch, salad/punch, and souffle.

The basic colors you will find are Black, Burgundy, Orange Red, Chartreuse, Chinese Yellow, Dark Blue, Gray, Ivory, Jade Green, Light Blue, Light Brown, Olive Green, Red Brown, Turquoise, and White.

Pricing

Burgundy, Dark Blue, Ivory, Orange Red, and White are at the high end of the price range. Add 50% for Black.

AD creamer	*$10–$15*
AD cup	*$30–$40*
AD saucer	*$20–$25*
AD sugar	*$18–$24*
Ashtray, 2″	*$20–$25*
Ball jug	*$65–$85*
Barrel jug	*$100–$150*
Barrel mug, 12 oz	*$50–$65*
Batter bowl, 1 qt	*$60–$80*
Batter bowl, 2 qt	*$45–$60*
Beating bowl, 1 qt	*$30–$40*
Beating bowl pitcher, 1 qt	*$40–$55*
Beer pitcher	*$150–$200*
Beer stein	*$50–$65*
Bowl, nesting, 6″	*$12–$16*
Bowl, nesting, 7″	*$15–$20*
Bowl, nesting, 8″	*$20–$25*
Bowl, nesting, 9″	*$30 $40*
Butter, ¼ lb	*$75–$100*
Butter dish, round	*$65–$85*
Candlestick, spool	*$30–$40*
Canister, 4½″	*$45–$60*
Canister, 6″	*$60–$80*
Canister, 6¾″	*$75–$100*
Carafe, metal handle	*$35–$45*

Ring ware: 14″ chop plate; dealer sign ($200–$250); Sombrero ashtray ($45–$60); 12-oz tumbler w/handle; 6-oz tumbler w/handle; barrel tumbler w/handle; 1-qt pitcher and round butter dish. *(Photo courtesy of Jack Chipman)*

Casserole, ind, 5½″	*$60–$75*
Casserole, metal holder, 6½″	*$35–$40*
Casserole, metal holder, 7½″	*$45–$60*
Casserole, metal holder, 8½″	*$55–$70*
Casserole, metal holder, 9½″	*$60–$80*
Chop plate, 12″	*$30–$40*
Chop plate, 14″	*$35–$45*
Chop plate, 17″	*$50–$65*
Cigarette jar	*$100–$150*
Coffee pot, 8 cup	*$125–$175*
Coffee server, wood handle, 6 cup	*$25–$30*
Coffee server, wood handle, 8 cup	*$35–$45*
Cookie jar	*$100–$150*
Creamer	*$12–$16*
Cup, coffee	*$15–$20*
Cup, tea	*$15–$20*
Custard	*$8–$12*
Dish, dessert, 4″	*$8–$12*
Dish, baking, w/lid, 4″	*$18–$24*
Dish, cereal, 4½″	*$18–$24*

Dish, fruit, 5″	$12–$16
Egg cup	$60–$80
Goblet	$60–$80
Gravy bowl	$35–$45
Jumbo cup	$35–$45
Mixing bowl, 1 pt	$12–$16
Mixing bowl, 1½ pt	$15–$20
Mixing bowl, 1 qt	$18–$24
Mixing bowl, 1½ qt	$20–$25
Mixing bowl, ½ gal	$30–$40
Mixing bowl, 1 gal	$40–$55
Mixing bowl, 1¼ gal	$75–$100
Mustard	$100–$150
Pedestal bowl, 14″	$150–$200
Pickle dish	$15–$20
Pie baker, no holder, 9″	$20–$25
Pitcher, 1½ pt	$20–$25
Pitcher, 1 qt	$25–$30
Pitcher, 2 qt	$30–$40
Pitcher, 3 qt	$40–$55
Pitcher, cream, 1 pt	$35–$45
Pitcher, ice lip, w/metal handle, 2 qt	$65–$85
Plate, 5″	$15–$20
Plate, 6″	$8–$12
Plate, 7½″	$15–$20
Plate, 9″	$15–$20
Plate, 10½″	$30–$40
Platter, oval, 9″	$20–$25
Platter, oval, 12″	$25–$30
Punch bowl, 14″	$150–$200
Punch cup	$15–$20
Ramekin, 4″	$8–$12
Refrigerator jar, open	$15–$20
Refrigerator set, 4 pieces	$75–$100
Relish, 5-part	$35–$45
Salad, low, 9″	$30–$40

Salad, low, 12"	$50–$65
Salad, low, 14"	$65–$85
Salad/Punch, 9"	$100–$150
Salad/Punch, 11"	$150–$200
Saucer, coffee/tea	$6–$8
Shaker, barrel-shape	$6–$8
Shaker, low	$6–$8
Shaker, sugar	$50–$65
Sherbet	$30–$40
Souffle dish	$125–$150
Soup, 7½"	$25–$30
Soup, lug, 6"/7"	$25–$30
Sugar	$20–$25
Teapot, 2 cup	$50–$65
Teapot, 6 cup	$50–$65
Teapot, wood handle, 6 cup	$65–$80
Tumbler, 3 oz	$10–$15
Tumbler, 6 oz	$10–$15
Tumbler, 12 oz	$20–$25
Tumbler, barrel shape, w/metal handle	$30–$40
Vase, cylinder, 6"	$20–$25
Vase, cylinder, 8"	$25–$30
Vase, cylinder, 10"	$35–$45
Vegetable, oval, 8"	$25–$30
Vegetable, oval, 10"	$35–$40
Vegetable, oval, divided	$45–$60

THE EDWIN BENNETT POTTERY

Baltimore, Maryland

In 1846 Edwin Bennett established his first pottery in East Liverpool, Ohio and began making stoneware and a type of majolica. Through the years a variety of products were made including parian, white granite, and semi-porcelain. The firm closed in 1936.

Marks

Most Bennett is backstamped with a variety of marks: "Bennett Bakeware," and "Bennett, S-V, Baltimore." "II Duce" will also appear on their kitchenware.

Dinnerware

Bennett produced a variety of shapes. Of greatest interest to collectors is their Cameo line. The process was brought to Bennett by a German immigrant, George Bauer, who later brought it to Harker (q.v.) when Bennett closed. Cameo was made in at least three colors: Apricot, Sky Blue, and Summer Yellow. A dark brown may show up.

Pricing

Cameo is at the high end of the range.

Butter dish	*$10–$12*
Casserole	*$15–$20*

Cameo creamer and sugar with undertray, barrel jug.

Creamer	$4–$6
Cup	$4–$6
Dish, 5½″	$1–$2
Gravy	$8–$10
Plate, 6″	$1–$2
Plate, 8″	$2–$4
Plate, 9″	$4–$5
Platter, rect	$5–$6
Saucer	$1
Soup, 7½″	$4–$5
Sugar	$8–$10
Vegetable, rect	$9–$10

Kitchenware

You will find a variety of silk-screen decorations, including polka-dots and stylized poppies. A French Provincial couple on a tan background is common also.

Bean pot	$15–$20
Cake plate	$4–$5
Cake server	$10–$15
Canister, small (spice jar)	$20–$25

Canister, large	$20–$25
Casserole	$15–$20
Casserole liner	$4–$5
Cookie jar, reed handle	$15–$20
Custard	$2–$3
Drip jar	$12–$15
Jug, barrel	$10–$12
Jug, batter	$20–$25
Jug, covered	$20–$25
Jug, syrup	$20–$25
Mixing bowl, small	$8–$10
Mixing bowl, medium	$10–$15
Mixing bowl, large	$15–$20
Mug, barrel	$8–$10
Pie baker	$6–$8
Salad bowl, sq	$9–$10
Salt box	$20–$25
Shaker, range	$6–$8
Shaker, tall	$10–$12
Stack set, rd, 4-piece	$35–$40
Stack set, sq, 3-piece	$25–$30
Tray, batter set	$10–$15

BRAYTON POTTERY

Laguna Beach, California

Begun in 1927 by Durlin Brayton, the company made dinnerware and novelty ware including figurines and cookie jars. Durlin Brayton died in 1951, and the company continued until 1968.

Many Brayton figurines show a high level of sophistication and are increasingly catching the eye of collectors.

Marks

Early mark is an incised "Laguna Pottery." Later mark is "Brayton Laguna Pottery" either incised or ink-stamped. Some Disney pieces are ink-stamped "Gepetto Pottery."

Animal Figures

Fish, ultra 50s, pair	*$115–$125*
Giraffes, necks intertwined, 18″, pair	*$190–$200*
Horse, "Ma"	*$35–$45*
Hound dog	*$15–$20*
Purple bull	*$60–$65*
Purple calf	*$25–$30*
Purple cow	*$40–$50*
Toucans, male/female, pair	*$140–$150*
Zebra, small	*$20–$25*
Zebra, medium	*$40–$45*
Zebra, large, head up, 11″	*$60–$65*
Zebra, large, head down	*$60–$65*

"Ma" horse, hound dog, purple calf, and purple cow. Hand-decorated figures designed by Andy Anderson. *(Photo courtesy of Jack Chipman)*

Cookie Jars

Circus Tent	*$95–$125*
Disney Coachman	*$250+*
Grandma	*$200–$225*
Mammy	*$300+*
Peasant Woman (at least 6 nationalities known)	*$225–$275*
Puppy	*$150–$175*

ND = price is not determined; item too rare to price.
+ = worth at least sum indicated, but could be higher.

Disney Figures (1939)

Figaro, begging	*$90–$100*
Figaro, feeding	*$90–$100*
Figaro, playing	*$90–$100*
Figaro, playing, tail up	*$90–$100*
Figaro, stretching	*$90–$100*
Geppetto, standing	*$200–$225*
Geppetto, w/Pinocchio on lap	*$275–$300*

Pinocchio, sitting	$200–$225
Pinocchio, walking	$225–$250

Figures

Arthur (boy w/chicken)	$30–$35
Blackamoor, w/cornucopia	$30–$35
Emily (girl w/purse)	$30–$35
Frances, flower holder	$25–$30
Jon	$30–$35
Man, abstract, w/cat, 21″	$225–$250
Mandy, flower holder, black girl	$200–$225
Miranda, 6½″	$30–$35
Peasant woman, flower holder	$30–$35
Sally, flower holder	$20–$25

"Jon" and "Miranda" figures; polychrome hand decoration. Designed by Frances Robinson. *(Photo courtesy of Jack Chipman)*

The Girls (3 girls, one w/doll)	$90–$100
Violets (2 black girls w/basket)	$140–$150
Woman's torso, abstract, 10½ "	$60–$65

Shakers

Chef & Jemima, pair	$50
Gingham dog & Calico cat, pair	$25
Pigs, pair	$20

BRUSH POTTERY

Roseville, Ohio

Brush Pottery began manufacturing in 1925. They made a variety of wares, including florist ware, kitchenware, and decorative items. The cookie jars have the greatest collector interest. The firm closed in 1982.

Marks

Will be found unmarked or with "USA" or a shape number impressed.

Pricing

Jars marked with an asterisk come in small and large sizes. Add 10% for the large sizes.

Cookie Jars

Boy w/Balloons	*$250+*
Chick on Nest	*$125–$150*
Circus Horse	*$250–$300*
Clock	*$125–$150*
Clown	*$125–$150*
Covered Wagon	*$200–$250*
Cow (Brown)	*$65–$75*
Cow (Blue, Purple or Black)	*$250+*

Humpty Dumpty with cowboy hat cookie jar. *(Photo courtesy of Dave Pritchard)*

Davy Crockett/*	*$150–$175*
w/gold/*	*$250+*
Dog w/Basket	*$65–$75*
Donkey w/Cart	*$95–$125*
Elephant, w/ice cream cone	*$100–$150*
Fish	*$200–$250*
Granny	*$95–$125*
Hen on Nest	*$55–$65*
Hobby Horse	*$200–$250*
House	*$55–$65*
Humpty Dumpty/Cowboy Hat	*$95–$125*
Humpty Dumpty/Beanie	*$95–$125*
Lantern	*$95–$125*
Little Angel	*$250+*

Little Boy Blue/*	*$225–$250*
w/gold/*	*$300+*
Little Girl	*$150–$175*
Little Red Riding Hood/*	*$225–$250*
w/gold/*	*$200+*
Old Woman's Shoe	*$55–$65*
Panda (Black & White)	*$95–$125*
Panda (Blue)	*$150–$195*
Peter Pan/*	*$225–$275*
w/gold/*	*$300+*
Peter Peter Pumpkin Eater	*$125–$150*
Pig in Tails, "Formal Pig"	*$125–$150*
w/gold	*$300+*
Praying Girl	*$35–$45*
Pumpkin Coach	*$125–$150*
Puppy Police	*$125–$150*
Rabbit	*$85–$95*
Raggedy Ann/*	*$125–$150*
Siamese Cat	*$150–$225*
Squirrel on Log	*$65–$75*
Squirrel	*$95–$125*
Teddy Bear, brown	*$45–$55*
Teddy Bear, green bib	*$75–$85*
Three Bears	*$55–$65*
Treasure Chest	*$65–$75*
Tulips	*$45–$55*

CAMARK POTTERY

Camden, Arkansas

Camark Pottery was established in 1926 as Camden Art and Tile Company for the production of Le-Camark art pottery, a wheel-thrown, hand-decorated line. The firm changed to molded industrial art ware in 1928. It was purchased by W. A. and Mary Daniel in 1962. Due to an overstocked inventory, very little was produced after 1968; a sales only policy prevailed through the 1970s. After Mrs. Daniel's death in 1982, the pottery closed.

The most collectible items are Le-Camark pieces, animal figurals, and pitchers with figural handles.

Note. The cat w/fish bowl ("Wistful Kitten") in the catalog, has been reproduced for the past several years.

Marks

The most common is an impressed "CAMARK."

Ashtray, Texas shape, (038)	$8
Bowl, cabbage leaf (051)	$8
Bowl, pumpkin, small (R59)	$8
Bowl, pumpkin, large (R58)	$14
Bowl, swans (521)/HD	$15
Dealer sign, Arkansas shape	$50
Figure, cat, climbing, small (N155)	$12
Figure, cat, climbing, medium (N138)	$18
Figure, cat, climbing, large (058)	$24
Figure, cat w/fish bowl	$25

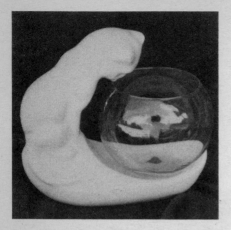

Cat with fish bowl. *(Photo courtesy of Burdell Hall)*

Figure, dog, reclining, (N130)/HD	$45
Flower frog, female dancer	$22
Flower frog, swans (318)	$18
Novelty, dog, miniature (694-50)	$6
Novelty, football, hog on top (N130)	$15
Novelty, lion, marked "Camden, Ark. Lions Club"	$12
Pitcher, bulbous w/cat handle	$40
Pitcher, pinch spout w/parrot handle	$55

Parrot-handled pitcher. *(Photo courtesy of Burdell Hall)*

Planter, basket w/bird on handle   *$18*
Planter, rooster (501)   *$15*
Planter, rolling pin (N1-51)   *$8*
Shakers, letters "S" and "P" (690)   *$10*
Shelf sitter, Humpty Dumpty (R33)   *$25*
Sugar/Creamer on single base (830)   *$12*
Wall pocket, Scoop w/embossed flowers (N45)   *$12*

All prices given are for items in *mint* condition. In general, discoloration, crazing, chipping, and repairs will fetch lower prices.

THE CANONSBURG
POTTERY COMPANY

Canonsburg, Pennsylvania

Founded in 1901, the company manufactured semi-porcelain dinnerware and toilet ware. Manufacturing ceased after a fire in 1975.

Marks

Canonsburg used a variety of backstamps often incorporating a picture of a cannon.

Priscilla plate and teapot.

Priscilla (1932)

Distinguished by a heavily embossed band on the rim and around the hollowware.

Casserole	*$15–$20*
Creamer	*$4–$6*
Cup	*$4–$6*
Plate, 6"	*$1–$2*
Plate, 7"	*$2–$3*
Plate, 9"	*$4–$5*
Saucer	*$1*
Sugar	*$8–$10*
Teapot	*$15–$20*

Westchester (1935)

An Art Deco shape. The AD pieces were used for a child's tea set and a Mary and Her Lamb decal will be found.

Casserole	*$15–$20*
Coffee pot, AD	*$20–$25*

Westchester platter, AD coffee pot, and teapot.

Creamer	*$4–$6*
Creamer, AD	*$4–$6*
Cup	*$4–$6*
Cup, AD	*$4–$6*
Plate, 6″	*$1–$2*
Plate, 7″	*$2–$4*
Plate, 9″	*$4–$5*
Platter, oval, lug, 11¾″	*$5–$6*
Saucer	*$1*
Saucer, AD	*$1–$2*
Sugar	*$8–$10*
Sugar, AD, open	*$4–$6*
Teapot	*$15–$20*

CATALINA
CLAY PRODUCTS
Pebbly Beach, California

In 1927 the pottery was established near Avalon, on Catalina Island, to make ceramic building products. Production of art ware, dinnerware, and garden products was added in 1930. The company was sold to Gladding-McBean (q.v.) in 1937 who closed the Island plant and moved production to Los Angeles.

Collector interest is strongest for (1) the red-bodied ware (Island clay) rather than the white body (mainland clay), and (2) hand-decorated art ware.

Marks

Prior to 1937, pieces were impressed with either "Catalina" or "Catalina Island," hand-inscribed or in block letters. After 1937, "Catalina Pottery" or "Catalina Rancho," either impressed or stamped in ink, were used by Gladding-McBean.

Art Ware

Bookends, monk design, pair	*$550–$600*
Candelabra, 3-tiered	*$190–$200*
Tray, embossed swordfish, 14"	*$325–$350*
Vase, Art Deco stepped design, 5"	*$225–$250*
Vase, fan-shaped, footed, 12"	*$190–$200*
Wall pocket, basket weave, 9½"	*$140–$150*

Hand-decorated plate, 10½″, macaw design, polychrome. *(Photo courtesy of Jack Chipman)*

Hand-Decorated Plates

Macaw, 11½″	*$400–$450*
Moorish, 11½″	*$350–$400*
Spanish Galleon, 12″	*$450–$500*
Submarine Garden, 10½″	*$400–$450*

Miscellany

These pieces were made before 1937.

Pricing

Add 25% for items made from Island clay.

Ashtray, Fish	*$75–$85*
Ashtray, Goat	*$90–$100*
Ashtray, Goofy goat	*$110–$125*
Ashtray, Seal	*$90–$100*

Ashtray, Siesta, decorated	*$150–$175*
Cruet, Gourd	*$40–$45*
Flower frog, Crane	*$60–$65*
Flower frog, Pelican	*$60–$65*
Marmalade, Gourd	*$40–$45*
Shaker, Cactus	*$65–$75*
Shaker, Gourd	*$20–$25*
Shaker, Peon	*$45–$50*
Shaker, Senorita	*$45–$50*
Shaker, Tulip	*$18–$20*

CERAMIC ARTS STUDIO

Madison, Wisconsin

Ceramic Arts Studio was begun in 1941 for the manufacture of hand-thrown flower pots and vases. The demand for novelties created by the banning of Japanese imports turned their attention to molded art pieces. Betty Harrington began designing many of the items that are now collectible. Due to declining sales, the company closed in 1955.

Marks

The words "Ceramic Arts Studio" stamped on a line or with the addition of "Madison, Wisconsin" stamped in a semi-circle. If there is room, the name of a piece might appear. If there is no room, a piece will be unmarked.

NOVELTIES

Ceramic Arts pieces come in a wide variety of colors, usually with one, two or three colors predominating. The same pieces were often decorated in a variety of color combinations. Some collectors like to collect pairs and sets in matching colors, others like to mix colors. Red, white, and black figures, as well as pink and black, are among the popular color combinations, as is maroon on some of the tall figures. Chartreuse is easy to find and not considered desirable.

Pricing

All prices are for pairs unless otherwise indicated. Shaker sets are marked with /S after the entry; add $5 when found as figurines.

Animals

Calico Cat/Gingham Dog/S	*$15–$20*
Cats, Puff/Muff	*$18–$20*
Cats, Siamese, large/small/S	*$15–$18*
Cocker sitting/standing	*$18–$20*
Colt, Balky, Frisky	*$30–$35*
Dogs, Fifi/Fufu	*$18–$20*
Fish, Twist-Tail, head up/down/S	*$15–$18*
Fox/Goose	*$30–$35*
Horse Heads/S	*$18–$20*
Lovebirds, one-piece	*$15 $18*
Ox/Covered Wagon/S	*$25–$30*
Parakeets/S	*$18–$20*
Parrots, Pete/Polly	*$45–$50*
Penguin, Mr. and Mrs./S	*$18–$20*
Pomeranian sitting/standing	*$18–$20*
Rabbit, Mother/Baby kissing/S	*$15–$18*
Roosters/S	*$18–$20*
Scotties/S	*$18–$20*
Skunk, Baby Boy/Girl, each	*$15–$20*
Skunk, Mother/Father, each	*$18–$20*
Tigers, fighting, head up/down	*$45–$50*
Wee Elephants/S	*$20–$25*

Childhood Favorites

Alice in Wonderland/White Rabbit	*$55–$60*
Archibald the Dragon	*$65–$70*
Bo Peep	*$25–$30*
Bo Peep's Sheep	*$18–$25*
Boy Blue	*$15–$18*
Cinderella/Prince	*$35–$40*
Hansel and Gretel (one-piece)	*$35–$40*
Lady Rowena	*$65–$70*
Little Jack Horner	*$15–$18*

Cinderella and Prince Charming. *(Photo courtesy of Dave Pritchard)*

Little Jack Horner/Miss Muffet #2	*$18–$25*
Mary/Lamb	*$25–$30*
Miss Muffet #1	*$15–$18*
Native Boy and Tiger/S	*$35–$40*
Peter Pan/Wendy	*$45–$50*
Pied Piper	*$30–$35*
Pied Piper children	
Boy, running	*$20–$25*
Girl, hands clasped	*$20–$25*
Girl, running	*$20–$25*
St. George	*$85–$90*
Tom Tom the Piper's Son w/Pig	*$40–$45*

Figures/Couples

Adonis/Aphrodite	*$250*
Bashful/Lover Boy/Willing, each	*$20–$25*
Bedtime Boy/Girl	*$25–$30*
Berty/Bobby, each	*$75*
Blythe/Pensive	*$90–$100*

Bride/Groom	*$50–$60*
Clonial Boy/Girl, dancing	*$35–$40*
Colonial Boy/Girl, sitting	*$35–$40*
Colonial Lady/Man	*$35–$40*
Comedy/Tragedy	*$75–$90*
Cowgirl/Cowboy	*$45–$50*
Fire Man/Woman	*$150*
Fishing Boy/Farmer Girl	*$30–$35*
Flame Man/Woman	*$150*
Gay 90s Lady/Man #2	*$35–$40*
Gay 90s Lady/Man #1	*$35–$40*
Harlequin Boy/Girl, w/mask	*$125–$150*
King's Jester, Flutist/Lutist	*$180*
Kissing Girl/Boy	*$35–$40*
Modern Dance Woman	*$50*
Pierrette/Pierrot, sitting	*$75–$80*
Pioneer Sam/Susie	*$35–$40*
Santa Claus/Evergreen Tree/S	*$20–$25*
Sitting Girl w/Cat/ *Sitting Boy w/Dog*	*$35–$40*
Sitting Girl/Boy	*$35–$40*
Southern Belle/Gentleman	*$35–$40*
Square Dance Boy/Girl	*$35–$40*
St. Francis, tall	*$75–$80*
Standing Boy/Girl	*$35–$40*
Victorian Lady/Man	*$35–$40*
Willy/Winney, each	*$60*

Figures/Couples (Foreign Nationalities)

Balinese Dance Boy/Girl	*$90–$100*
Chinese Boy/Girl, standing/kneeling	*$25–$30*
Chinese Man/Woman/S	*$18–$20*
Chinese Sitting Girl/Boy	*$15–$20*
Cuban Child	*$20–$22*
Cuban Woman	*$25–$30*

Dutch Boy/Girl/S	$18–$20
Dutch Boy/Girl, dancing #1	$70–$75
Dutch Boy/Girl, dancing #3	$70–$75
Dutch Boy/Girl, sitting	$22–$25
Dutch Boy Hans/Girl Gretel	$45–$50
Dutch Love Boy/Girl	$30–$35
Gypsy Tambourine Girl/Violin Boy	$100–$150
Hindu Boys/S	$30
Mexican Boy/Girl #1	$55–$60
Polish Boy/Girl	$30–$35
Russian Boy/Girl	$55–$60
Spanish Dance Man/Woman	$75
Temple Dancer	$150
Wee Chinese/S	$18–$22
Wee Dutch/S	$18–$22
Wee Eskimos/S	$18–$22
Wee French/S	$18–$22
Wee Indians/S	$18–$22
Wee Scotch/S	$18–$22
Wee Swedish/S	$18–$22
Zulu Man/Woman, kneeling/standing	$90–$100

Figure Sets

Balinese Dancers	
Bali Gong	$30–$35
Bali Hai	$30–$35
Bali Kris	$30–$35
Bali Lao	$30–$35
Ballet	
Arabesque	$30–$35
Attitude	$30–$35
Ballet En Pose	$30–$35
Ballet En Repose	$30–$35
Daisy	$25–$30
Pansy	$25–$30
Rose	$25–$30
Violet	$25–$30

Four Seasons

Autumn Andy	*$18–$25*
Spring Sue	*$18–$25*
Summer Sally	*$18–$25*
Winter Willy	*$18–$25*

Legend of Hiawatha

Birchbark Canoe (planter)	*$25–$30*
Chipmunk	*$20–$25*
Hiawatha	*$20–$25*
Minnehaha	*$20–$25*
Rabbit	*$20–$25*
Seagull	*$20–$25*
Standing Fawn	*$20–$25*
Wee Indian Girl/S	*$12–$15*
Wee Indian Boy/S	*$12–$15*

Orchestra

Accordion Boy	*$65–$70*
Banjo Girl	*$40–$45*
Bass Viol Boy	*$40–$45*
Drummer Girl	*$40–$45*
Flute Girl	*$40–$45*
Guitar Boy	*$40–$45*
Harmonica Boy	*$40–$45*
Saxophone Boy	*$40–$45*

Sultan on Pillow, w/2 harem girls	*$55*

Woodland Fantasy

Frog	*$18–$20*
Pixie	*$18–$20*
Pixie Boy on Snail	*$18–$20*
Pixie Girl on Lilypad	*$18–$20*
Pixie on Toadstool	*$18–$20*
Pixie under Toadstool	*$18–$20*
Toadstool	*$18–$20*

Miscellany

There should be a bell to pair with Lillibelle.

Bank, Barber Head	*$50–$60*
Bank, Mr. Blankety Blank	*$50–$60*
Bank, Mrs. Blankety Blank	*$50–$60*

Head vases: Manchu, Mei-Ling, Svea, and Sven. *(Photo courtesy of Dave Pritchard)*

Bell, Lillibelle	$45–$55
Bell, Summer Belle/Winter Belle, each	$45–$55
Planter, heads, Manchu/Mei-Ling, each	$60–$75
Planter, heads, Svea/Sven	$50–$65
Planter, Lorelei w/Harp on Seashell	$50–$55
Vase, Lu-Tang/Wing-Sang	$40–$50

Vases: Lu-Tang and Wing-Sang. *(Photo courtesy of Dave Pritchard)*

Plaques

Attitude/Arabesque	*$50–$60*
Chinese Lantern Man/Woman	*$50–$60*
Cockatoos	*$45–$50*
Columbine/Harlequin	*$65–$70*
Comedy/Tragedy	*$65–$70*
Dutch Boy/Girl, dancing	*$30–$40*
Goosey Gander	*$45–$50*
Grace/Greg	*$45–$50*
Hamlet/Ophelia, masks	*$75–$80*
Lotus/Manchu	*$60–$65*
Shadow Dancer, Man/Woman	*$45–$50*
Zor/Zorina	*$45–$50*

Snuggles/Lap-Sitters

These items fit together in various ways, one figure sitting on another's lap or back, or a dog in a doghouse.

Baby Chick in Nest/S	*$18–$25*
Bear, Mother/Baby/S	*$18–$25*
Boy/Chair/S	*$18–$25*
Clown and Clown Dog/S	*$18–$25*
Cow, Mother/Baby/S	*$18–$25*
Dog/Doghouse/S	*$18–$25*
Elephant and Native Boy/S	*$25–$30*
Girl/Chair/S	*$18–$25*
Kangaroo, Mother/Baby/S	*$18–$25*
Kitten and Pitcher/S	*$18–$25*
Monkey, Mother/Baby/S	*$18–$25*
Mouse and Cheese/S	*$18–$25*
Native Boy on Alligator/S	*$30–$35*
Oak Sprite sitting on Leaf/S	*$18–$25*
Oak Sprite straddling Leaf/S	*$18–$25*
Seahorse and Coral/S	*$18–$25*
Skunk, Mother/Baby/S	*$18–$25*
Suzette on Pillow/S	*$18–$25*

CLIFTWOOD ART POTTERIES, INC.

Morton, Illinois

One of six interrelated potteries in Morton, Cliftwood was begun in 1920 for the manufacture of miniature animals and toys. In 1925 art ware—vases, lamps, figurines—were added to the line. The company was sold in 1940 and renamed the Midwest Pottery Company. Midwest made items similar to Cliftwood and the two are usually considered together. Midwest closed in 1944.

Marks

"Cliftwood Potteries" incised in script. Midwest used a paper label only.

Figurines (Cliftwood)

Bald eagle, natural, 8½"	$75
Billikin doll, cobalt, 7½"	$50
Billikin doll, Rockingham, 11"	$85
Buffalo, natural, 6¼" × 10"	$200
Bull dog, sitting, gray, 11"	$80
Cat, reclining, cobalt, 4½" × 1½"	$25
Cat, reclining, gray drip, 6" × 2"	$30
Cat, reclining, blue drip, 8½" × 3"	$36
Cat, sitting, brown drip, 5¾"	$35
Elephant, trumpeting, gray drip, 4" × 7"	$25

Elephant, trumpeting, burgundy, 7½" × 9" $35
Elephant, trumpeting w/top carrier, brown drip, 5½" × 8" $60
Elephant, trunk down w/side carrier, brown drip, 6" × 4" $40
Lion, brown and tan, 8" × 14" $55
Lioness, brown and tan, 7" × 12" $50
Police dog, reclining, white, 6" × 9" $35
Police dog, reclining, brown drip, 8" × 12" $70
Police dog, reclining, brown drip, 8½" × 3" $125

Figurines (Midwest)

Blue heron, blue & yellow w/gold, 11" $35
Bird on stump, blue bird, 4½" $12
Bird on stump, blue jay, 6½" $15
Bird on stump, canaries, pair, 4½" $25
Bird on stump, wild turkey, 11½" $30
Camel, tan, 8½" $18
Cowboy on bronco, black w/gold, 7½" $25
Crane, matte turquoise, 6" $14
Deer, leaping, cobalt, 8" $14
Deer, stylized, gray-green, 12" $25
Fighting cock, blue-mauve, 6½" $12
Miniatures
    Camel, brown, 2½" $8
    Frog, green, 1" $7
    Goose, white w/blue head, 2" $6
    Goose, white w/gold 2¼" $4
    Hen, white/brown, 2¼" $5
    Polar bear, white, 1¾" $8
    Rabbit, white/pink ears, 2½" $6
    Rabbits/kissing, white/gold, 2½" $20
    Rooster, white/brown, 2¼" $5
    Sailing ship, yellow/blue sails, 2" $7
    Squirrel, brown, 2" $6
    Swan, matte white, 2" $5
    Turtle, green, 1" $7
Polar bear, white, 8½" × 12" $30
Pony, white/brown spots, 3½" × 4½" $8

Race horse on base, mahogany & black, 7¼″	$50
Road Runner, stylized, white w/gold, 8″	$12
Road Runner, stylized, gray	$22
Spaniel, white w/gold, 6 × 4″	
Stallion, rearing, green, 6″	$10
Stallion, rearing, 18K gold, 10¾″	$22
Tiger, natural, 7″ × 12″	$40
Woman, bust, Art Deco, white w/platinum hair	$60
Woman, dancing, Art Deco, white w/gold, 8½″	$20
Woman, nude, holding seaweed garland, 14K gold, 11½″	$95
Woman w/Russian wolfhound, gold & platinum, 11″	$110

Miscellany

Cliftwood

Beer set, pitcher/6 mugs, drip brown	$140
Bookend, tree trunk w/woodpeckers, drip brown	$85
Bookend, elephants, blue mulberry	$85
Desk lamps, lion/lioness, brown & tan, pair	$125
Flower frog, Lorelei on rocks, blue mulberry	$45
Vase, hndld, bust of Lincoln embossed on front, drip brown	$100
Vase, #113, blue-gray drip, 14½″	$25
Vase, #132 (handles are snakes swallowing fish), cobalt blue, 18¼″	$80

Midwest

Cow creamer, brown & white, 4¾″	$15
Honey jug, gold w/platinum lining, 5″	$20
Pitcher, duck, cattail handle, tan & gray, 10″	$22
Pitcher, fish, green, 9½″	$20
Shelf sitter, Oriental man/woman, black & white w/gold, 3½″	$25
Wall masks, African man/woman, black, pair, 9″ × 4″	$60

THE CRONIN
CHINA COMPANY

Minerva, Ohio

In 1934, Cronin, which had been located in New Cumberland, West
Virginia, bought and modernized the Owens China Company plant in
Minerva. They manufactured semi-porcelain dinnerware and kitch-
enware until they closed in 1956.

Marks

Dinnerware had a variety of backstamps, the most common of which
is a circular Union mark. Kitchenware usually had the raised mark
"Bake Oven" in a rectangular box.

Zephyr (1938)

A lightly banded, angular-handled shape. It was decorated in decals
and solid colors including Medium Blue, Mango Red, Turquoise, Maroon, and Medium Green.

Dinnerware

Creamer	$4–$6
Cup	$4–$6
Custard, 3½"	$2–$3
Dish, 5¼"	$1–$2
Dish, lug, 6½"	$1–$2

Pottery Guild "Teapot" teapot, "Mexican" Zephyr pie baker, Zephyr sugar and creamer (red and black flower), and Zephyr ball jug.

Plate, 6¼"	*$1–$2*
Plate, 9"	*$4–$5*
Plate, chop, lug, 10"	*$5–$7*
Plate, chop, lug, 11½"	*$5–$7*
Platter, 11½"	*$5–$6*
Platter, 13¼"	*$6–$7*
Saucer	*$1*
Shaker	*$3–$4*
Shirred egg, lug, 6½"	*$2–$4*
Soup, 7¾"	*$4–$5*
Sugar	*$8–$10*
Teapot	*$15–$20*
Vegetable, rd, 9½"	*$9–$10*

Kitchenware

Casserole, 7½"	*$15–$20*
Casserole, ind, 4½"	*$10–$12*
Jug, ball	*$12–$15*

Jug, disk, refrigerator	*$12–$15*
Mixing bowl, 4"	*$2–$3*
Mixing bowl, 5"	*$3–$5*
Mixing bowl, 6¼"	*$3–$5*
Mixing bowl, 7½"	*$5–$8*
Mixing bowl, 9"	*$8–$10*
Pie baker, 9"	*$6–$8*
Pie baker, 9¾"	*$6–$8*
Salad bowl, 9"	*$9–$10*

Pottery Guild

Cronin made a variety of items for this distributor. In addition to items above, you will also find:

Jug, batter	*$20–$25*
Jug, syrup	*$20–$25*
Tray, batter set	*$10–$15*

World's Fair

Cake plate	*$60–$75*
Cake server	*$20–$25*

THE CROOKSVILLE CHINA COMPANY

Crooksville, Ohio

Founded in 1902, Crooksville manufactured semi-porcelain dinnerware and kitchenware. The firm closed in 1959.

Marks

A variety of backstamps were used. The mark shown is the general dinnerware mark.

Dartmouth (1939)

An Art Deco shape.

Casserole, 7½"	$20–$25
Cookie jar	$15–$20
Creamer	$4–$6
Cup	$4–$6
Gravy	$8–$10
Jug, syrup	$15–$20
Mixing bowl, 4"	$4–$5

Dartmouth: Petitpoint Leaf sugar and creamer, "Nursery Rhyme" cookie jar, Carnival gravy, and "Mexican" jug.

Mixing bowl, 6"	*$5–$8*
Mixing bowl, 8"	*$10–$12*
Mixing bowl, 9"	*$12–$15*
Plate, 6"	*$1–$2*
Plate, 9"	*$4–$5*
Plate, 10"	*$4–$5*
Saucer	*$1*
Shaker	*$6–$8*
Sugar	*$8–$10*
Teapot	*$15–$20*

Euclid (1935)

An embossed fruit and leaf design. Many pieces of Euclid will be found marked "Pantry Bak-in Ware." The 9" plate is used as the casserole underplate and the 11 1/2" platter is the tray for the batter set.

Euclid: Autumn plate, "Vegetable Medley" coffee pot, "Flower Shop" batter set.

Easily found decals are Autumn (sepia flowers and leaves) and "Vegetable Medley."

Casserole, 8"	*$15–$20*
Coaster, 4"	*$6–$10*
Coffee pot	*$20–$25*
Creamer	*$4–$6*
Cup	*$4–$6*
Custard cup	*$2–$3*
Jug, batter	*$20–$25*
Jug, syrup	*$15–$20*
Mixing bowl, 6½"	*$5–$8*
Mixing bowl, 8½"	*$10–$12*
Mixing bowl, 10½"	*$15–$18*
Pie baker, 10"	*$6–$8*
Plate, 6"	*$1–$2*
Plate, 9"	*$4–$5*
Plate, 9¾"	*$4–$5*
Platter, rect, 11½"	*$5–$6*
Platter, rect, 15½"	*$8–$10*
Pudding dish	*$4–$5*
Saucer	*$1*

Sugar	*$8–$10*
Tea tile	*$18–$20*
Vegetable, rect, 9¼"	*$9–$10*

Pantry Bak-in Ware (1931)

Pink body, ivory body, or yellow glaze.

Bean pot	*$15–$20*
Cake plate	*$4–$5*
Canister, small (spice jar)	*$20–$25*
Canister, large	*$20–$25*
Casserole, 4"	*$15–$20*
Casserole, 6"	*$15–$20*
Casserole, 8"	*$15–$20*
Casserole, oval	*$15–$20*
Coffee pot, china drip	*$25–$35*
Cookie jar	*$15–$20*
Custard	*$2–$3*

Silhouette Pantry Bak-In Ware: cookie jar, teapot, canister, "Pelican" batter and syrup jugs.

Jug, batter, "Pelican"	*$20–$25*
Jug, refrigerator, flat top	*$20–$25*
Jug, syrup, "Pelican"	*$20–$25*
Juice pitcher, small	*$8–$10*
Juice pitcher, large	*$10–$12*
Leftover, rd, 4″	*$4–$5*
Leftover, rd, 6″	*$6–$8*
Leftover, rd, 8″	*$8–$10*
Leftover, split oval w/lid	*$20–$25*
Mixing bowl, 6″	*$5–$8*
Mixing bowl, 8″	*$8–$10*
Mixing bowl, 10″	*$10–$15*
Mixing bowl, 11″	*$15–$20*
Mixing bowl, 12″	*$20–$25*
Pie baker, 10″	*$6–$8*
Reamer (for juice pitcher)	*$40–$50*
Teapot	*$15–$20*
Tray, batter set, rd, pierced lug	*$10–$15*
Tray, casserole, sq, 9″	*$4–$5*
Tumbler	*$8–$10*

DEDHAM POTTERY

Dedham, Massachusetts

Dedham Pottery was an offshoot of the previous Chelsea Ceramic Art Works begun by the Robertson family of Chelsea, Massachusetts. Initially, the pottery was known for tiles and classically designed redware vases with soft and glossy glazes. In 1876, the "Dragon's blood" vases at the Korean exhibit of the Centennial Exposition inspired Hugh Robertson. In trying to emulate those glazes, he found the formula for the crackleware process, a commercial success which supported the pottery and his further experiments. In 1891 the Chelsea Pottery, U. S. opened. In 1896 they moved to Dedham, changed their name, and manufactured there until they closed in 1943.

Crackle Dinnerware

The ware was handmade in molds and free-hand decorated in Cobalt Blue. Decal and stencils were not used. In its catalog of 1938, patterns were listed in two categories: regular and special.

The regular patterns are: azalea, butterfly, clover, duck, grape, horse chestnut, iris, magnolia, polar bear, rabbit, snow tree, turkey, and water lily.

The special patterns are: birds in potted orange tree, chicken, crab, dolphin, elephant, lion, lobster, owl, swan, and turtle.

This distinction still exists today; the regular are still common and the special are the most sought after. The exceptions are the clover and the polar bear. Animals, in general, are considered desirable, more so than the simpler stylized vegetation. There are also custom order patterns which are highly desirable.

Marks

Mark 1 was used ca. 1895 to 1932. Mark 2 was used ca. 1896 to 1943.
The word "Registered" was added to mark 2 in 1929 and used alternately with it.

Note. Rabbit decorated reproductions have been made for several
years. They are easy to recognize, as they do not have the Dedham
mark.

Pricing

Because the pottery is hand made and molded, and then hand painted,
there are variations in quality between pieces. The clarity of drawing,
the color blue, and the regularity of the form are all factors. These
differences affect pricing; two plates of the same size and pattern can
be substantially different in price. Get your eye accustomed to quality
by comparing pieces. Become familiar with the patterns and types of
hollowware available. In general, teapots, bowls, and candlesticks are
more expensive than the more common plate. However, a plate with
a rare pattern can bring more than a Rabbit teapot.

Bowl, Elephant, 4″	*$250–$300*
Bowl, Rabbit, 6″	*$150–$250*
Bowl, Rabbit, 9″	*$350–$500*
Candlestick, pair, Rabbit, 3″	*$250–$300*
Celery, oblong, Rabbit, 10″	*$250–$300*
Chocolate pot, pear-shape, Rabbit	*$450–$650*
Cup/Saucer, Elephant	*$400–$500*
Cup/Saucer, Polar Bear	*$400–$500*
Cup/Saucer, Rabbit	*$150–$250*

All prices given are for items in *mint* condition. In general,
discoloration, crazing, chipping, and repairs will fetch lower
prices.

Rabbit cup and saucer, butterfly plate, rabbit marmalade, clover plate and rabbit celery dish. *(Photo courtesy of Skinner Inc.)*

Marmalade w/lid, Grape	*$250–$350*
Jug, cylindrical, Rabbit, 5″	*$300–$350*
Jug, Oak Block	*$800–$1200*
Shaker, pair, Elephant	*$500–$700*

Desirable decorations: turtle, elephant, poppy (center poppy), crab, clover, and lobster. *(Photo courtesy of Skinner Inc.)*

Plate Chart

Pattern	6"	8½"	10"
Azalea	$100–$150	$150–$250	$200–$300
Birds in			
Orange Tree	$300–$500	$400–$600	$600–$800
Butterfly	$150–$250	$200–$300	$400–$600
Crab	$300–$500	$500–$600	$700–$900
Duck	$200–$250	$200–$300	$300–$500
Elephant	$400–$600	$500–$700	$700–$900
Grape	$150–$250	$150–$250	$250–$350
Horse			
Chestnut	$150–$200	$200–$300	$250–$350
Iris	$125–$175	$200–$300	$250–$350
Lobster	$300–$500	$500–$700	$700–$900
Magnolia	$150–$250	$200–$250	$200–$300
Mushroom	$200–$300	$250–$300	$300–$500
Owl (flying)	$700–$800	$1000–$1500	
Pineapple	$250–$350	$400–$600	
Polar Bear	$600–$800	$600–$800	$800–$1200
Pond Lily	$150–$250	$200–$300	$300–$400
Poppy			
(central)	$400–$600	$500–$700	
Rabbit	$100–$150	$125–$175	$150–$250
Snowtree	$200–$250	$250–$350	
Strawberry	$1000–$1500		
Swan	$250–$350	$400–$600	
Tapestry Lion	$800–$1200	$1200–$1500	
Turkey	$250–$350	$300–$400	$600–$800
Turtle	$500–$700	$500–$700	
Special Patterns			
Clover	$400–$600		$600–$800
Scottie Dog		$1200–$1800	

FLORENCE
CERAMICS COMPANY
Pasadena, California

In 1942, Florence Ward, a ceramic hobbyist, began commercial production of her designs. She started her operations in a garage, expanded and moved several times, and by 1949 had established one of the most modern plants in California. The glazes on her semi-porcelain ware were fired with the body. Overglaze decoration completed the pieces. The company was sold in 1964.

Most of the production consisted of figurines; picture frames, plaques, flower holders, bowls, and other accessories were also made.

Marks

Names of the figures are usually embossed on the bottom, although some are unnamed. In addition, a backstamp, usually in ink, but sometimes in gold, will be found. Six backstamps are known and all contain some combination of "Florence," "Florence Ceramics," "Pasadena, California," and "Copyrighted" in a circle or on a line.

Figurines

The figurines were glazed in a large variety of colors. They were then hand painted in rich colors to represent features and clothing detail and fired a second time. Some had elaborate decorations that included applied flowers (usually roses), bows, lace, ringlets, and tresses, as well as gold trim.

In addition, a number of figures have articulated fingers. Note that some figures have never been found with these separated fingers, some only found with them, and some both ways.

There was also an economy line with none of the above decoration.

The colors included gray, beige, maroon, aqua, pink, royal red, royal purple, rose, yellow, white, blue, and several shades of green. The first four colors, often touched with green or maroon, are the colors usually found on the economy figures. Yellow is hard to find. Some colors will be found in an iridescent mother-of-pearl finish. These are hard to find. A figurine can come in more than one color of dress or hair.

Alternate name spellings are indicated in parentheses. Some names were used for two different figurines. These are indicated with (2). (Y) after a name indicates a Young figure; (G) after a name indicates authentic Godey costume.

Pricing

Florence collecting is still so new that consistent national prices have not been established. In some areas, they have risen very high very fast; some people feel they must fall. The prices given here reflect neither abnormally high prices nor the low prices of the uninformed. A range is given; the more special decoration, the higher the price. Some figures were made both with or without articulated fingers; these are priced two ways, as "plain" and as "fancy."

For those who want to group their pieces, the following figurines are made to go with each other: John Alden and Priscilla, Blue Boy and Pinkie, Blynken and Wynken, Douglas and the smaller Godey girls, Edward with Elizabeth and Victoria, Leading Man and Prima Donna, Mme. Pompadour and Louis XV, Marie Antoinette and Louis XVI, Scarlett, Rhett, Melanie, and Sue Ellen (there may be an Ashley), and the boy with life preserver and girl with pail. Yulen, Shen, She-Ti, Kiu, Chinese Girl and Boy, Blossom Girl, and Lantern Boy are the Chinese figures group. The two Madonnas, the Madonna Bust, the three Choir Boys, and the Angel are the Religious figures. The three Mermaids, called Merrymaids in the catalog, go with the Shell bowls. Note that Cinderella and Prince Charming are one piece.

ND = price is not determined; item too rare to price.
+ = worth at least sum indicated, but could be higher.

Abigail (G)	*$80–$90*
Adeline	*$90–$95*
Alden, John	*$60–$80*
Amber/Parasol	*$175–$195*
Amelia (G)	*$90–$110*
Angel	*$30–$40*
Ann	*$30–$60*
Annabel	*$120–$140*
Annette	*ND*
Ballerina Child 1	*$65–$85*
Ballerina Child 2	*$65–$85*
Barbara	*ND*
Beth	*$50 $60*
Betsy (Y)	*$70–$90*

Amber, Carol, and Lady Diane. *(Photo courtesy of Jeanne Fredericks)*

Betty (Merrymaid)	$80–$100
Birthday Girl	$100–$125
Blossom Girl	$50–$60
Blue Boy	$125–$150
Blynken	$40–$65
Boy w/bass fiddle	$75–$95
Boy w/cone	$75–$95
Boy w/life preserver	$85–$100
Boy w/white tuxedo	$70–$80
Bride	$300–$350
Bryan	ND
Camille	$60–$100
Carol	$175–$200
Catherine	$125–$150
Charles	$75–$90
Charmaine	
Plain	$65–$75
Fancy	$90–$100
Chinese Boy	$35–$45
Chinese Girl	$35–$45
Choir Boys (3), each	$40–$50
Cinderella/Prince Charming	$500
Cindy	
Plain	$40–$50
Fancy	$60–$75
Clarissa (2)	
Plain	$50–$60
Fancy	$90–$100
Claudia	$80–$90
Coleen	$50–$55
Cynthia	$175–$200
David (Y)	$50–$60
Dear Ruth	ND
Deborah	ND
Delia	$60
Denise	$150–$170
Diane	$80–$90
Dolores	$90–$100
Doralee	ND
Douglas	$60–$70
Edith	$50–$60
Edward	$100–$125
Elaine (G)	$30–$40

Catherine, Elizabeth, and Edward. *(Photo courtesy of Jeanne Fredericks)*

Elizabeth	*$125–$140*
Ellen	*$60–$70*
Ethel	*$50–$60*
Eugenie (Eugenia) (G)	*$150–$180*
Evangeline	*$40–$50*
Eve	*ND*
Fair Lady	*$250–$300*

Martin, Fair Lady, and Vivian. *(Photo courtesy of Jeanne Fredericks)*

Lisa, Dear Ruth, and Karla. *(Photo courtesy of Jeanne Fredericks)*

Fall (Y)	$30–$40
Gary	$60–$75
Genevieve	$90–$100
Georgette	ND
Girl in pinafore	$75–$90
Girl w/pail	$85–$100
Grace	$50–$60
Grandmother and I	$250–$275
Haru	$80–$90
Her Majesty	$60–$70
Irene (G)	$40–$50
Jane (Merrymaid)	$80–$100
Jeanette (2)	$60–$70
Jennifer	$110–$130
Jim	$40–$50
Josephine	$60
Joy	$40
Joyce	$175–$190
Julie	$60–$70
Karla (Ballerina)	$150

Kay	$50–$55
Kiu	$40–$50
Lady Diana	$125–$150
Lantern Boy	$35–$45
Laura	$90–$100
Lavon	ND
Leading Man	$125–$150
Lillian (G)	$80–$90
Lillian Russell	$300
Linda Lou (Y)	$60–$70
Lisa (Ballerina)	$150
Lisa	$75
Lorry (Y)	$100–$125
Louis XV	$175
Louis XVI	$125–$150
Louise (G)	$90–$100
Madonna Plain	$40–$50
Madonna w/child	ND
Margaret	ND
Margot	$175–$190
Marie Antoinette	$125–$150
Marsie	$60–$70
Martin	$150–$175
Mary	ND
Master David	ND
Matilda (G)	$90–$100
Meg	ND
Melanie	
Plain	$50
Fancy	$90
Memories	ND
Mikado	$125–$150
Mike	$40
Misha	$80–$90
Mme. Pompadour	$175
Musette	$90–$100
Nancy	$40–$50
Nell Gwynn	ND

Nita	*$60–$70*
Our Lady of Grace	*$40–$50*
Pamela (Y)	*$60–$70*
Pat	*ND*
Patricia	*$80–$90*
Peasant Girl/2 baskets	*$50–$60*
Peter	*ND*
Pinkie	*$125–$150*
Prima Donna	*$225–$250*
Princess	*$150–$175*
Priscilla	*$50–$60*
Rebecca	*$90–$100*
Rhett	
Plain	*$70–$80*
Fancy	*$90-$100*
Richard	*ND*
Roberta	*$75–$90*
Rosalie	*$80–$90*
Rose Marie	*$170–$180*
Rose Marie (Y)	*$80–$100*
Rosie (Merrymaid)	*$80–$100*
Sally	*$50–$60*
Sarah	*$50–$60*
Sarah Bernhardt	*$350–$400*

Children. *(Photo courtesy of Jeanne Fredericks)*

Mme. Pompadour, Blue Boy, Pinky, and Louis XV. *(Photo courtesy of Jeanne Fredericks)*

Scarlett	*$125–$150*
Shen	*$40*
Sherri	*$125–$150*
She-Ti	*$40–$50*
Shirley	*$100–$125*
Stephen	*ND*
Story Hour	*$200–$225*
Story Hour w/Boy	*$225–$250*
Sue	*$40–$50*
Sue Ellen	*$65–$80*
Susan (Susann)	*$185–$200*
Suzanna	*ND*
Taka	*$100–$125*
Tess	*ND*
Toy	*$50–$60*
Victor	*$100–$110*
Victoria	*$175–$200*
Vivian (G)	*$100–$125*

Wynken	$40–$65
Yulan	ND
Yvonne	
Plain	$70–$80
Fancy	$160–$175

Birds

Several birds have turned up in the regular Florence style. These are listed below. There is also a later line of stylized birds and animals.

Parakeet	$55–$65
Pheasant, tail up	$60–$70
Pheasant, tail down	$60–$70
Pouter pigeon	$60–$70

Busts

Modern busts done in Satin White; traditional busts done in iridescent.

Boy, modern	$70–$80
Boy, traditional	$70–$80
Girl, modern	$70–$80
Girl, traditional	$70–$80
La Petite	ND
Madonna w/Child	$60–$70
Mme. DuBarry	ND

Fashions in Brocade

Hand fashioned in metallic brocade, these were top-of-the-line items with carefully detailed faces and hands and genuine feather hair ornaments. An old catalog lists four dress combinations: Metallic gold with either Green, Vermouth, Mint, or Strawberry Vermouth.

Amelia	$300
Anita	$300

Caroline	*$300*
Georgia	*$300*
Marleen	*$300*
Virginia	*$300*

Flower Holders

Also called Flower Containers in old catalogs. Many of these were designed to look like figurines only, when not in use.

Ava	*$90–$100*
Bee	*$20–$30*
Belle	*$30–$40*
Beth	*$30–$40*
Blossom Girl	*$30–$40*
Chinese Boy	*$25–$30*
Chinese Girl	*$25–$30*
Emily	*$20–$30*
Fern	*$20–$30*
Jule	*ND*
June	*$20–$30*
Kay	*$20–$30*
Lantern Boy	*$30–$40*
Lea	*$30–$40*
Lyn	*$30–$40*
May	*$20–$30*
Mimi	*$20–$30*
Molly	*$20–$30*
Patsy	*$20–$30*
Peg	*$20–$30*
Polly	*$20–$30*
Sally	*$20–$30*
Suzette	*$25–$30*
Violet	*$20–$30*
Wendy	*$20–$30*

Lamps

Shades were made of ninon (oval and round with lace trim), taffeta (skirted or ruffled), and pleated chiffon with velvet trim to match the figurines. Bases were hardwood or polished brass.

Camille	*$100–$150*
Clarissa	*$100–$150*
Claudia	*$100–$150*
Dear Ruth (TV)	*$100–$150*
Delia	*$100–$150*
Elizabeth	*$100–$150*
Genevieve	*$100–$150*
Marie Antoinette	*$100–$150*
Musette	*$100–$150*
Scarlett	*$100–$150*
Vivian	*$100–$150*

Shadow Boxes

One of the higher-priced lines, the boxes were backed in velvet and the hats were made with fabrics, feathers, and trimmings.

Bernice (Poke Bonnet)	*$100–$150*
Jacqueline (Pill Box Hat)	*$100–$150*

Miscellany

The shell pieces accessorized the Merrymaids. In addition to the pieces listed below, Florence made a line of art ware that included bonbons, cigarette sets, clocks, trays, and bowls.

Diana, powder box	*$50–$60*
Shell ashtray	*$10–$20*
Shell bowl, 11 ½"	*$20–$30*
Shell bowl, 15 ½"	*$30–$40*
Shell wall vase	*$30–$40*

FRANKOMA POTTERY

Sapulpa, Oklahoma

In 1927 John Frank moved to Norman, Oklahoma, to establish a new ceramics department for the University of Oklahoma. In 1933, while still working at the university, he established Frank Potteries in Norman, using a light clay he had found near the town of Ada. In 1934, the name was changed to Frankoma Potteries and in 1936, he left the university to work at the pottery full time. The business was moved to Sapulpa, in 1938, and renamed Frankoma Pottery. In 1953, a new, desirable clay, brick red, was found nearby and by 1954, the transition to its use was complete. Frankoma is still in business; see Traveler's Directory.

Marks

Most pieces will have the name "Frankoma" impressed in the bottom of the piece; some early pieces will have the name stamped in black. From 1936 to 1938 an impressed panther in front of a vase was placed over the name.

Pricing

Items marked "Ada" are priced for the earlier, more desirable clay. They will also be found in red clay, for which you can expect to pay less.

Bookends

Bucking Bronco	$75
Charger Horse (Ada)	$75
Dreamer Girl	$85
Leopard	$80
Mallard Head	$100
Mountain Girl	$65
Rearing Clydesdale	$250
Red Irish Setter (Ada)	$85
Seahorse	$225

Figures

Cowboy	$175
Fan Dancer	$125
Fan Dancer (Ada)	$185
Flower Girl	$60

Cowboy. *(Photo courtesy of Phyllis and Tom Bess)*

Torch Singer. *(Photo courtesy of Phyllis and Tom Bess)*

Gardener Boy, w/overalls	*$85*
Gardener Boy, w/pants	*$90*
Gardener Girl	*$65*
Harlem Hoofer	*$400*
Indian Bowl Maker (Ada)	*$85*
Indian Chief (Ada)	*$85*
Monk w/Basket	*$100*
Torch Singer	*$400*

Miniature Animals

Bull	*$40*
Elephant, walking	*$60*
English Setter, 2⅞"	*$35*
Flower Holders	
Fish	*$100*
Hobby Horse	*$100*

Puma	*$30*
Swan	*$30*
Trojan Horse	*$35*

Sculptures

Circus Horse (Ada)	*$65*
Cocker Spaniel	*$75*
Gannet	*$250*
Pacing Leopard	*$185*
Pekingese	*$175*
Prancing Colt	*$250*
Puma w/Prey	*$185*
Reclining Puma (Ada)	*$75*
Seated Puma (Ada)	*$75*

Shakers

Priced per pair.

Barrel	*$12*
Dutch Shoes	*$20*
Elephant	*$50*
Jug	*$15*
Oil Derrick	*$10*
Puma	*$45*
Teepee	*$15*
Wheat Shock	*$15*

Dinnerware

All of Frankoma's dinnerware lines, Mayan-Aztec (1945), Lazybones, Plainsman (1948), Wagon Wheels (1941), and Westwind were designed by John Frank. They are still in production, although Wagon Wheels, which was discontinued in 1983, can only be special ordered. Some of the pieces listed are no longer being made; those that are currently in the catalog are marked /C. Individual and 5-quart bakers are hard to find.

All lines were made in Prairie Green and Desert Gold. You will find certain pieces in a variety of other colors as well, although a complete set in any of these colors will not be possible to assemble.

Note

Because this is a composite list, not all pieces will be found in all lines.

Pricing

Double the price for pieces made from Ada clay.

AD creamer/C	*$3.25*
AD cup	*$5*
AD saucer	*$3*
AD sugar/C	*$3.25*
Ashtray/Candleholder	*$18*
Baker, ind	*$25*
Baker, 2 qt/C	*$9.25*
Baker, 3 qt/C	*$13.25*
Baker, 5 qt	*$50*
Bowl, 8 oz/C	*$2.75*
Bowl, 14 oz/C	*$3.25*
Bowl, 20 oz/C	*$3.75*
Bowl, divided, 13″/C	*$7.75*
Bowl, rd, 8″/C	*$6.50*
Bowl, rd, lug, 9″/C	*$4.75*
Bowl, 4½ qt/C	*$17.50*
Butter/C	*$6.50*
Chop plate, ftd, 15″/C	*$25*
Corn dish/C	*$2.50*
Creamer, old style	*$15*
Creamer, restyled/C	*$3.25*
Creamer, small	*$10*
Cup/C	*$2.75*
Custard/C	*$2.75*
Gravy boat	*$10*
Gravy, 2-spout/C	*$6.50*

Horseshoe	$8
Lazy Susan	$50
Mug, 8 oz	$5
Mug, coffee, 12 oz/C	$3.25
Mug, 14 oz/C	$4.50
Pitcher, 1 qt/C	$6.50
Pitcher, 2 qt/C	$9.25
Pitcher, 3 qt/C	$12.50
Plate, 7"/C	$3.50
Plate, 9"/C	$4
Plate, 10"/C	$6
Platter, oval, shallow, 17"/C	$17.50
Platter, oval, deep, 13"	$20
Platter, oval, deep, lug, 13"/C	$7.75
Platter, oval, deep, 17"	$35
Platter, rect, shallow, 9"/C	$3.75
Platter, rect, shallow, 11"/C	$4.50
Platter, rect, shallow, 13"/C	$5
Platter, rect, deep, 13"/C	$7.75
Platter, rect, deep, 17"/C	$17.50
Salad, crescent/C	$2.50
Saucer/C	$2.75
Shaker, pair/C	$4.75
Sugar/C	$5
Sugar, small/C	$3.25
Taco holder, pair/C	$10
Teapot, rd, 2 cup/C	$6.50
Teapot, rd, 6 cup/C	$9.25
Teapot, tall, 2 cup	$20
Teapot, tall, 6 cup	$35
Teapot, 12 cup/C	$13
Tray, rect, 9"/C	$3.75
Tumbler, 6 oz/C	$3.25
Tumbler, 12 oz/C	$3.75
Vegetable, 1 qt/C	$4.75
Warmer/C	$7.25

THE FRENCH-SAXON
CHINA COMPANY

Sebring, Ohio

The Saxon China Company began in 1911 and over the years had close ties to the French China Company, as both were owned by the Sebring family. Both companies were part of the American Chinaware Company merger of 1929 and ceased to exist when that company declared bankruptcy in 1932. W. V. Oliver purchased the old Saxon plant, named his company French-Saxon, and began making semi-porcelain dinnerware and kitchenware. He died in 1963 and Royal China bought the company in 1964.

Marks

French-Saxon used a knight and shield graphic backstamp which was a variant of an old Saxon mark, as well as a circular Union mark. Romany and Rancho will be found with only their names stamped.

Zephyr (1938)

The easiest pieces to find are the shaker, sugar, creamer, and plates. Hardest are the teapot and casserole. Zephyr was decorated with decals and in solid colors. There are two solid color lines, Romany (called ''Grenada'' by some collectors) and Rancho. Romany colors are red, yellow, dark blue, and green. Black was used as a contrasting color on lids, odd pieces, and service items. Pastel shades will also be found. Rancho comes in maroon, gray, chartreuse, and dark green.

Zephyr: tall shakers, small shakers, chop plate, and gravy.

Pricing

Use the low end of the range for decal-decorated pieces and Rancho colors; the high end for Romany colors. Add 10% for red.

Bowl, 36s	*$4–$5*
Coffee pot	*$20–$25*
Creamer, open handle	*$4–$6*
Creamer	*$4–$6*
Cup	*$4–$6*
Dish, 5 ¼"	*$1–$2*
Dish, 6"	*$1–$2*
Gravy boat	*$8–$10*
Plate, 6"	*$1–$2*
Plate, 7"	*$2–$4*
Plate, 9"	*$4–$5*
Plate, 10"	*$4–$5*

Plate, chop, 13″	*$6–$8*
Plate, lug, 7″	*$2–$4*
Plate, lug, 10¾″	*$5–$6*
Saucer	*$1*
Shaker	*$3–$5*
Shaker, tall	*$3–$5*
Soup, 7¾″	*$4–$5*
Sugar	*$8–$10*
Vegetable, rd, 8½″	*$9–$10*

All prices given are for items in *mint* condition. In general, discoloration, crazing, chipping, and repairs will fetch lower prices.

THE W. S. GEORGE POTTERY COMPANY

East Palestine, Ohio

In 1898 William S. George leased the East Palestine Pottery Company from the Sebring brothers. He bought the pottery, ca. 1903, and renamed it. Semi-porcelain dinnerware was produced until the company closed, about 1960.

A curious fact is that W. S. George seems never to have produced any kitchenware, which its competitors were making.

Marks

A wide variety of backstamps, many particular to the shape, were used.

Bolero (mid-1933)

Be aware that Bolero has been restyled a number of times. Hard-to-find pieces are the old style items; the compote is rare.

Many decal decorations were used; Pink Cherry Blossom from the late thirties, early forties is the most easily found. Three colors, called Bolero Faience, were added in 1934: alabaster, lemon yellow, and turquoise (with and without decal). These colors are rare.

Casserole	*$15–$20*
Casserole, straight side	*$15–$20*
Compote	*$12–$15*
Creamer	*$4–$6*

Creamer, old style	*$6–$7*
Cream soup, w/lid	*$10–$12*
Cup	*$4–$6*
Custard cup	*$2–$3*
Dish, lug, 6½"	*$1–$2*
Gravy, double lip	*$10–$12*
Pickle	*$3–$4*
Plate, 6¾"	*$1–$2*
Plate, 8"	*$3–$4*
Plate, 9¼"	*$4–$5*
Platter, oval, 11¾"	*$5–$6*
Platter, rd, lug, 12"	*$6–$7*
Relish, shell shape	*$6–$8*
Saucer	*$1*
Shaker	*$5–$6*
Soup, lug	*$4–$5*
Sugar	*$8–$10*
Sugar, old style	*$10–$12*
Teapot	*$15–$20*
Vegetable, oval	*$9–$10*
Vegetable, rd, 9"	*$9–$10*

Elmhurst (1938)

A bit thinner body, not much Elmhurst is found. Elmhurst was decorated in decals and solid colors. Decals include: Pergola, Gracia (Mexican), and Wing (birds on flower trellis). Pastel colors were introduced in 1939: apple green, blue, maple sugar, pink, turquoise, and yellow.

Bowl, 36s	*$4–$5*
Casserole	*$15–$20*
Creamer	*$4–$6*
Cup	*$4–$6*
Cup, AD	*$4–$6*
Dish, 5"	*$1–$2*
Dish, 6"	*$1–$2*

Apple Blossom Bolero teapot, "Catkin" Elmhurst platter, and Shortcake Ranchero coffee.

Gravy	*$8–$10*
Gravy faststand	*$10–$12*
Pickle	*$3–$4*
Plate, 8¼"	*$2–$4*
Plate, 9"	*$4–$5*
Platter, 11"	*$5–$6*
Platter, 13"	*$6–$7*
Platter, 15½"	*$8–$10*
Saucer	*$1*
Saucer, AD	*$1–$2*
Soup, lug	*$4–$5*
Sugar	*$8–$10*
Teapot	*$15–$20*
Vegetable, oval	*$8–$10*
Vegetable, rd	*$9–$10*
Vegetable, rd, w/lid	*$15–$20*

Georgette (1933)

Called "Petal" by collectors. Decorated originally in decals; I believe colors were added later as those used are the pastels of the late thirties and more somber colors of the forties. Colors are most easily found: aqua, chartreuse, dark green, gray, light green, maroon, medium blue, pink, and yellow. Many decals were used but few are found: Peasant, Jolly Roger (pirate ships), and Federal (eagle and stars) are the most interesting.

Bowl, 36s	*$4–$5*
Creamer	*$4–$6*
Cup	*$4–$6*
Cup, AD	*$4–$6*
Cup, jumbo	*$5–$7*
Dish, 5 ½ "	*$1–$2*
Dish, 6 ½ "	*$1–$2*
Gravy	*$8–$10*
Plate, 6 ½ "	*$1–$2*
Plate, 8 ½ "	*$3–$4*
Plate, 9 ¼ "	*$4–$5*
Plate, 10 ¼ "	*$4–$5*
Saucer	*$1*
Saucer, AD	*$1–$2*
Saucer, jumbo	*$2–$3*
Sugar	*$8–$10*
Vegetable, oval, 9 "	*$8–$9*

Lido (1932)

Candlesticks are rare. An experiment with horizontal cup handles, called Streamline (also Nes-Teas), was tried. I have not seen one.

Decal decorations on a white or Canary-Tone glaze include Breakfast Nook (picket fence below window w/bird cage), Gaylea (stylized floral basket), and Prim (pot of geraniums next to window).

Ashtray	*$6–$8*
Bowl, 36s	*$4–$5*
Butter dish	*$15–$20*

Candlestick	*$15–$18*
Casserole, lug	*$15–$20*
Casserole, 9½"	*$15–$20*
Creamer	*$4–$6*
Cup	*$4–$6*
Cup, AD	*$4–$6*
Dish, 5½"	*$1–$2*
Dish, 6⅜"	*$1–$2*
Egg cup	*$5–$7*
Gravy	*$8–$10*
Gravy, faststand	*$10–$12*
Pickle tray, 7½"	*$3–$4*
Plate, 6½"	*$1–$2*
Plate, 7½"	*$2–$4*
Plate, 9½"	*$4–$5*
Plate, 10¼"	*$4–$5*
Platter, 11¾"	*$5–$6*
Platter, 13¼"	*$6–$7*
Saucer	*$1*
Saucer, AD	*$1–$2*
Shaker	*$5–$6*
Soup, 7¾"	*$4–$5*
Sugar	*$8–$10*
Sugar, no handle	*$8–$10*
Teapot	*$15–$20*
Vegetable, 9"	*$8–$10*

Rainbow (1934)

Casserole, candleholder, and gravy are hard to find. The lid for the sugar and creamer is interchangeable.

Decorated in decals and solid color. Decals: Cross Stitch (Colonial motifs in black w/red), Iceland Poppy, Reflection (a willow and its reflection), and Santa Rosa (a floral bouquet with a tulip projecting). Colors: blue, green, pink, tan, and yellow. In mid-1935, Petit Point, an embossed needlecraft effect, was introduced on the Rainbow shape

Iceland Poppy and Petitpoint Rainbow plates, Breakfast Nook Rainbow candleholder, Cross Stitch Rainbow chocolate cup, Georgette plate and gravy.

in the following colors: cobalt blue, light green, yellow, and chocolate brown.

Bowl, 36s	*$4–$5*
Candleholder	*$15–$18*
Casserole	*$15–$20*
Chocolate cup	*$8–$10*
Compote	*$12–$15*
Creamer	*$4–$6*
Cup	*$4–$6*
Dish, 5¼"	*$1–$2*
Egg cup	*$5–$7*
Gravy	*$8–$10*
Plate, 6¼"	*$1–$2*
Plate, 7¼"	*$2–$3*
Plate, 8¼"	*$2–$4*
Plate, 9¼"	*$4–$5*
Platter, oval, 10"	*$4–$5*
Platter, oval, 11¼"	*$5–$6*
Relish	*$5–$6*

Saucer	*$1*
Sugar	*$8–$10*
Vegetable, 8 3/4"	*$9–$10*

Ranchero

The line was designed by Simon Slobodkin. The egg cup and teapot are hard to find.

The following decals on a golden glaze background are most easily found: Wampum (in predominant shades of Iroquois red, Cherokee blue, or Navajo brown), Shortcake (strawberries), Rosita (roses), Indian Corn, and Fruit Fantasy. Some solid-color pieces with initials will turn up.

Butter, 1/4 lb	*$12–$15*
Casserole	*$15–$20*
Coffee pot	*$20–$25*
Creamer	*$4–$6*
Cup	*$4–$6*
Cup, AD	*$4–$6*
Dish, 5 1/2"	*$1–$2*
Egg cup	*$5–$7*
Gravy, 2-spout	*$10–$12*
Plate, 6 1/4"	*$1–$2*
Plate, 9"	*$4–$5*
Platter	*$6–$7*
Saucer	*$1*
Saucer, AD	*$1–$2*
Shaker	*$5–$6*
Sugar	*$8–$10*
Sugar, no handle	*$8–$10*
Teapot	*$15–$20*
Vegetable, rd	*$9–$10*

GLADDING, McBEAN & COMPANY

Los Angeles, California

The company began in 1875 to produce sewer pipes. Architectural terra cotta was added in 1884 and other building materials followed. The Franciscan line, an earthenware body for art ware and dinnerware, was introduced in 1934; initially bright and pastel-colored dinnerware, it grew to include decal decorations and the embossed, hand-painted underglaze line that is still popular. Catalina Clay Products (q.v.) was bought in 1937 and several lines were produced under the name "Catalina Pottery." In 1963 the company name was changed to the Interpace Corporation. It was sold to Wedgwood (England) in 1979 which continued to manufacture in America until 1985 (production fully phased out by 1986), at which time the Glendale plant was closed and all Franciscan production transferred to England.

Marks

Gladding used a large variety of backstamps and decals. "GMB" in an oval is common. For Franciscan, an "F" in a box, "Franciscan Ware" forming a circle or a variant of the decal below. "England" is in the backstamp of pieces currently produced there.

Coronado

Coronado was decorated in both high gloss and matte shades of apple green (gloss only), coral, ivory, light blue, maroon, turquoise, and yellow.

Pricing

Maroon is at the high end. Add 20% for apple green.

Ashtray	*$3–$4*
Butter, ¼ lb	*$18–$20*
Casserole, ind, 5½″	*$8–$12*
Casserole, 10½″	*$20–$25*
Cigarette box	*$20–$25*
Coffee pot, AD	*$25–$30*
Creamer, flat	*$4–$6*
Creamer, ftd	*$8–$10*
Cream soup	*$8–$10*
Cream soup saucer	*$6–$8*
Cup	*$3–$5*
Cup, AD	*$6–$8*
Cup, jumbo	*$6–$8*
Custard/sherbet	*$4–$6*
Dish, 5″	*$3–$5*
Dish, 6″	*$4–$6*
Dish, crescent	*$6–$8*
Gravy, faststand	*$12–$14*
Jug	*$18–$25*
Nut cup, ftd	*$6–$8*
Party plate	*$10–$12*
Plate, 6½″	*$1–$3*
Plate, 7½″	*$3–$5*
Plate, 8½″	*$4–$6*
Plate, 9½″	*$4–$6*
Plate, 10½″	*$8–$10*
Plate, chop, 12½″	*$12–$15*
Plate, chop, 14″	*$15–$18*

Platter, oval, 10"	*$8–$10*
Platter, oval, 13"	*$10–$12*
Platter, oval, 15½"	*$18–$22*
Relish, handled	*$8–$10*
Salad bowl, 10"	*$20–$22*
Saucer	*$1–$2*
Saucer, AD	*$2–$4*
Saucer, jumbo	*$3–$5*
Shaker	*$4–$6*
Soup, 8"	*$8–$10*
Sugar, flat	*$8–$10*
Sugar, ftd	*$10–$12*
Teapot, flat	*$25–$30*
Teapot, ftd	*$30–$40*
Vegetable, oval, 10"	*$10–$12*
Vegetable, rd, 9"	*$8–$10*

Franciscan Classics

This was Gladding-McBean's name for Apple (1940), Desert Rose (1941), and Ivy (1948), the three most popular patterns in their embossed, hand-painted underglaze dinnerware line made in the forties. They remain the three most popular patterns with collectors today. Rare pieces are the AD coffee and the toast cover.

Although all Franciscan Classics are microwave safe (per the company), three pieces were made as a microwave set. See M after the listing. Gladding also made 6" square tiles and glassware to match these lines.

Note

Apple and Desert Rose have been in continuous production since their introduction, though some items were made for a limited time.

Pricing

Prices are for all three patterns. Some pieces are found in one or two patterns only; these are indicated by letters after each listing.

Ivy teapot, Apple pitcher, and Desert Rose coffee pot. *(Photo courtesy of Dave Pritchard)*

Baker, rect, 1½ qt (M)	*$35–$45*
Baker, sq, 1 qt (M)	*$25–$35*
Batter bowl (A)	*$30–$40*
Buffet plate, rd, divided (D)	*$10–$15*
Butter, ¼ lb	*$15–$20*
Candleholder (A/D)	*$8–$12*
Casserole, 1½ qt	*$35–$45*
Casserole, 2½ qt (D)	*$45–$60*
Casserole, ind (A)	*$10–$15*
Cheese server	*$30–$40*
Cigarette box (AD)	*$35–$40*
Coaster (A)	*$6–$10*
Coffee pot, 8 cup	*$30–$40*
Compote	*$20–$30*
Compote, low (D)	*$30–$40*
Cookie jar (A/D)	*$60–$75*
Creamer	*$10–$14*
Creamer, AD (A/D)	*$8–$12*
Cup	*$6–$8*
Cup, AD (A/D)	*$8–$10*

Cup, jumbo	*$12–$14*
Cup, tall (D)	*$10–$15*
Dish, cereal	*$8–$10*
Dish, fruit	*$6–$8*
Egg cup (A/D)	*$8–$12*
Goblet (D)	*$18–$25*
Gravy faststand	*$15–$20*
Jug, small (new) (A/D)	*$8–$12*
Jug, syrup, 1 pt	*$8–$12*
Jug, 1 qt (A/D)	*$18–$24*
Jug, 2½ qt	*$20–$45*
Ladle, plain	*$8–$10*
Long and narrow, 15″ (D)	*$35–$45*
Marmalade (A/D)	*$30–$40*
Mixing bowl, small	*$25–$30*
Mixing bowl, medium	*$35–$40*
Mixing bowl, large	*$45–$50*
Mug, 7 oz (A/D)	*$8–$12*
Mug, 10 oz (D)	*$10–$15*
Mug, 12 oz	*$12–$18*
Party plate, rd	*$12–$15*
Plate, 6½″	*$4–$8*
Plate, coupe, 7½″ (A/D)	*$8–$12*
Plate, 7½″	*$6–$10*
Plate, 9½″	*$8–$12*
Plate, 10½″	*$10–$14*
Plate, chop, 12″ (A/D)	*$18–$25*
Plate, chop, 14″	*$30–$35*
Platter, 12″	*$20–$25*
Platter, 14″	*$25–$35*
Platter, 17″	*$65–$95*
Porringer (A/D)	*$10–$15*
Relish	*$10–$15*
Relish, divided	*$18–$20*
Salad	*$35–$45*
Salt/Pepper Mill (A/D)	*$60–$75*

Saucer	$4–$6
Saucer, AD (A/D)	$4–$5
Saucer, jumbo	$4–$8
Shaker, small	$8–$12
Shaker, jumbo (A/D)	$12–$15
Sherbet	$10–$12
Side salad (crescent)	$8–$12
Snack plate, sq (M)	$12–$15
Soup, flat	$10–$14
Soup, ftd	$8–$12
Sugar	$12–$18
Sugar, AD (A/D)	$10–$14
Teapot, 6 cup	$30–$40
Tray, heart (D)	$8–$12
Tray, 3-compartment (A)	$14–$20
Trivet, sq	$6–$10
Trivet, rd (A/D)	$6–$10
Tumbler, 6 oz (A/D)	$8–$10
Tumbler, 10 oz	$10–$15
Tureen, small (A)	$75–$125
Tureen, large	$75–$125
TV plate, oval	$20–$30
Two-tier tidbit	$24–$35
Vegetable, small (A/I)	$16–$20
Vegetable, medium	$18–$22
Vegetable, large	$18–$24
Vegetable, divided	$20–$25

Franciscan Classics Giftware

Ashtray, sq (A/D)	$6–$8
Ashtray, ind	$4–$6
Bell (D)	$14–$20
Box, heart (D)	$15–$18
Box, oval (D)	$15–$18
Box, rd (A/D)	$12–$15

Bud vase (D)	*$10–$14*
Candy dish, oval (A/D)	*$10–$12*
Ginger jar (A/D)	*$20–$25*
Hurricane lamp (D)	*$12–$15*
Napkin ring (A/D)	*$4–$8*
Piggy bank (A/D)	*$20–$25*
Tea canister	*$30–$35*
Thimble (A/D)	*$10–$12*
Tile, sq, 6″	*$6–$10*
Tile, rd (A/D)	*$6–$10*

Metropolitan (1940)

Metropolitan was designed by Morris Sanders for an exhibit of industrial design at the Metropolitan Museum of Art in New York, hence the name. All shapes are square or rectangular.

It was originally produced in satin finish colors of Ivory, Ivory and Coral, Ivory and Turquoise, and Ivory and Gray. In the combinations, Ivory was used as a lining and for the lid and handles. Both Mauve and Chocolate Brown, lined with Ivory, were also made. There is evidence of early decal decoration, but no indication that these were produced. Trio, a fifties decal decoration of three stylized leaves, *was*

Metropolitan.

produced. From 1949 to 1954, the shape was the basis of the Tiempo line in solid gloss colors, some of which are Copper, Hot Chocolate, Leaf (dark green), Mustard, Pebble, Sprout (light green), Stone (light gray), White and a pink and a tan, one of which may be Pebble.

Ashtray/coaster	*$10–$12*
Butter, ¼ lb	*$20–$25*
Casserole, ind	*$18–$20*
Coffee pot, 6 cup	*$35–$45*
Creamer	*$10–$12*
Cup	*$6–$8*
Dish, fruit/cereal	*$4–$8*
Gravy	*$15–$18*
Jug, 1½ qt	*$35–$40*
Plate, 6″	*$4–$6*
Plate, 8″	*$6–$8*
Plate, 10″	*$8–$10*
Plate, chop, sq, 13″	*$18–$20*
Platter, rect, 14″	*$12–$14*
Relish	*$12–$15*
Salad, 10″	*$20–$25*
Saucer	*$2–$4*
Shaker	*$8–$10*
Soup	*$10–$12*
Sugar	*$15–$18*
Teapot, 6 cup	*$30–$40*
Tumbler	*$12–$15*
Vegetable, divided	*$20–$25*
Vegetable, covered	*$30–$35*
Vegetable, rect	*$18–$20*

Miscellany

Add 50% for brown-tinted ''terra-cotta'' body.

Samoan Mother and Child	*$50*
Samoan Girl, reclining	*$35*
Vase, Bust, Peasant Girl	*$25*

Ox-Blood (1935)

You will also find candlesticks, ashtrays, and a box with a white lid.

105/Vase, bottle, 6″	*$45*
114/Vase, flare top, 8¾″	*$65*
115/Vase, 10½″	*$65*
116/Vase, bottle, 9½″	*$65*
122/Vase, ball, 8¼″	*$125*
123/Vase, large, 11″	*$200*
132/Vase, rd, 4½″	*$35*
141/Vase, beaker, 7¼″	*$65*
C278/Vase, Japanese, 6″	*$85*
C279/Vase, sq, 4½″	*$35*
C281/Vase, ftd, 6″	*$75*
C284/Vase, 8¼″	*$100*
C286/Vase, tall w/flange, 11″	*$175*
C289/Vase, wide mouth, 9″	*$100*
C290/Vase, 11″	*$100*
C293/Vase, large rd, 5½″	*$50*
C300/Vase, small, 5″	*$35*

Rancho-Ware (1937)

There is Rancho-Ware in old California colors. In 1939, the firm added Duotone: white outside with linings of coral, yellow, blue, or green.

Bowl	*$12–$15*
Creamer	*$8–$10*
Cup	*$12–$15*
Jug	*$40–$45*
Plate (5 sizes)	*$5–$25*
Platter, oval	*$12–$15*
Saucer	*$3–$5*
Sugar	*$12–$15*
Teapot	*$55–$65*

THE HAEGER POTTERIES
Dundee and Macomb, Illinois

Haeger began in 1871 as a brick yard. In 1914 art pottery was introduced under the guidance of Martin Stangl. In 1938 the Royal Haeger line, designed by Royal Hickman, was introduced. It is still in production today.

Haeger made many lines, including dinnerware and florist ware, but it is the Royal Haeger line, specifically the hundreds of designs by Royal Hickman, that is most collectible today.

Marks

"Royal Haeger by Royal Hickman" with the shape number, all raised.

Note

All pieces listed are from the Royal Haeger line. Shape numbers are given where known.

Pricing

As Haeger becomes more collectible, certain colors will gain greater popularity with collectors than others. For now, the bright red and glossy black introduced in the mid-forties are certainly of interest and are at the high end of the price range. In addition, be alert for two hard-to-find finishes: Boko (or Boco) which looks like the glaze has been bubbled over the surface of the piece, and D'Este, which resembles rough, horizontal grooving. Add 50% to the prices for these finishes.

Ashtrays

Some ashtrays are also figurines; these are noted in parentheses.

Cat, leopard, 8 ½ ″/632	*$20–$25*
Cog wheel/230	*$6–$8*
Deer, fawn, 8 ½ ″/1283	*$20–$25*
Diamond, 9″/1215	*$6–$8*
Dog, boxer (figurine), 13″/1399	*$30–$35*
Dog, cocker, standing, 12″/1443	*$30–$35*
Dog, poodle, 12″/1441	*$30–$35*
Elephant, 4″/668	*$12–$15*
Heart, 7 ½ ″/1184	*$6–$8*
Heart, double, 9″/1363	*$6–$8*
Leaf, 5″/449	*$6–$8*
Leaf, 6″/597	*$6–$8*
Leaf, 8″/567	*$8–$10*
Palette, 9 ½ ″/811	*$6–$8*

Bookends

Some bookends are also planters. These are noted in parentheses.

Calla lily/475	*$15–$18*
Cat, leopard (planter), 15″/638	*$40–$45*
Cat, lion head, 7 ½ ″/700	*$20–$25*
Horse, stallion (planter), 8 ½ ″/641	*$20–$25*
Horsehead (figurine), 7″/1365	*$20–$25*
Indian (planter)/741	*$40–$45*
Ram, 9″/132	*$25–$30*
Ram's head, 5 ½ ″/718	*$18–$20*
Water lily, 5″/1144	*$15–$18*

Bowls

Oyster shell, 15″/985	*$10–$15*
Petunia/737	*$8–$10*

Sailfish planter bowl, 11″/1191	*$30–$35*
Star fish, 14″/967	*$15–$18*
Swan, 11″/955	*$15–$18*
Swan flower, 12″/1218	*$30–$35*
Violin, 17″/293	*$20–$25*

Candleholders

Apple, 2½″/1206	*$8–$10*
Butterfly, 6½″/1208	*$12–$15*
Chinese figures, 5″/622	*$10–$12*
Cornucopia/312	*$6–$8*
Fish, 5″/183	*$18–$20*
Fish (2)/203	*$20–$25*
Leaf, 5″/437	*$6–$8*
Plume/295	*$6–$8*
Star fish, 6″/968	*$8–$10*
Swan, 5¼″/959	*$12–$15*

Dishes

Calla lily, 7½″/431	*$16–$18*
Cat, leopard, 7″/631	*$20–$25*
Dolphin, 7½″/512	*$20–$25*
Elephant (3), 8¼″/625	*$20–$25*
Horse head, 7″/685	*$20–$25*
Polar bear, 7½″/664	*$20–$25*
Turtle, 9¼″/684	*$25–$30*

Figures

Bird, parrot/macaw, 14″/180	*$20–$25*
Bird, pouter pigeon, 7″/233	*$12–$15*
Buddha, 10½″/694	*$20–$25*
Cat, black panther, 18″/683	*$20–$25*

Figure: Giraffe and Young (1301). *(Photo courtesy of Dave Pritchard)*

Cat, black panther, 24″/495		*$60–$65*
Cat, Egyptian, tall/758		*$65–$75*
Cat, Egyptian, head down, 6½″/493		*$10–$12*
Cat, Egyptian, head up, 7½″/494 ·		*$10–$12*
Cat, lion/695		*$25–$30*
Cat, sitting, 6″/898		*$15–$18*
Cat, sleeping, 7″/896		*$15–$18*
Cat, standing, 7″/897		*$15–$18*
Cat, tiger, 11″/314		*$18–$20*
Cat, tigress, 8″/313		*$15–$18*
Cowboy on bucking horse, 13″/424		*$50–$60*
Deer, does (2), bust, 14½″/624		*$20–$25*
Deer, fawn, kneeling, 7½″/413		*$10–$12*
Deer, fawn, standing, 11½″/412		*$12–$15*
Dog, cocker pup, begging, 4″/779		*$8–$10*
Dog, cocker pup, rolling, 6″/778		*$8–$10*

Dog, cocker pup, sleeping, 6″/776	$8–$10
Dog, cocker pup, standing, 4¾″/777	$8–$10
Dog, collie/734	$35–$40
Dog, dachshund, 14½″/736	$25–$30
Dog, Miss Peke/781	$15–$18
Dog, Mister Scot/780	$15–$18
Dog, Russian wolfhound, head down, 7″/318	$15–$18
Dog, Russian wolfhound, head up, 7″/319	$15–$18
Dog, Shetland puppies (3)/782	$18–$20
Ducks (3), wings down, 11″/237	$20–$25
Elephant, 5″/785	$18–$20
Elephant, 9″/539	$40–$45
Fish (3), noses down, 10″/157A	$25–$30
Garden Girl, 14″/1179	$35–$40
Giraffe (2), 15″/218	$70–$80
Giraffe & Young (bust)/740	$20–$25
Giraffe & Young, 13½″/1301	$55–$70
Girl, Gypsy, 16½″/1224	$40–$50
Girl w/2 bowls, 13″/1225	$35–$40
Hen, 4″/401	$12–$15
Horse, dappled, 5″/402	$15–$18
Horse, 7″/103	$15–$18
Horse, 13″/415	$40–$45
Horse, racing, 9″/1130	$18–$20
Horse, racing (2), 10″/408	$40–$45
Horse & Colt (bust)/739	$20–$25
Horse, Mare & Foal, standing, 9″/451	$40–$45
Indian on Horse/721	$45–$50
Little Brother, 11½″/1254	$20–$25
LittleLittle Sister, 11½″/1253	$20–$25
Man, Chinese musician, 11″/711	$15–$18
Man, peasant, 16½″/382	$35–$40
Mermaid on Sailfish, 20″/1178	$85–$100
Neptune on Sailfish, 20″/1177	$85–$100
Nude, 14″/181	$30–$35
Pheasant cock, 6″/165	$15–$18

Pheasant hen, 6″/164	*$10–$12*
Polar bear, standing, 5½″/376B	*$15–$18*
Polar bear, 7″/375B	*$15–$18*
Polar bear, 16″/702	*$40–$45*
Polar bear cub, sitting, 3″/375A	*$8–$10*
Polar bear cub, standing, 2½″/376A	*$8–$10*
Prospector, large/722	*$25–$30*
Prospector w/Burros, 11½″/479	*$20–$25*
Rooster, 5″/400	*$12–$15*
Stag, resting, 14½″/880	*$25–$30*
Woman's head, Russian, 12″/472	*$40–$45*

Frogs

Bird, 7″/820	*$12–$15*
Bird, flying, 17½″/125	*$40–$45*
Birds (2), 11″/359	*$18–$20*
Birds (3), on branch, 7″/361	*$18–$20*
Deer, standing, 11½″/104	*$18–$20*
Fish, tropical (2), 11″/360	*$20–$25*
Fish, trout, leaping, 7″/169B	*$15–$18*
Fish (3), noses down, 12½″/157B	*$30–$35*
*Jockey/*788	*$25–$30*
Nude on Fish, 10″/363	*$30–$35*
Nude, sitting, 6″/189	*$12–$15*
Nude w/Seal, 13″/364	*$25–$30*
*Stag/*772	*$18–$20*

Leaves

Banana, 13″/909	*$8–$10*
Banana, 18″/910	*$8–$10*
Elephant ear, 11″/916	*$8–$10*
Elephant ear, 13″/915	*$8–$10*
Lily, 11″/908	*$8–$10*

Tropical, 10″/914	*$8–$10*
Tropical, 14″/913	*$8–$10*
Wine, 10″/911	*$8–$10*
Wine, 15″/912	*$8–$10*

Miscellany

Bird house, w/2 birds, 9½″/287	*$12–$15*
Fish bowl stand, mermaid, 11½″/656	*$20–$25*
Pitcher, fish, 9″/595	*$20–$25*
Wall pocket, grape vine/745	*$12–$15*
Wall pocket, rocking horse/724	*$12–$15*

Planters

Cat, leopard/760	*$20–$25*
Deer, fawn, 17″/1351	*$15–$20*
Donkey cart, 11¼″/754	*$10–$12*
Elephant, 10½″/563	*$20–$25*
Fish, 8½″/752	*$15–$18*
Fish, large/719	*$20–$25*
Gazelle, 18″/869	*$20–$25*
Gondolier, 19½″/657	*$20–$25*
Horse, racing (2), 18″/883	*$25–$30*
Horse, colt, 14½″/875	*$20–$25*
Turtle, 11″/834	*$12–$15*

Table Lamps

Some lamps are also planters; these are noted in parentheses. Expect to pay about 30% more for lamps with original shades.

Acanthus leaf/5349	*$30–$35*
Bison, bird finial/5171	*$60–$70*
Cabbage rose, 24″	*$25–$30*
Cat, leopard on rock	*$60–$70*

Deer, fawns (2)/5195	*$30–$35*
Deer, fawn (planter), 18 ½ ″	*$10–$12*
Deer, running	*$45–$55*
Duck, flying	*$45–$55*
Fighting cock	*$45–$55*
Fish, flying/5351	*$50–$60*
Fish on Wave	*$50–$60*
Horse head, horse head finial	*$50–$60*
Horses, racing (2)	*$60–$70*
Horses, mare and foal	*$50–$60*
Mermaid/5398	*$50–$60*
Plume (3)/5292	*$30–$35*
Plume, square base/5024	*$30–$35*

TV Lamps

Bronco	*$20–$25*
Comedy & Tragedy	*$20–$25*
Dog, cocker	*$20–$25*
Fish, angel (2)	*$25–$30*
Gazelle, 10 ½ ″	*$20–$25*
Gazelle, leaping	*$20–$25*
Greyhound (planter), 13 ″/6202	*$20–$25*
Horse, colt	*$20–$25*
Horses, racing (2)	*$25–$30*
Panther	*$20–$25*
Peacock	*$20–$25*

Vases

Angel, 7 ″/1141	*$18–$20*
Ballet, female, 13 ½ ″/1216	*$15–$18*
Ballet, male, 13 ½ ″/1215	*$15–$18*
Bird, peacock, 10 ″/453	*$20–$25*
Bird, peacock, all styles/31	*$20–$25*
Bird of Paradise, 12 ¾ ″/186	*$20–$25*

Bird, seagulls (3), wings up, 16"/208	*$50–$60*
Butterfly, 7½"/1221	*$12–$15*
Cornucopia w/nude, 8"/426	*$12–$15*
Cornucopia, double, 16"/246	*$12–$15*
Cornucopia, double shell, 7½"/322	*$15–$18*
Deer, running, 15"/706	*$12–$15*
Deer, standing, 15"/707	*$12–$15*
Duck, flying, 9"/903	*$15–$20*
Duck, flying, 14"/1465	*$20–$22*
Duck, setting, 9"/904	*$15–$20*
Fan, 9½"/714	*$10–$12*
Feather, 8½"/723	*$10–$12*
Fish, 6½"/1136	*$15–$18*
Fish, sail fish, 9"/271	*$15–$18*
Fish, sword fish, 6"/901	*$15–$18*
Fish, trout, 7"/284	*$20–$25*

Vase: Pegasus (393). *(Photo courtesy of Dave Pritchard)*

*Fish/Waves/*742	*$15–$20*
Gazelle, 13″/115	*$12–$15*
Goose Quills, 17½″/888	*$12–$15*
Leaf, single, 12½″/138	*$12–$15*
Leaf, elm, 12″/320	*$12–$15*
Pegasus, bust, 11¼″/393	*$40–$45*
Peter Pan, 10″/917	*$18–$20*
Pine cone, 9″/1189	*$10–$12*
Pine cone, 12″/1190	*$12–$15*
Sea shell, 11″/701	*$15–$18*
Shell, conch, 8″/321	*$15–$18*
Swan, 8″/430	*$12–$15*
Swan, 13″/856	*$20–$25*
Swan, both styles, 15½″/36	*$30–$35*
Swan, head down/414	*$18–$20*
Tulip, 8″/646	*$10–$12*

All prices given are for items in *mint* condition. In general, discoloration, crazing, chipping, and repairs will fetch lower prices.

THE HALL
CHINA COMPANY

East Liverpool, Ohio

Robert Hall had been a director of the East Liverpool Pottery Company. In 1901 that company and four others attempted a merger that did not succeed. In 1903 he bought the pottery, renamed it the Hall China Company, and continued making the semi-porcelain dinnerware and toilet ware the old company had produced. He died in 1904 and his son began a search for a one-fire process (body and glaze fired at the same time) for making vitrified china. Long experimentation paid off in 1911 and Hall still makes vitrified hotel and restaurant ware. In 1920, the first gold-decorated teapots were introduced, for retail sale, which are now almost synonymous with the Hall name. And in 1931, decal-decorated kitchenware and dinnerware, much of it for premium sales, were introduced. Hall is still going strong today.

Hall is unique among the potteries that made semi-porcelain or vitreous ware in that almost all its lines are collectible: teapots, decal-decorated ware (especially Autumn Leaf), refrigerator ware, and its kitchenware.

Marks

Mark 1 (H/2) Mark 2 (H/3) Mark 3 (H/4)

MADE IN
U. S. A.

Mark 4 (HSQK)

Mark 5 (HD)

Mark 1 (H/2) was used in the twenties. Mark 2 (H/3) was used from ca. 1930. Mark 3 (H/4) has been supplanting mark 2 since 1972; both are still in use. Mark 4 (HSQK) dates to 1932 and was used on kitchenware only. Mark 5 (HD) or a variant is found on dinnerware. Abbreviations after each one are the codes collectors use in mail-order advertisements.

Note

For the last few years, Hall has been reissuing many of its pieces, including some classic designs, in its new Americana line. They are all decorated in solid colors (none of the decals or gold decorations have been reissued and there is no intention of doing so) and are generally marked with the H4 mark. Many are in new colors, sometimes in color combinations, which is another way to identify them. Because of this reissue, prices have dropped slightly on a few items.

Autumn Leaf

Aladdin teapot, 7 cup	*$35–$40*
Ball jug, #3	*$20 $30*
Bud vase	*$150–$175*
Butter, ¼ lb	*$125–$150*
Butter, MJ, ¼ lb	*$350–$500*
Butter, Hallcraft, ¼ lb	*$350–$500*
Butter, 1 lb	*$175–$200*
Cake plate	*$12–$15*
Candy dish	*$250–$300*

Casper shaker	*$6–$7*
Clock, battery	*$150–$200*
Clock, electric	*$350–$400*
Conic mug	*$45–$50*
Flute French baker, 10 oz	*$8–$10*
Flute French baker, 2 pt	*$45–$50*
Flute French baker, 3 pt	*$12–$15*
Ft. Pitt baker	*$65–$75*
Irish coffee mug	*$75–$85*
Jordan drip coffee, 5 cup	*$175–$200*
J-Sunshine coffee pot, 8 cup	*$25–$30*
J-Sunshine coffee pot, 9 cup	*$30–$35*
J-Sunshine creamer	*$14–$16*
J-Sunshine jug	*$12–$15*
J-Sunshine sugar	*$18–$20*
J-Sunshine teapot	*$45–$50*
Marmalade, 3-piece	*$40–$45*
MaryLou stack set	*$50–$60*
MJ electric coffee maker	*$225–$250*
Mustard, 3-piece	*$40–$45*
New England bean pot, 1 handle	*$300–$350*
New England bean pot, 2 handle	*$80–$100*
Newport teapot, old, 7 cup	*$85–$100*
Newport teapot, new, 7 cup	*$75–$90*
Pie baker	*$18–$20*
Range shaker	*$9–$10*
Ruffled-D line	
Cream soup	*$15–$18*
Creamer	*$8–$10*
Cup	*$6–$8*
Dish, 5½″	*$4*
Dish, 6½″	*$8–$9*
Gravy	*$15–$18*
Pickle dish	*$18–$22*
Plate, 6″	*$4*
Plate, 7¼″	*$4*
Plate, 8″	*$8–$9*

Ruffled-D
cream soup

Jewel candy dish

Clock

Fort Pitt baker

St. Denis
cup & saucer

Jordan
drip coffee

MaryLou
stack set

Tootsie
covered drip

M. J.
electric percolator

Round warmer

Tootsie
casserole

Zeisel bean pot
(cookie jar)

Ruffled-D
pickle dish

Irish coffee mug

Conic mug

Ruffled-D gravy

Ruffled-D covered
oval vegetable

Ruffled-D
three-tier tidbit

Plate, 9"	$7–$8
Plate, 10"	$8–$10
Platter, oval, 11½"	$12–$15
Platter, oval, 13½"	$15–$18
Saucer	$3
Soup, 8½"	$8–$10
Sugar	$10–$12
Tidbit, 2-tier	$55–$60
Tidbit, 3-tier	$35–$45
Vegetable, divided	$50–$55
Vegetable, oval, covered	$35–$40
Vegetable, rd	$55–$70
Vegetable, oval	$15–$18
Salad bowl	$12–$15
St. Denis cup	$20–$22
St. Denis saucer	$5–$7
Sunshine bowl, #1	$4–$6
Sunshine bowl, #3	$10–$12
Sunshine bowl, #4	$12–$15
Sunshine bowl, #5	$15–$18
Tootsie casserole	$25–$30
Tootsie cookie jar	$80–$100
Tootsie covered drip	$12–$15
Warmer base, oval	$120
Warmer base, rd	$100
Zeisel "cookie jar"	$80–$90

Banded

The bowls are hard to find. There is a 6-cup teapot and a 9-cup coffee pot that are found with decal decorations, but they have not been seen in solid colors.

Pricing

Prices are for all colors. Chinese Red (the most often found color) and Cobalt are the most popular colors.

Batter bowl	$30–$35
Bowl, 6"	$10–$12

Bowl, 7³⁄₈″	$12–$15
Bowl, 8³⁄₄″	$15–$20
Carafe	$90–$110
Casserole	$25–$30
Cookie jar	$40
Jug, 1½ pt	$10–$12
Jug, 2 qt	$15–$20
Shaker	$8–$10
Syrup	$50–$75

Beer Sets

Barrel mug, solid color	$6–$8
Flagon mug, decal	$18–$20
Flagon mug, solid color	$8–$10
Pretzel jar, decal	$75–$100
Tankard pitcher, decal	$75–$100
Tankard pitcher, solid color	$40–$50

Blue Blossom/Blue Garden

Silk-screened decal on Cobalt blue glaze. No piece is easy to find, although the Saf-handle casserole, #4, turns up with a little more frequency than the other pieces. Prices are soaring on these very popular patterns.

Pricing

The "B" and/or "G" that follows each entry indicates the decoration the piece has been found in. Price given is for either decoration.

Aladdin teapot (G)	$125–$150
Airflow teapot (B/G)	$125–$150
Ball jug, #1 (B/G)	$40–$50
Ball jug, #2 (B/G)	$40–$50
Ball jug, #3 (B/G)	$30–$40
Ball jug, #4 (B/G)	$30–$40
Banded batter bowl (B)	$60–$75

Blue Blossom Streamline teapot, Autumn Leaf bud vase, and Crocus Bingo water bottle.

Banded casserole (B)	*$45–$50*
Banded cookie jar (B/G)	*$100–$125*
Banded jug, 1½ pt (B)	*$20–$30*
Banded jug, 2 qt (B)	*$35–$45*
Banded shaker (B)	*$18–$20*
Banded syrup (B)	*$75–$85*
Big Lip bowl, 6″ (B/G)	*$25–$30*
Big Lip bowl, 7½″ (B/G)	*$30–$35*
Big Lip bowl, 8⅝″ (B/G)	*$35–$40*
Big Lip casserole, knob handle (B)	*$45–$50*
Big Lip covered drip (B/G)	*$35–$40*
Big Lip custard (B/G)	*$15–$18*
Bingo butter (B/G)	*$100–$150*
Bingo leftover (B)	*$100–$150*
Bingo water bottle (G)	*$175–$200*
Cereal set canister (B/G)	*$125–$150*
Cereal set shaker (B/G)	*$35–$45*
Doughnut jug (B)	*$60–$75*
1188 drip (B/G)	*$20–$30*
Handled shaker (B/G)	*$18–$20*

Loop handle jug (B/G)	*$50–$60*
Loop handle leftover (B/G)	*$40–$60*
Morning set creamer (B/G)	*$25–$30*
Morning set sugar (B/G)	*$30–$35*
Morning set teapot (B/G)	*$100–$125*
New England bean pot, #4 (B/G)	*$65–$75*
New York creamer (B/G)	*$35–$40*
New York sugar (B/G)	*$40–$50*
New York teapot, 6 cup (G)	*$150–$175*
100 casserole, oval, w/handle (B)	*$40–$50*
Saf-handle batter bowl (B/G)	*$80–$100*
Saf-handle casserole, #1 (B/G)	*$40–$45*
Saf-handle casserole, #4 (B/G)	*$35–$40*
Saf-handle coffee server (B/G)	*$150–$200*
Saf-handle cookie jar (B/G)	*$150–$200*
Saf-handle syrup (B/G)	*$75–$85*
Saf-handle teapot, 6 cup (B/G)	*$125–$150*
68 casserole, rd, no handle (G)	*$35–$45*
76 casserole, rd, no handle (B)	*$35–$45*
77 casserole, rd, no handle (B)	*$35–$45*
Streamline teapot, 6 cup (B/G)	*$125–$150*
Sunshine bowl (G)	*$25–$30*

Blue Bouquet

Use Taverne prices.

Coffee Pots

Solid color pots are in the $25 to $30 range, less if small. Decal-decorated coffee pots are in the $45 to $60 range, except the common drip-o-lators, which are around $35. Drip coffees with china drip sections are in the $100 to $125 range, higher price for decals and Chinese Red, lower price for other solid colors.

Crocus

Aladdin teapot	*$100–$125*
Art Deco creamer	*$12–$15*
Art Deco sugar	*$15–$18*
Ball jug, #3	*$35–$45*
Banded coffee pot	*$40–$50*
Beverage mug	*$35–$40*
Big Lip soup tureen	*$150–$175*
Bingo butter	*$175–$200*
Bingo leftover	*$150–$175*
Bingo water bottle, 7"	*$200–$225*
Boston teapot	*$50–$75*
Cake plate	*$20–$25*
Classic jug	*$70–$80*
Clover soup tureen	*$125–$150*
Colonial casserole	*$35–$45*
Colonial creamer	*$12–$15*
Colonial sugar	*$15–$18*
Colonial teapot, 6 cup	*$35–$40*
Crest drip-o-later	*$35–$45*
Dinnerware	
Cup	*$7–$8*
Dish, 5⅝"	*$4–$5*
Dish, 6"	*$5–$7*
Plate, 6⅛"	*$6–$8*
Plate, 7¼"	*$5–$7*
Plate, 8¼"	*$5–$7*
Plate, 9⅛"	*$7–$9*
Plate, 10¼"	*$12–$15*
Platter, small, 11¼"	*$12–$15*
Platter, lg, 13¼"	*$15–$18*
Saucer	*$2–$3*
Soup, 8½"	*$12–$15*
Tidbit server	*$25–$35*
Vegetable, rd, 9⅛"	*$18–$20*
Vegetable, oval, 10¼"	*$15–$18*
D-line gravy	*$18–$20*

ND = price is not determined; item too rare to price.
+ = worth at least sum indicated, but could be higher.

Doughnut teapot	*$500+*
Egg drop shaker	*$12–$15*
1188 open drip	*$20–$25*
Flute French baker	*$18–$20*
Handled shaker	*$12–$15*
Jordan drip coffee pot	*$150–$175*
J Sunshine jug	*$25–$35*
Kadota drip coffee pot	*$100–$125*
MaryLou creamer	*$8–$10*
MaryLou leftover, rect	*$25–$30*
MaryLou leftover, sq	*$30–$40*
MaryLou sugar	*$10–$12*
Meltdown creamer	*$15–$18*
Meltdown sugar	*$18–$20*
New England bean pot, #4	*$55–$65*
New England bean pot, #5	*$65–$70*
New York creamer	*$18–$20*
New York sugar	*$20–$25*
New York teapot, 2 cup	*$50–$60*
New York teapot, 6 cup	*$45–$50*
New York teapot, 8 cup	*$50–$60*
New York teapot, 12 cup	*$70–$80*
Pie baker	*$20–$22*
Pretzel jar	*$70–$80*
Salad bowl	*$15–$20*
St. Denis cup	*$15–$18*
St. Denis saucer	*$10–$12*
Step-down coffee pot, lg	*$35–$40*
Step-down coffee pot, small, w/decaled china drip	*$90–$100*
Step-down coffee pot, small, w/metal drip	*$40–$50*

Streamline teapot	*$200–$250*
Sunshine bowl, #1	*$10–$12*
Sunshine bowl, #2	*$20–$25*
Sunshine bowl, #3	*$12–$15*
Sunshine bowl, #4	*$15–$18*
Sunshine bowl, #5	*$18–$20*
Sunshine casserole	*$30–$35*
Sunshine covered drip	*$20–$25*
Sunshine jug, #4	*$20–$25*
Sunshine jug, #5	*$20–$30*

Fantasy

Most pieces are hard to find and desirable. Price 20% less than Blue Blossom.

#488

Use Crocus prices.

Meadow Flower

Meadow Flower pieces, as with Fantasy, are hard to find and desirable. Price 20% less than Blue Blossom.

Pink Morning Glory

Currently popular, add 25% to Taverne prices.

Poppy

Ball jug, #3	*$30–$35*
Bellevue coffee pot	*$100–$125*
Bellevue teapot	*$100–$125*
Boston teapot	*$50–$60*

Meadow Flower Banded cookie jar, Fantasy Sunshine casserole, and #488 Sunshine teapot.

Cake plate	*$15–$20*
Cake server	*$60–$75*
Dinnerware	
Cup	*$8–$10*
Dish, 5⅝″	*$4–$5*
Dish, 6″	*$6–$7*
Plate, 6⅛″	*$5–$6*
Plate, 7¼″	*$6–$7*
Plate, 9⅛″	*$9–$10*
Platter, oval, 11¼″	*$12–$15*
Platter, oval, 13¼″	*$15–$18*
Saucer	*$3–$5*
Soup, 8½″	*$12–$15*
Vegetable, rd, 9⅛″	*$12–$15*
Doughnut teapot	*$150–$175*
Flute French baker	*$12–$15*
Fork	*$65–$75*
Golden Key coffee pot	*$40–$45*

Golden Key creamer	*$10–$12*
Golden Key sugar	*$12–$15*
Handled shaker	*$10–$12*
Loop Handle leftover	*$40–$45*
Melody teapot	*$90–$115*
New England bean pot, #4	*$50–$60*
100 oval casserole	*$20–$25*
101 oval casserole	*$30–$40*
103 oval casserole	*$95–$110*
Pie baker	*$18–$20*
Pretzel jar	*$40–$50*
Salad bowl	*$12–$15*
76 round casserole	*$25–$30*
S-Lid coffee pot	*$40–$45*
Spoon	*$50–$60*
Streamline teapot	*$75–$100*
Sunshine bowl, #1	*$3–$4*
Sunshine bowl, #3	*$8–$10*
Sunshine bowl, #4	*$10–$12*
Sunshine bowl, #5	*$12–$15*
Sunshine bowl, #6	*$20–$25*
Sunshine bulge shaker	*$40–$50*
Sunshine casserole	*$30–$35*
Sunshine Cereal set canister	*$100–$125*
Sunshine Cereal set shaker	*$40–$50*
Sunshine covered drip	*$18–$22*
Sunshine jug, #4	*$25–$30*
Sunshine jug, #5	*$15–$20*
Three-piece mustard	*$40–$50*
Windshield teapot	*$90–$100*

Poppy and Wheat

Use Crocus prices.

Poppy & Wheat New England bean pot #3, Taverne coffee pot, and Poppy Doughnut teapot.

Red Poppy

Aladdin teapot	*$45–$55*
Ball jug, #3	*$30–$35*
Cake plate	*$15–$18*
Dinnerware	
Cup	*$4–$6*
Dish, 5⅝"	*$3–$4*
Gravy	*$18–$20*
Plate, 6¼"	*$3–$4*
Plate, 7¼"	*$4–$6*
Plate, 8¼"	*$6–$7*
Plate, 9⅛"	*$5–$7*
Platter, 11¼"	*$12–$15*
Platter, 13¼"	*$15–$18*
Saucer	*$1–$2*
Soup, 8½"	*$8–$10*
Vegetable, oval, 10½"	*$10–$12*
Vegetable, rd, 9⅛"	*$10–$12*
Egg drop shaker	*$6–$10*
1188 open drip	*$20–$25*
Flute French baker	*$12–$15*

Handled shaker	*$10–$12*
MaryLou creamer	*$7–$8*
MaryLou leftover, rect	*$35–$40*
MaryLou leftover, sq	*$45–$50*
MaryLou sugar	*$8–$9*
New York teapot	*$35–$45*
Pie baker	*$15–$18*
Rickson coffee	*$20–$25*
Rickson creamer	*$6–$8*
Rickson milk jug	*$20–$25*
Rickson sugar	*$8–$10*
Salad bowl	*$12–$15*
Sunshine bowl, #1	*$4–$5*
Sunshine bowl, #3	*$8–$10*
Sunshine bowl, #4	*$10–$12*
Sunshine bowl, #5	*$12–$15*
Sunshine casserole	*$20–$25*
Sunshine covered drip	*$16–$18*
Sunshine jug, #5	*$12–$15*

Refrigerator Ware (ca. 1940)

Many of these pieces match the design of the refrigerators they originally came with.

Pricing

All water servers are priced with lids or china-tipped corks. Bottoms alone are worth only 40% of total price.

Aristocrat

Butter	*$16–$18*
Leftover	*$10–$15*
Leftover, tan or ivory	*$15–$18*
Water server, Cobalt	*$60–$75*
Water server, Tan	*$80–$90*
Water server, tilt top	*$100–$125*

Bingo
Butter	$65–$75
Leftover	$50–$60
Water bottle, 27 oz, 7″ hi	$55–$60
Water bottle, 48 oz, 7⅝″ hi	$50–$55

Emperor
Butter	$12–$15
Leftover	$10
Water server, Delphinium	$35–$40
Water server, green	$40–$45

Hotpoint
Leftovers
Rectangular	$20–$25
#1 round	$15–$18
#2 round	$18–$20
#3 round	$20–$25
#1 square	$10–$16
#2 square	$10–$16
#3 square	$15–$20
#4 square	$20–$25
#5 square	$20–$25
Water server	$40–$50

Left to Right. Emperor, Patrician, and Aristocrat water servers.

Norris
    Water server, w/o lid   *$12–$15*

Patrician
    Butter   *$10–$15*
    Leftover   *$8–$10*
    Water server, Cobalt   *$100–$125*
    Water server, Delphinium   *$30–$35*
    Water server, Garden   *$35–$40*
    Water server, odd green   *$40–$50*

Plaza
    Water server   *$55–$65*
      w/cork   *$85–$95*

Rose Parade

Rose Parade is easy to find. It usually has a blue flower decal; occasionally you'll find a pink or pink and yellow flower decal.

Pricing

Add 20% for hard-to-find decals.

Flute French baker	*$20–$25*
Jordan drip coffee pot	*$100–$125*
Salad bowl	*$15–$18*
Sani-Grid bowl, 6⅛"	*$10–$12*
Sani-Grid bowl, 7½"	*$12–$15*
Sani-Grid bowl, 8⅞"	*$15–$18*
Sani-Grid creamer	*$8–$10*
Sani-Grid jug, small	*$15–$18*
Sani-Grid jug, medium	*$18–$20*
Sani-Grid jug, large	*$20–$25*
Sani-Grid shaker	*$10–$15*
Sani-Grid sugar	*$8–$10*
Sani-Grid teapot, 3 cup	*$30–$35*
Sani-Grid teapot, 6 cup	*$30–$35*
Straightside bowl, #1	*$10–$12*
Straightside bowl, #3	*$15*

Straightside bowl, #4	$20
Straightside bowl, #5	$25
Tab handle bean pot	$35–$40
Tab handle casserole	$25–$30
Tab handle covered drip	$15–$18

Saf-Handle

Batter bowl	$50–$60
Casserole, #1	$30–$35
Casserole, #4	$25–$30
Coffee server	$100–$125
Cookie jar	$100–$150
Sugar	$15–$18
Syrup	$40
Teapot, 8 oz	$25–$30
Teapot, 10 oz	$25–$30
Teapot, 6 cup	$60–$65

Cookie jar

Coffee server

Taverne

Ball jug, #3	$40–$45
Banded coffee pot, 9 cup	$35–$40
Banded shaker	$10–$12
Banded teapot, 6 cup	$35–$40
Beverage mug	$25–$35

Bobby berry	*$15–$18*
Bobby nappy	*$10–$15*
Classic jug	*$55–$65*
Colonial bowl, #3	*$12–$15*
Colonial bowl, #4	*$15–$20*
Colonial bowl, #5	*$20–$25*
Colonial casserole	*$25–$30*
Colonial coffee pot, 9 cup	*$35–$45*
Colonial covered drip	*$15–$18*
Colonial creamer	*$10–$12*
Colonial drip coffee	*$100–$125*
Colonial jug, #2	*$15–$18*
Colonial jug, #3	*$18–$20*
Colonial shaker	*$12–$15*
Colonial sugar	*$12–$15*
Colonial teapot, 6 cup	*$30–$35*
Dinnerware	
Cup	*$8–$10*
Dish, 5⅝″	*$5–$7*
Dish, 6″	*$6–$7*
Plate, 6⅛″	*$5–$6*
Plate, 7¼″	*$7–$8*
Plate, 9⅛″	*$8–$10*
Plate, 10″	*$10–$12*
Platter, 11¼″	*$12–$15*
Platter, 13¼″	*$15–$18*
Saucer	*$3*
Soup, 8½″	*$12–$14*
Vegetable, oval, 10½″	*$15*
Egg drop shaker	*$20–$25*
Flute French baker	*$12–$15*
Handled shaker	*$18–$20*
Kadota drip coffee pot	*$100–$125*
MaryLou creamer	*$10*
MaryLou leftover, rect	*$18–$25*
MaryLou leftover, sq	*$25–$30*
MaryLou sugar	*$12*
New England bean pot, #4	*$80–$90*

New York teapot, 6 cup	*$75–$85*
Pie baker	*$20–$25*
Pretzel jar	*$55–$65*
Salad bowl	*$12–$15*
St. Denis cup	*$12–$15*
St. Denis saucer	*$10–$12*
Streamline teapot, 6 cup	*$85–$95*
Sunshine bowl, #3	*$15–$18*
Sunshine bowl, #4	*$20–$25*
Sunshine bowl, #5	*$30–$35*
Sunshine casserole	*$35–$40*
Sunshine covered drip	*$25–$30*
Tea tile, rd, 6″	*$80–$100*

Teapots

It's important to have some experience with which colors are more common and which are more scarce. For example, a Canary yellow Parade isn't worth the low end of the range, and Maroon and Rose Windshields are the most readily found, but you'd go a long ways before you'd see any teapot in Orchid.

	Chinese Red	Gold Decorated
Airflow, 6 cup	$40–$50	$40–$50
Airflow, 8 cup	$40–$50	$40–$50
Aladdin	$40–$50	$25–$35
Albany	$75–$85	$25–$40
Automobile	$350–$400	$350–$400
Baltimore	$75–$85	$35–$45
Basket	$110–$125	$60–$90
Basketball	$350–$400	$350–$400
Birdcage	$300–$350	$150–$275
Boston	$50–$75	$20–$35
Cleveland	$85–$110	$35–$45
Doughnut	$175–$185	$150–$175
Football	$350–$400	$350–$400
French	$50–$65	$25–$40

	Chinese Red	*Gold Decorated*
Globe	$85–$95	$75–$85
Hollywood	$75–$85	$25–$50
Hookcover	$40–$45	$25–$45
Illinois	$125–$150	$100–$125
Indiana	$150–$200	$100–$150
Kansas	$150–$200	$100–$150
Los Angeles	$55–$65	$25–$40
Melody	$100–$110	$100–$110
Moderne	$65–$75	$15–$25
Nautilus	$125–$135	$55–$85
New York	$50–$75	$25–$40
Ohio	$125–$150	$100–$125
Parade	$50–$55	$25–$40
Philadelphia	$50–$75	$25–$40
Rhythm	$110–$125	$85–$120
Saf-handle	$75–$85	$55–$75
Sani-grid	$20–$25	$35–$45
Star	$150–$200	$25–$55
Streamline	$35–$45	$35–$45
Surfside	$125–$135	$55–$85
Windshield	$75–$85	$20–$35
World's Fair		$400

Wildfire

Use Taverne prices.

THE HARKER
POTTERY COMPANY

*East Liverpool, Ohio and
Chester, West Virginia*

The Harker Pottery Company was incorporated in 1890, but various Harkers had been in the pottery business before 1850. Harker produced semi-porcelain dinnerware, toilet ware, hotel ware, kitchenware, and advertising pieces. In 1931, it bought the old E. M. Knowles plant in Chester and abandoned its East Liverpool operations. The company closed in 1972.

The Cameoware line and the Hotoven kitchenware are of greatest interest to collectors.

Marks

This arrow backstamp is the common dinnerware mark.

Cameoware (1940)

The Cameoware process was brought to the United States by George Bauer, a German immigrant. It was first made here at the Bennett

153

Cameoware: Dainty Flower Octagonal tea tile, Swirl creamer and sugar; Pear Swirl salad bowl (special salad set); White Rose Skyscraper covered drip; Dainty Flower tall refrigerator jug.

Pottery in Baltimore. When that company closed, Bauer took the process to Harker which initially used it for kitchenware and specialty items. Dinnerware was added in 1941.

Cameoware was made in Blue and Pink. Some pieces have turned up in yellow. Black has been rumored but not substantiated. Harker called the common decoration Dainty Flower, and this is found on most pieces.White Rose decoration will be found on a limited number of pieces.

Cameoware decoration will be found on the Hotoven, Plain Round, Swirl, and Virginia shapes. Specialty items are listed below.

Baby feeder (rd or hex)	*$15–$20*
Jumbo cup	*$12–$15*
Jumbo saucer	*$3–$5*
Kiddo set	
Bowl	*$3–$5*
Mug	*$8–$10*
Plate	*$2–$3*

"GC"

Raised lines descend partway down the sides of these kitchenware pieces.

Bowl, 5⅜″ × 3¾″ H	$4–$5
Custard	$2–$3
Mixing bowl, 9″	$8–$10
Refrigerator jug, squat	$20–$25
Tall custard	$3–$4
Teapot	$15–$20
Tureen	$15–$20

Hotoven Kitchenware (1926)

Harker claimed this was the first decal-decorated line of ovenware made. Along with the general pieces listed here, you will find pieces from other shapes, including Zephyr, with the Hotoven mark.

Batter bowl, rope/arch, 9″	$10–$15
Batter bowl, paneled, 9¾″	$10–$15
Bean pot, ind	$3–$5
Cake server, all styles	$12–$15
Casserole, paneled, 7½″	$15–$20
Casserole, plain, 7½″	$15–$20
Casserole, plain, 8½″	$15–$20
Custard, regular	$2–$3
Custard, tall	$3–$5
Drip jar, Skyscraper	$12–$15
Flour scoop	$20 $25
Fork, all styles	$25–$35
Jug, Arches	$15–$20
Jug, Gargoyle, small	$10–$12
Jug, Gargoyle, medium	$12–$15
Jug, Gargoyle, large	$15–$20
Jug, Ohio, batter	$15–$20
Jug, Ohio, syrup	$15–$20

Kitchenware: *Left to Right. Back row:* "Carnivale" "Arches" jug, Oriental Poppy "Ribbed collar" jug, and Tulip "Gargoyle" jug. *Front row:* Ohio syrup jugs with three different lids: Cameoware (flat lid), Wampum (Deco finial), and "Wild Poppies" (open finial).

Jug, refrigerator, modern	*$20–$25*
Jug, refrigerator, rd	*$15–$20*
Jug, refrigerator, sq	*$15–$20*
Jumbo cup	*$6–$7*
Jumbo saucer	*$2–$3*
Leftover, paneled, large	*$12–$15*
Mixing bowl, 9″	*$10–$15*
Mixing bowl, 9¾″	*$10–$15*
Mixing bowl, rope/arch, 9″	*$10–$15*
Pie plate, 9″	*$6–$8*
Pie plate, 10″	*$6–$8*
Rolling pin	*$35–$45*
Shaker, Skyscraper	*$6–$8*
Spoon, all styles	*$15–$18*
Stack set, 3-piece	*$25–$30*
Stack set, 4-piece	*$35–$40*
Tea tile, oct	*$18–$20*
Teapot	*$15–$20*

Modernage

This line is characterized by a narrow, oval body; the finial on the lid is like a lifesaver. In order to expand the Modernage line, Harker put this finial on lids from other shapes, Zephyr for one, but these pieces seldom show up. The teapot, sugar, creamer, and cookie jar are usually found.

Fruits, Petitpoint, and Modern Tulip are the easily found decals.

Cake server	$12–$15
Cake tray, lug, 11½"	$4–$5
Casserole, 6"	$15–$20
Casserole, 8¾"	$15–$20
Cookie jar	$15–$20
Creamer	$4–$6
Custard	$2–$3
Drip jar	$12–$15
Fork	$25–$30
Jug, batter	$20–$25
Jug, syrup	$15–$20
Mixing bowl, 11"	$15–$18
Platter, rd, 11½"	$6–$7
Shaker, Zephyr, small	$5–$7
Spoon	$15–$18
Sugar	$8–$10
Teapot	$15–$20

"Plain Round"

This is the shape usually found with White Rose Cameoware.

Coupe soup, 7½"	$4–$5
Dish, 6"	$2–$3
Dish, 5½"	$1–$2
Dish, 5¼", thin rim	$1–$2
Dish, lug, 6"	$2–$3
Plate, 6¼"	$1–$2

Plate, 9 1/4″	$4–$5
Plate, 6 1/4″, thin rim	$1–$2
Platter, oval, 11 3/4″	$5–$6
Platter, oval, 13 1/2″	$6–$8
Saucer, 6″	$1
Vegetable, rd, 8 3/4″	$9–$10

Royal Gadroon

This line is distinguished by a gadroon edge. Many solid colors and decals were used over its long life. The colors included Chesterton (silver-mist gray), Corinthian (teal green), Celadon (Chinese gray-green), Charcoal (gray-black), Pink cocoa (beige), Celeste (sky blue), Chartreuse, Chocolate brown, light blue, pink, and yellow. Ivy is perhaps the most common decal.

Ashtray, 4 3/4″	$6–$8
Ashtray, 5 1/4″	$6–$8
Creamer	$4–$6
Cup	$4–$6
Cup, AD	$4–$6
Dish, 6″	$2–$3
Dish, covered	$6–$8
Fruit	$1–$2
Gravy	$8–$10
Onion soup	$6–$8
Pickle	$4–$6
Plate, 6 1/4″	$1–$2
Plate, 7 1/4″	$2–$4
Plate, 9 1/4″	$4–$5
Plate, 10 1/4″	$4–$5
Plate, chop	$6–$8
Plate, party, sq, 8 1/2″	$5–$6
Plate, sq, 8 1/4″	$3–$5
Platter, emb handle, 11″	$5–$6
Platter, emb handle, 13 1/2″	$6–$8
Platter, emb handle, 15 1/2″	$8–$10

Salad bowl	*$9–$10*
Saucer	*$1*
Saucer, AD	*$1–$2*
Shaker	*$5–$6*
Soup, 8½″	*$4–$5*
Sugar	*$8–$10*
Teapot	*$15–$20*
Triple-tier tidbit	*$10–$12*
Vegetable, 9″	*$9–$10*

Swirl

This shape was used primarily for Cameo Shellware, but other decorations will be found.

Bowl, lug, 6¼″	*$3–$5*
Creamer	*$4–$6*
Cup	*$4–$6*
Plate, saucer (no cup ring), 6″	*$1*
Plate, 7⅜″	*$2–$4*
Salad, rd, 9″	*$9–$10*
Sugar	*$8–$10*

Virginia

A square shape. The lug-handle platter will be found unsigned with many different decorations; a number of these may have been done by the Stetson China Company.

Ashtray	*$6–$8*
Bowl, 36s	*$4–$5*
Casserole	*$15–$20*
Creamer	*$4–$6*
Cup	*$4–$6*
Cup, AD	*$5–$8*
Dish, 5″	*$1–$2*
Dish, lug, 6⅝″	*$2–$3*

"Cottage" Virginia platter, Petitpoint Rose square refrigerator jug, and "Fruit Basket" round refrigerator jug.

Plate, 6½"	*$1-$2*
Plate, 8½"	*$3-$4*
Plate, 9½"	*$4-$5*
Platter, rect, lug, 11¼"	*$5-$6*
Platter, rect, 13¾"	*$6-$7*
Platter, sq, lug, 10¾"	*$6-$7*
Platter, sq, lug, 12¾"	*$7-$8*
Saucer	*$1*
Saucer, AD	*$1-$2*
Soup, 7¾"	*$4-$5*
Sugar	*$8-$10*
Vegetable, 8¼"	*$7-$8*

White Clover (1951)

White Clover was designed by Russel Wright. Ashtray and divided vegetable were later additions to the line.

The line was made in four colors: Golden Spice, Coral Sand, Meadow Green, and Charcoal. The Cloverleaf decoration will be found on items followed by /C. The other items are solid color only.

Ashtray/C	*$30–$35*
Casserole, covered, 2 qt/C	*$30–$35*
Chop plate, 9 1/4"	*$7–$8*
Chop plate, 10"	*$8–$10*
Chop plate, 11"/C	*$10–$12*
Clock, GE	*$60–$70*
Creamer/C	*$12–$15*
Cup/C	*$7–$9*
Dish, cereal/soup/C	*$5–$6*
Dish, fruit/C	*$3–$4*
Gravy/C	*$15–$18*
Pitcher, covered, 2 qt/C	*$35–$40*
Plate, 6"	*$4–$5*
Plate, 7 5/8"	*$5–$6*
Plate, 9 1/4"	*$6–$7*
Plate, 10"/C	*$8–$10*
Plate, 11"	*$14–$16*
Platter, 13 1/4"/C	*$16–$18*
Saucer	*$1–$2*
Shaker, either size/C	*$8–$10*
Sugar	*$10–$12*
Vegetable, divided/C	*$25–$30*
Vegetable, covered, 8 1/4"	*$25–$30*
Vegetable, 7 1/4"	*$15–$18*

Zephyr

Zephyr covered pieces will be found with two different finials, a ball knob or a deco-like wing finial.

Casserole, 1 1/2 qt, 7 1/2"	*$15–$20*
Casserole, 2 qt, 8 1/2"	*$15–$20*
Casserole, Au Gratin	*$15–$20*
Casserole tray, 8 1/4"	*$4–$5*
Casserole tray, 10 1/4"	*$4–$5*
Cheese tray, rd	*$6–$8*
Cheese box, covered	*$12–$15*

Coffee maker, 4 cup	$15–$20
Coffee maker, 6 cup	$15–$20
Coffee maker, 8 cup	$15–$20
Cookie jar	$15–$20
Custard	$2–$3
Leftover, rd, 4"	$4–$5
Leftover, rd, 5"	$6–$8
Leftover, rd, 6"	$8–$10
Mixing bowl, 10"	$15–$18
Serving bowl, 6"	$3–$5
Serving bowl, 7"	$5–$8
Serving bowl, 8"	$10–$12
Serving bowl, 9"	$12–$15
Shaker	$5–$6
Stack set, 3-piece	$25–$30
Teapot, 5 cup	$15–$20

THE HOMER LAUGHLIN
CHINA COMPANY

*East Liverpool, Ohio and
Newell, West Virginia*

Incorporated in 1896 as the Homer Laughlin China Company, the pottery started production in 1874 as the Laughlin Brothers Pottery, but Homer's brother, Shakespeare, withdrew in 1877. In 1905, a plant was built in Newell and operations grew until, in 1929, the East Liverpool plant was closed. Homer Laughlin has produced semi-porcelain dinnerware, kitchenware, and novelties. In 1959, vitreous dinnerware and institutional ware lines were introduced. The company, one of the largest in the world, is still manufacturing today.

Due to its Fiesta line, and related products, Homer Laughlin's name is synonymous with brightly colored dinnerware. Although not an originator in this field, Laughlin's superior sales organization enabled it to become a leader. Many other lines are of interest to collectors, including dinnerware designed by Frederick Rhead, head designer from 1928 to 1942, and Don Schreckengost, head designer from 1945 to 1960.

Marks

A variety of backstamps were used. The above is more common.

Americana (1949–1956)

Americana is a hybrid in terms of shape. A number of pieces were taken from the Britanny and Empress shapes, and the AD cup and saucer and the teapot were designed specifically for this line.

The only decoration consists of a series of pink underglaze American scenes based on Currier & Ives prints. The line was probably inspired by Vernon Kilns' "Our America." There is also a line called Historical American Subjects—16 in all—based on the art of Joseph Boggs Beale. It is priced the same as Americana.

Creamer	*$5–$7*
Cup	*$5–$7*
Cup, AD	*$5–$7*
Dish, 4"	*$2–$3*
Egg cup	*$10–$12*
Gravy	*$10–$12*
Pickle	*$5–$6*
Plate, 6"	*$2–$3*
Plate, 7"	*$3–$4*
Plate, 9"	*$4–$5*
Plate, 10"	*$5–$6*
Plate, chop, 13"	*$8–$10*
Plate, sq, 8"	*$4–$5*
Platter, 11"	*$6–$8*
Platter, 13"	*$8–$10*
Platter, 15"	*$12–$15*
Saucer	*$1–$2*
Saucer, AD	*$2–$3*
Soup, 9"	*$10–$12*
Sugar	*$10–$12*
Teapot	*$20–$25*

All prices given are for items in *mint* condition. In general, discoloration, crazing, chipping, and repairs will fetch lower prices.

Vegetable, covered, 9″	*$15–$20*
Vegetable, oval, 8″	*$10–$12*
Vegetable, rd	*$10–$12*

Carnival

A very short line made for Quaker Oats. There is interest because it is glazed in solid colors similar to Fiesta (although a rare decal will be found).

Cup	*$2–$3*
Dish, fruit	*$2–$3*
Dish, cereal	*$2–$3*
Plate, 6″	*$1–$2*
Plate, 9″	*$3–$4*
Saucer	*$1–$2*

Century/Riviera (1931)

Century is one of the earliest square shapes in dinnerware. Some pieces will be found with either square or oval wells. The butter dish is an early piece that was replaced by the 1-lb oblong. The disk jug and six juice tumblers made up a juice set.

When the Riviera line was created in the late thirties, it was based on the Century shape with the addition of the disk jug, mug, tumbler, and quarter-pound butter, which were designed for this line, and the shakers which were taken from the Tango shape. These extra pieces, marked with /R, have not been found with decals. Riviera was decorated in solid colors of green, ivory, mauve blue, red, and yellow. Cobalt blue pieces will be found.

Pricing

Red is at the high end of range. Add 20% for ivory without the Century mark. Hacienda and Mexicana decals are at the upper end of the range.

Butter, ¼ lb/R	*$75–$95*
Butter, ½ lb	*$65–$95*
Casserole	*$65–$75*

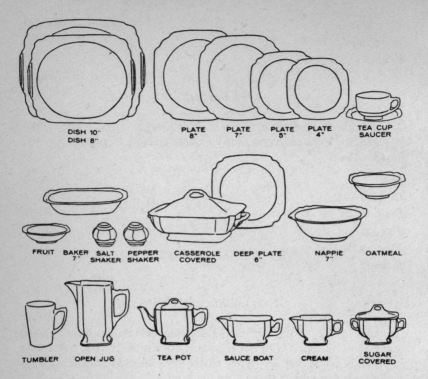

DISH 10"
DISH 8"

PLATE 8" PLATE 7" PLATE 5" PLATE 4" TEA CUP SAUCER

FRUIT BAKER 7" SALT SHAKER PEPPER SHAKER CASSEROLE COVERED DEEP PLATE 6" NAPPIE 7" OATMEAL

TUMBLER OPEN JUG TEA POT SAUCE BOAT CREAM SUGAR COVERED

Century (Riviera) shape.

Cream soup	*$40–$50*
Cream soup saucer	*$18–$20*
Creamer	*$6–$10*
Cup	*$8–$10*
Dish, 5"	*$6–$8*
Dish, 6"	*$28–$32*
Gravy	*$15–$18*
Gravy faststand	*$25–$30*
Jug, batter	*$95–$125*
Jug, disk/R	
Mauve	*$125–$145*
Red	*$150–$185*
Yellow	*$75–$90*

Jug, syrup	*$85–$95*
Pickle tray	*$15–$18*
Plate, 6½″	*$5*
Plate, 7″	*$8–$10*
Plate, 9″	*$12–$14*
Plate, 10″	*$35–$45*
Platter, 11″	*$15–$18*
Platter, 13″	*$18–$24*
Platter, 15″	*$25–$30*
Platter, sq	*$20–$25*
Saucer	*$4–$6*
Shaker (Tango)/R	*$8–$10*
Soup, 7¾″	*$12–$15*
Sugar	*$12–$15*
Teapot	*$75–$95*
Tumbler/R	*$45–$50*
Ivory	*$95–$125*
Turquoise	*$95–$125*
Tumbler, handled/R	*$65–$85*
Vegetable, oval, 9″	*$18–$22*
Vegetable, rd, 9″	*$22–$25*

Epicure

This shape was designed by Don Schreckengost and glazed in solid colors of Charcoal, Pink, Turquoise, and White.

Casserole	*$45–$50*
Coffee pot	*$40–$50*
Creamer	*$8–$10*
Cup, coffee	*$12–$15*
Dish	*$12–$15*
Gravy	*$12–$15*
Ladle	*$18–$20*
Plate, 6½″	*$6–$8*
Plate, 8½″	*$8–$10*
Plate, 10½″	*$12–$15*

Century gravy FS, Epicure coffee pot, and Mexicana Century teapot.

Saucer	*$3–$5*
Shaker, pair	*$18–$20*
Soup	*$12–$15*
Sugar	*$18–$20*

Fiesta (1936)

Fiesta was designed by Frederick H. Rhead. Some pieces were restyled in the late sixties.

The shape was introduced in Blue, Green, Ivory, Red, and Yellow. Turquoise was added in 1937, Chartreuse, Forest Green, Gray, and Rose after World War II, and Medium Green in the late fifties.

Note

Reissued in 1986, Fiesta will be found in seven colors: Apricot, Black, Cobalt, Pale Yellow, Rose (bright pink), Turquoise, and White. A number of pieces were restyled from the original and are still available and selling well as of this writing.

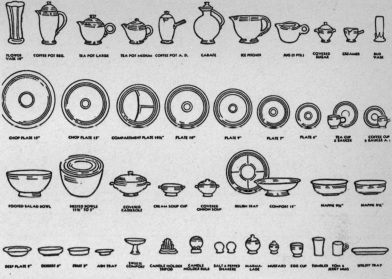

The original Fiesta assortment.

Pricing

Light Green, Turquoise, and Yellow are at the low end of the range, Cobalt and Ivory at the high end. Add 20% for Red. Add 30% to the low end for Chartreuse and Forest Green, 40% to the high end for Rose and Gray, and 60% for Medium Green.

Ashtray	*$25–$30*
Bowl, serving, 8½″	*$25–$28*
Bowl, serving, 9½″	*$32–$35*
Cake plate, flat	*$250–$350*
Candle holder, bulb	*$25–$30*
Candle holder, tripod	*$100–$110*
Carafe	*$115–$125*
Casserole	*$75–$85*
Casserole, French	*$165–$175*
Coffee pot	*$90–$95*
Coffee pot, AD	*$165–$175*
Compote, 12″	*$75–$85*
Compote, sweets	*$35–$40*

Covered onion soup	$200–$225
Cream soup	$25–$30
Creamer	$12–$14
Creamer, ind (specialty)	$45–$50
Red	$75–$85
Creamer, stick-handle	$25–$30
Cup	$18–$22
Cup, AD	$35–$40
Dish, dessert, 6″	$18–$20
Disk water pitcher	$55–$60
Egg cup	$25–$30
Fruit, 4¾″	$12
Fruit, 5½″	$12–$14
Fruit, 11¾″	$125–$145
Gravy boat	$25–$30
Grill plate, 10½″	$18–$20
Grill plate, 12″	$25–$30
Jug, ice lip	$70–$75
Jug, disk, 2 pt	$45–$50
Juice pitcher	$30–$35
Marmalade	$100–$110
Mixing bowl, #1	$60–$65
Mixing bowl, #2	$35–$40
Mixing bowl, #3	$40–$45
Mixing bowl, #4	$40–$45
Mixing bowl, #5	$55–$60
Mixing bowl, #6	$90–$100
Mixing bowl, #7	$110–$125
Mixing bowl lids, each	$175–$200
Mug	$45–$50
Mustard	$90–$95
Plate, 6″	$4–$6
Plate, 7″	$6–$8
Plate, 9″	$10–$12
Plate, 10″	$20–$22
Plate, chop, 13″	$25–$30

Plate, chop, 15″	*$30–$35*
Platter, 12½″	*$20–$25*
Relish tray (lazy Susan), 5-part	*$125–$135*
Salad, ftd, 11½″	*$225–$250*
Salad, ind, 7½″	*$45–$60*
Salad (specialty), 9½″	*$85–$95*
Saucer	*$3–$5*
Saucer, AD	*$10–$15*
Shaker	*$8*
Soup, 8¾″	*$22–$25*
Sugar	*$22–$25*
Sugar, ind (specialty)	*$70–$80*
Syrup	*$125–$135*
Teapot, medium	*$90–$95*
Teapot, large	*$125–$135*
Tray for ind cream/sugar	
Cobalt	*$85–$95*
Turquoise	*$185–$200*
Tray, utility	*$20–$22*
Tumbler, juice	*$18–$20*
Tumbler, water	*$40–$45*
Vase, 8″	*$225*
Vase, 10″	*$375*
Vase, 12″	*$400*
Vase, bud	*$40–$45*

Harlequin

Harlequin was sold as an inexpensive alternative to Fiesta, exclusively through Woolworth's. The handle is reminiscent of Salem's Tricorne shape. The butter is the Century shape.

Harlequin was decorated in solid colors which changed over the years: chartreuse, dark green, gray, light green, maroon, mauve blue, medium green, red, rose, spruce green, turquoise, and yellow.

Note

Harlequin was reissued for a few years in the early eighties.

Pricing

Add 20% for light green, maroon, medium green, red, and spruce green.

Ashtray	*$25–$30*
Ashtray, "Basketweave"	*$20–$25*
Ashtray saucer	*$45–$50*
Ball jug	*$35–$40*
Bowl, 36s	*$20–$22*
Butter, ½ lb	*$65–$95*
Candle holder	*$70–$75*
Casserole	*$60–$65*
Creamer	*$8–$10*
Creamer, "high lip"	*$25–$30*
Creamer, ind	*$10–$12*
Creamer, "novelty"	*$15–$18*
Cream soup	*$12–$15*
Cup	*$6–$7*
Cup, AD	*$15–$18*
Cup, large, tankard	*$55–$60*
Dish, 5½″	*$6–$8*
Dish, 6½″	*$18–$20*
Egg cup	*$10–$12*
Gravy	*$12–$15*
Jug, milk, 22 oz	*$20–$25*
Marmalade	*$100–$110*
Nut dish, ind	*$8–$10*
Plate, 6″	*$4*
Plate, 7″	*$6–$7*
Plate, 9″	*$8–$10*
Plate, 10″	*$20–$22*
Platter, 10″	*$20–$22*
Platter, 13″	*$22–$25*
Relish tray, 4-part	*$175–$195*
Saucer	*$2*
Saucer, AD	*$10–$12*
Shaker	*$7–$8*

Soup, 8″	$12–$14
Sugar	$12–$15
Syrup	$175–$195
Teapot	$55–$65
Tumbler	$25–$28
Vegetable, oval, 9″	$15–$18
Vegetable, rd, 9″	$18–$22

Harlequin Animals

Cat	$80–$85
Donkey	$70–$75
Duck	$60–$65
Fish	$70–$75
Lamb	$70–$75
Penguin	$60–$65

Kitchen Kraft (1937)

Kitchen Kraft was designed by Frederick H. Rhead and was officially called Kitchen Kraft Ovenserve. The fork, spoon, and cake server are from the Ovenserve line. The jug was sold both open and lidded. There is a reference in company records to a Salad Nappy.

The shape was decorated in both decals and Fiesta colors (1938) of blue, green, red, and yellow. A Serenade casserole in pastel colors was made but only the bottom has been found. This is not surprising since company records indicate that perhaps only one lid was made for every hundred bottoms.

Pricing

Red should be 20% higher. In decals, use the prices below for Mexicana and Kitchen Bouquet. Add 20% for Sun Porch and Conchita, and deduct 50% for other decals.

The mixing bowls were also glazed in Chartreuse, Forest Green, and Harlequin Yellow as an exclusive for J. C. Penney; add 20%. And they were glazed in the Jubilee colors of Celadon, Gray, and Pink; add 20%.

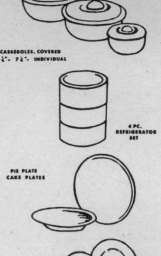

Kitchen Kraft.

Cake plate	$40–$45
Cake server	$50–$75
Casserole, ind	$95–$125
Casserole, 7 1/2 "	$65–$75
Casserole, 8 1/2 "	$65–$75
Covered jar, small	$125–$150
Covered jar, medium	$135–$165
Covered jar, large	$125–$150
Fork	$75–$90
Jug w/lid	$175–$200
Mixing bowl, 6 "	$40–$55
Mixing bowl, 8 "	$55–$65
Mixing bowl, 10 "	$65–$75
Pie baker, 9 "	$35–$40

Pie baker, 10″	*$40–$45*
Platter, oval, 13″	*$40–$50*
Refrigerator stack set, 4-piece	*$130–$165*
Shaker	*$25–$30*
Spoon	*$65–$75*

Ovenserve (1933)

Ovenserve was Homer Laughlin's first kitchenware line. The long spoon, which is hard to find, was made especially for Woolworth's.

Ovenserve was decorated in two solid colors: Melon Yellow and Orange (pumpkin). (Note: The 6″ oval bowl will be found in a variety of colors, marked both Homer Laughlin and Taylor, Smith & Taylor, because Quaker Oats commissioned both companies to manufacture this piece.)

The most common decoration is an underglaze green hand painted over the raised decoration (blue is occasionally found). You will also find a four-color underglaze polychrome decoration, as well as a decal; both applied directly over the raised design.

Bean pot	*$15–$20*
Cake server	*$15–$20*
Casserole	*$15–$20*
Casserole, French, open	*$12–$15*
Creamer	*$6–$8*
Cup	*$4–$6*
Custard	*$1–$2*
Fork	*$20–$25*
Jug	*$10–$12*
Leftover, 4 ½″	*$4–$5*
Leftover, 5 ¼″	*$6–$8*
Pie baker, oval	*$6–$8*
Pie baker, rd	*$6–$8*
Plate, 6 ½″	*$1–$2*
Plate, 7″	*$3–$4*
Plate, 9 ¼″	*$4–$5*
Saucer	*$1–$2*
Shirred egg, 6″	*$2–$4*

Shirred egg, 7"	*$2–$4*
Spoon	*$15–$20*
Spoon, long, 12"	*$20–$25*
Sugar	*$10–$12*

Rhythm

This shape was designed by Don Schreckengost. The covered vegetable bottom is the same as the open vegetable. Company records show that the Swing-shape shaker was used with Rhythm, but another shaker has also turned up.

Rhythm was decorated in solid colors of Burgundy, Chartreuse, Gray, Green (dark green), and Harlequin Yellow. Black may be found. Also decals: American Provincial (a Pennsylvania Dutch design by Don Schreckengost—the first silk-screened decal used at Homer Laughlin) and Rhythm Rose are easily found.

Creamer	*$4–$6*
Cup	*$4–$6*
Dish, 5½"	*$1–$2*
Dish, ftd, 5½"	*$2–$3*
Gravy	*$8–$10*
Jug, 2 qt	*$10–$12*
Pickle, 9"	*$4–$5*
Plate, 6"	*$1–$2*
Plate, 7"	*$2–$3*
Plate, 8"	*$3–$4*
Plate, 9"	*$4–$5*
Plate, 10"	*$4–$5*
Platter, oval, 11½"	*$5–$6*
Platter, oval, 13½"	*$6–$7*
Platter, oval, 15½"	*$8–$10*
Saucer	*$1*
Shaker (Swing)	*$4–$5*
Soup, 8"	*$4–$5*
Spoon rest	
Dark green/Yellow	*$95–$135*
Turquoise	*$145–$175*

DINNER PLATE, 10"

LUNCHEON PLATE, 9"

SALAD PLATE, 8"

PIE PLATE, 7"

TEA SAUCER

TEA CUP

BREAD & BUTTER PLATE, 6"

COVERED TEA POT -

CREAM PITCHER

COV'D. SUGAR

CEREAL SOUP, 5½"

SAUCE BOAT

WATER JUG, 2 qts.

ROUND VEGETABLE, 8½"

COUPE SOUP, 8"

COVERED CASSEROLE

FRUIT, 5¼"

SALT

PEPPER

OVAL PLATTER, 15½"

OVAL PLATTER, 13½"

OVAL PLATTER, 11½"

SAUCEBOAT STAND, or PICKLE, 9"

Rhythm dinnerware.

Sugar	*$8–$10*
Teapot	*$15–$20*
Vegetable, rd, 9″	*$9–$10*
Vegetable, covered	*$15–$20*

Riviera

See Century.

Serenade (1939)

A lightly embossed wheat sheaf decorates the shoulders and rims of this shape.

It was decorated in matte glaze pastels of blue, green, pink, and yellow.

Casserole	*$15–$20*
Creamer	*$4–$6*
Cup	*$4–$6*
Dish, 6″	*$1–$2*
Gravy	*$8–$10*
Pickle, 9″	*$4–$5*
Plate, 6¼″	*$1–$2*
Plate, 7″	*$2–$3*
Plate, 9″	*$4–$5*
Plate, 10″	*$4–$5*
Plate, chop, 13″	*$8–$10*
Platter, oval, 12½″	*$6–$7*
Saucer	*$1*
Shaker	*$6–$8*
Soup, 8″	*$5–$6*
Sugar	*$8–$10*
Teapot	*$15–$20*
Vegetable, rd, 9″	*$9–$10*

Swing (1938)

Swing has delicate round handles and finials that are easily broken.

This shape was decal decorated; the solid color shakers, easily found, were intended to go with the Rhythm shape.

Butter dish	*$10–$12*
Casserole	*$15–$20*
Coffee pot, AD	*$15–$20*
Creamer	*$4–$6*
Creamer, AD	*$5–$7*
Cream soup	*$10–$12*
Cream soup saucer	*$3–$5*
Cup	*$4–$6*
Cup, AD	*$1–$2*
Egg cup	*$5–$7*
Muffin cover	*$15–$20*
Plate, 6"	*$1–$2*
Plate, 7"	*$2–$3*
Plate, 8"	*$2–$3*
Plate, 9"	*$4–$5*

Swing AD coffee pot, Tango bowl and egg cup, and American Provincial Rhythm teapot.

Plate, 10″	*$4–$5*
Platter, 11″	*$5–$6*
Platter, 13″	*$5–$6*
Saucer	*$1*
Saucer, AD	*$1–$2*
Shaker	*$4–$5*
Soup, 8″	*$4–$5*
Sugar	*$8–$10*
Sugar, AD	*$4–$6*
Teapot	*$15–$20*
Vegetable, oval, 9″	*$9–$10*

All prices given are for items in *mint* condition. In general, discoloration, crazing, chipping, and repairs will fetch lower prices.

Tango

There was not very much Tango made but the solid color decoration on this shape makes it popular with collectors. You will find burgundy, green, mauve, blue, red, and yellow.

Casserole	*$20–$25*
Creamer	*$6–$8*
Cup	*$5–$7*
Dish, 6″	*$3–$4*
Egg cup	*$20–$25*
Plate, 6″	*$2–$3*
Plate, 7″	*$3–$4*
Plate, 9″	*$5–$7*
Plate, 10″	*$5–$7*
Platter, 11½″	*$8–$10*
Saucer	*$1–$2*
Shaker	*$6–$8*
Soup	*$8–$10*

Sugar	*$10–$12*
Vegetable, oval, 9″	*$10–$12*
Vegetable, rd, 8¾″	*$10–$12*

Virginia Rose (1933)

This is a shape name, but collectors can be misled into thinking it is the decoration name because of the Wild Rose decal most often found on this shape. The open jugs (made only for J. J. Newberry), cream soup/saucer, and shaker (made only in the fifties) are hard to find. A Century-shape butter (called oblong in company records) is often found in sets of Virginia Rose, as is the Cable-shape egg cup which was often mixed with other shapes.

Virginia Rose was produced over 20 years and you will find many decals.

Bowl, 36s	*$4–$5*
Casserole	*$15–$20*
Cream soup	*$10–$12*
Cream soup saucer	*$3–$5*
Creamer	*$4–$6*
Cup	*$4–$6*
Dish, 6″	*$1–$2*
Gravy	*$8–$10*
Gravy faststand	*$10–$12*
Jug, batter, open	*$15–$20*
Jug, syrup, open	*$15–$20*
Pickle, 9″	*$3–$4*
Plate, 6¼″	*$1–$2*
Plate, 7″	*$2–$4*
Plate, 8″	*$2–$4*
Plate, 9″	*$4–$5*
Plate, 10″	*$4–$5*
Plate, lug, 11″	*$4–$5*
Platter, 11½″	*$5–$6*
Platter, 13½″	*$6–$7*
Platter, 15½″	*$8–$10*

Saucer	*$1*
Shaker	*$5–$6*
Soup, 8½"	*$4–$5*
Sugar	*$8–$10*
Vegetable, oval, 8"	*$9–$10*
Vegetable, oval, 10"	*$9–$10*
Vegetable, rd, 9½"	*$9–$10*

Wells (1930)

Designed by Frederick Rhead, Wells is distinguished by a thin rim and open-work handles.

It was decorated in solid colors, known as Art Glazes, of Green, Peach, Rust, Vellum Ivory, and Yellow. Colors will vary, and decal decorations are a little less commonly found; look for Tulip and Palm Tree.

Ashtray	*$6–$8*
Bowl, 36s	*$4–$5*
Casserole	*$15–$20*
Coffee pot, AD	*$15–$20*

Virginia Rose batter set, Serenade gravy, Wells teapot, and Wells batter jug.

Covered toast	*$15–$20*
Creamer	*$4–$6*
Cream soup	*$10–$12*
Cream soup saucer	*$3–$5*
Cup	*$4–$6*
Cup, AD	*$4–$6*
Dish, 5"	*$1–$2*
Egg cup	*$5–$7*
Gravy	*$8–$10*
Jug, batter	*$20–$25*
Jug, syrup	*$20–$25*
Pickle	*$3–$5*
Plate, 6"	*$1–$2*
Plate, 7"	*$2–$4*
Plate, 8"	*$2–$4*
Plate, 9"	*$4–$5*
Plate, 10"	*$4–$5*
Plate, sq	*$4–$5*
Platter, 11½"	*$5–$6*
Platter, 13½"	*$6–$7*
Platter, 15½"	*$8–$10*
Saucer	*$1*
Saucer, AD	*$1–$2*
Soup	*$4–$5*
Sugar	*$8–$10*
Sugar, flat handles	*$8–$10*
Teapot	*$15–$20*
Vegetable, rd, 8¼"	*$9–$10*
Vegetable, rd, 9¼"	*$9–$10*

Yellowstone (late twenties)

Yellowstone is an octagonal shape made in an Ivory body. It was decal decorated. "Maxicana" (similar to Mexicana) is the most interesting decal; the Mexican sleeping against the cactus is Maxicana.

Bowl, 36s	*$4–$5*
Butter dish	*$10–$12*
Casserole	*$15–$20*
Creamer	*$4–$6*
Cup	*$4–$6*
Cup, AD	*$4–$6*
Cup, coffee	*$4–$6*
Dish, 5⅛"	*$1–$2*
Gravy	*$8–$10*
Jug, batter	*$15–$20*
Jug, syrup	*$15–$20*
Plate, 6"	*$1–$2*
Plate, 7"	*$2–$3*
Plate, 8¾"	*$3–$4*
Plate, lug, 10¼"	*$4–$5*
Platter, 10"	*$4–$5*
Platter, 11½"	*$5–$6*
Saucer	*$1*
Saucer, AD	*$1–$2*
Saucer, coffee	*$1–$2*
Soup, 7½"	*$4–$5*
Sugar	*$8–$10*
Teapot	*$15–$20*
Vegetable, oval, 9"	*$9–$10*
Vegetable, rd, 9½"	*$9–$10*

World's Fair/Expositions

Four Seasons plate	*$35–$45*
George Washington pitcher, 2"	
Bisque	*$25–$30*
Ivory	*$20–$25*
George Washington pitcher, 5"	*$35–$40*
Golden Gate ashtray	*$45–$50*
Golden Gate plate	*$45–$50*

Martha Washington pitcher, 2"	
Bisque	*$35–$40*
Ivory	*$30–$35*
Martha Washington pitcher, 5"	*$45–$50*
New York World's Fair plate	*$85–$95*
Potter's plate	*$30–$35*
Vase, 6"	*$90–$100*
Vase, 8"	*$90–$100*
Vase, 10"	*$90–$100*
Zodiac cup/saucer	*$55–$60*

THE A. E. HULL POTTERY COMPANY

Crooksville, Ohio

The company was started in 1905 for the manufacture of stoneware. In 1907, Hull purchased the Acme Pottery Company which made semi-porcelain dinnerware. Art ware, florists ware, kitchenware, and tile were added to the lines, and in the late thirties, Hull began introducing the matte-finished pastel art pottery for which it is best known. Production of this ware continued through the fifties. Hull is still open but no longer manufactures.

When known, the shape numbers have been included in the listings. Note that for some lines every shape and size has a separate number, and in others, the same shape in different sizes will have the same number.

Marks

Early marks include a capital "H" in either a circle or a diamond, impressed. Later marks include the words "Hull," "Hull Art," or "Hull Ware" with "USA," in block letters or script, as well as the shape number and size, either raised or impressed.

ART POTTERY

Blossom Flite

Multicolored flowers over a basketweave background of high gloss pink with blue lattice decor and green interior, or black decor with pink interior.

Pricing

Add 10% for gold trim.

Basket, T2, 6″	*$22–$28*
Basket, T4, 8½″	*$35–$50*
Basket, low, T8, 8″ × 9″	*$40–$60*
Bowl, low, handled, T9, 10″	*$40–$60*
Candleholder, pair, T11	*$25–$35*
Console bowl, T10	*$35–$45*
Cornucopia, T6, 10½″	*$35–$45*
Creamer, T15	*$20–$22*
Ewer, T13, 13½″	*$70–$100*
Honey jug, T1	*$15–$20*
Pitcher, T3, 8½″	*$35–$45*
Planter/Flower bowl, T12	*$30–$45*
Sugar, T16	*$20–$25*
Teapot, T14	*$40–$55*
Vase, handled, T7, 10½″	*$40–$50*

Bow-Knot (1949)

Bow-Knot was decorated with high-relief multicolored flowers and bows in matte finish on a background of either pink with blue, or blue with blue or turquoise. Hull was reaching perfection in detail and creativity with this most collectible line. Unfortunately, the 1950 fire destroyed the molds. The large basket, ewer, jardiniere, and vase are rare.

Basket, B25, 6½″	*$85–$95*
Basket, B12, 10½″	*$300–$400*
Basket, B29, 12″ rare	*$600–$750*
Candleholders, pair, B17	*$60–$80*
Console bowl, B16, 13½″	*$100–$125*
Cornucopia, B5, 7½″	*$40–$50*
Cornucopia, double, B13, 13″	*$80–$90*
Creamer, B21	*$40–$50*
Ewer, B1, 5½″	*$50–$60*
Ewer, B15, 13½″	*$600–$750*

Flower pot/saucer, B6	*$65–$80*
Jardiniere, B18, 5³/₄″	*$65–$75*
Jardiniere, B19, 9³/₈″	*$300–$450*
Plate/Wall plaque, B28	*$400–$500*
Sugar, B22	*$40–$50*
Teapot, B20	*$150–$200*
Vase, B2, 5″	*$40–$50*
Vase, B3, 6¹/₂″	*$45–$50*
Vase, B4, 6¹/₂″	*$55–$60*
Vase, B7, 8¹/₂″	*$70–$80*
Vase, B8, 8¹/₂″	*$65–$75*
Vase, B9, 8¹/₂″	*$70–$80*
Vase, B10, 10¹/₂″	*$125–$150*
Vase, B11, 10¹/₂″	*$125–$150*
Vase, B14, 12¹/₂″	*$350–$450*
Wall pocket, cup/saucer, B24	*$65–$85*
Wall pocket, iron, no mark	*$85–$100*
Wall pocket, pitcher, B26	*$65–$75*
Wall pocket, whisk broom, B27	*$65–$75*

Butterfly

Pink and blue flowers and butterflies with black decorate either cream-colored matte with turquoise interiors or glossy all-white pieces.

Pricing

Glossy pieces are not as popular as matte; subtract 10% to 20%.

Ashtray, heart-shape, B3	*$15–$22*
Basket, B13, 8″	*$35–$45*
Basket, B17, 10¹/₂″	*$60–$80*
Bowl, fruit, B16	*$30–$40*
Bud vase, pitcher-shape, B1	*$20–$25*
Candleholders, pair, B22	*$25–$35*
Candy dish, bonbon, B4	*$12–$15*
Candy dish, urn-shape, open, B6	*$20–$25*

Console bowl, 3 feet, B21	*$35–$45*
Cornucopia, B2, 6½"	*$20–$25*
Cornucopia, B12	*$30–$40*
Creamer, B19	*$20–$25*
Ewer, B15, 13½"	*$75–$100*
Flower dish, rect, B7	*$20–$25*
Jardiniere, B5, 6"	*$20–$25*
Lavabo set, B24/B25, 16"	*$60–$75*
Pitcher/Vase, handled, B11	*$30–$40*
Sugar, B20	*$22–$28*
Teapot, B18	*$50–$75*
Tray, divided, B23	*$40–$50*
Vase, B10, 7"	*$20–$30*
Vase, B9, 9"	*$20–$30*
Vase, B14, 10½"	*$30–$45*
Window box, B8	*$20–$30*

Calla Lily (Also called Jack-in-the-Pulpit)

Calla Lily is distinguished by embossed flowers in matte-color combinations of green, maroon, turquoise, brown, and purple, with green leaves.

Pricing

Solid purple is the most desirable; add 10% to the prices below.

Bowl, 500–32, 10"	*$60–$80*
Candleholders, pair, no mark	*$50–$75*
Console bowl, 590–33, 13"	*$60–$85*
Cornucopia, 570–33, 8"	*$35–$40*
Ewer, 506, 10"	*$100–$150*
Vase, 530–33, 5"	*$40–$50*
Vase, 504–33, 6"	*$40–$50*
Vase, 540–33, 6"	*$40–$50*
Vase, 501–33, 6½"	*$50–$60*
Vase, 502–33, 6½"	*$40–$50*

Vase, 530–33, 7″	*$50–$60*
Vase, 500–33, 7″	*$50–$60*
Vase, 550–33, 7½″	*$40–$50*
Vase, 500–33, 8″	*$50–$60*
Vase, 510–33, 8″	*$50–$70*
Vase, 520–33, 8″	*$40–$60*
Vase, 530–33, 9½″	*$175–$200*
Vase, 560–33, 10″	*$70–$100*
Vase, 570–33, 13″	*$80–$125*

Camellia

See Open Rose.

Dogwood

Decorated with raised dogwood flowers (wild rose) on matte backgrounds of blue/peach, all peach or turquoise/peach, Dogwood's popularity has been rapidly increasing. The tall ewer is rare.

Note

The teapot without a lid is sometimes sold as a watering can; value $65–$85.

Basket, 501, 7½″	*$100–$145*
Bowl, low, 521, 7″	*$45–$60*
Candleholders, pair, 512, 4″	*$70–$85*
Console bowl, 511, 11½″	*$90–$120*
Cornucopia, 522, 4″	*$25–$28*
Ewer, 520, 4¾″	*$40–$45*
Ewer, 505, 8½″ (marked 6½″)	*$70–$90*
Ewer, 519, 13½″	*$300–$400*
Jardiniere, 514, 4″	*$35–$45*
Teapot, 507, 6½″	*$150–$175*
Vase, 516, 4¾″	*$30–$40*
Vase, 517, 4¾″	*$30–$40*

Vase, 509, 6½"	*$40–$50*
Vase, 513, 6½"	*$50–$60*
Vase, 502, 6½"	*$70–$85*
Vase, 503, 8½"	*$80–$100*
Vase, 504, 8½"	*$80–$100*
Vase, 515, 8½"	*$80–$100*
Vase, 510, 10½"	*$100–$120*
Window box, 508, 10½"	*$75–$100*

Ebbtide

This line can be identified by glossy fish and seashell designs on backgrounds of chartreuse and rose or peach and turquoise.

Ashtray, Mermaid, E8	*$35–$45*
Basket, E5, 9⅛"	*$35–$45*
Basket, E11, 16½"	*$75–$85*

Ebbtide vase. *(Photo courtesy of Dave Pritchard)*

Candleholder, pair, E13, 2½″	*$15–$20*
Console bowl, E12, 15¾″	*$50–$65*
Cornucopia, E3, 7½″	*$35–$45*
Cornucopia, E9, 11¾″	*$35–$45*
Creamer, E15	*$20–$30*
Pitcher vase, E4, 8¼″	*$35–$45*
Pitcher vase, E10, 14″	*$85–$125*
Sugar, E16	*$20–$30*
Teapot, E14	*$70–$85*
Vase, bud, E1, 7″	*$20–$25*
Vase, twin fish, E2, 7″	*$20–$30*
Vase, angel fish, E6, 9¼″	*$35–$45*
Vase, fish, E7, 11″	*$40–$50*

Iris

Embossed iris flowers decorate this line on matte-finished bodies of blue and rose, all peach or rose, and peach combinations. The solid peach pieces do not seem to be as sought after as the multicolored pieces, but values are similar. The small advertising plaque is hard to find and the large one is rare.

Advertising plaque 2″ × 5″	*$350–$450*
Advertising plaque 5″ × 11″	*$800–$1000*
Basket, 408, 7″	*$85–$125*
Bud vase, 410, 7½″	*$40–$45*
Candleholders, pair, 411, 5″	*$60–$80*
Console bowl, 409, 12″	*$100–$125*
Ewer, 401, 5″	*$35–$45*
Ewer, 401, 8″	*$75–$85*
Ewer, 401, 13½″	*$175–$225*
Jardiniere, 413, 5½″	*$40–$50*
Jardiniere, 413, 9″	*$125–$160*
Rose bowl, 412, 4″	*$30–$35*
Rose bowl, 413, 7″	*$50–$60*
Vase, 402, 4¾″	*$30–$35*
Vase, 403, 4¾″	*$30–$35*

Vase, 404, 4¾"	*$30–$35*
Vase, 405, 4¾"	*$30–$35*
Vase, 407, 4¾"	*$30–$35*
Vase, 402, 7"	*$45–$55*
Vase, 403, 7"	*$45–$55*
Vase, 404, 7"	*$45–$55*
Vase, 405, 7"	*$45–$55*
Vase, 406, 7"	*$45–$55*
Vase, 407, 7"	*$45–$55*
Vase, 402, 8½"	*$65–$85*
Vase, 403, 8½"	*$65–$85*
Vase, 404, 8½"	*$65–$85*
Vase, 405, 8½"	*$65–$85*
Vase, 406, 8½"	*$65–$85*
Vase, 407, 8½"	*$65–$85*
Vase, 403, 10½"	*$110–$135*
Vase, 404, 10½"	*$110–$135*
Vase, 405, 10½"	*$110–$135*
Vase, 414, 10½"	*$110–$135*
Vase, 414, 16"	*$300–$350*

Magnolia [Matte] (1943)

This line has embossed magnolia flowers on backgrounds of either pink and blue or rose (often resembles brown) and yellow. Prices are usually identical though some collectors seem to prefer pink/blue.

Basket, 10, 10½"	*$100–$150*
Candleholders, pair, 27, 4½"	*$40–$50*
Console bowl, 26, 12½"	*$60–$70*
Cornucopia, 19, 8½"	*$30–$35*
Cornucopia, double, 6, 12½"	*$50–$65*
Creamer, 24	*$20–$22*
Ewer, 5, 7"	*$40–$50*
Ewer, 18, 13½"	*$100–$135*
Ewer, 14, 4¾"	*$22–$28*

Lamp base, 12 ½ "	*$200–$300*
Sugar, open, 25	*$20–$22*
Teapot, 23	*$60–$75*
Vase, 13, 4 ¾ "	*$18–$20*
Vase, 4, 6 ¼ "	*$20–$25*
Vase, 11, 6 ¼ "	*$20–$25*
Vase, 12, 6 ¼ "	*$25–$30*
Vase, 15, 6 ¼ "	*$20–$25*
Vase, 1, 8 ½ "	*$35–$45*
Vase, 2, 8 ½ "	*$35–$45*
Vase, 3, 8 ½ "	*$35–$45*
Vase, 7, 8 ½ "	*$40–$50*
Vase, 8, 10 ½ "	*$55–$65*
Vase, 9, 10 ½ "	*$55–$70*
Vase, 17, 12 ¼ "	*$70–$85*
Vase, 22, 12 ½ "	*$75–$90*
Vase, 21, open handles, 12 ½ "	*$75–$100*
Vase, 21, closed handles, 12 ½ "	*$90–$110*
Vase, 16, floor vase, 15 "	*$150–$200*
Vase, 20, floor vase, 15 "	*$175–$225*

Magnolia (Glossy)

Most of the shapes in the glossy line are the same as the matte; they consist of hand-painted pink or blue flowers on a solid pink glossy background.

Basket, H14, 10 ½ "	*$75–$110*
Cornucopia, H10, 8 ½ "	*$30–$40*
Cornucopia, double, H15, 12 "	*$40–$50*
Creamer, H21	*$18–$22*
Ewer, H11; 8 ½ "	*$35–$40*
Ewer, H19, 13 ½ "	*$135–$175*
Sugar, H22	*$18–$22*
Teapot, H20	*$50–$60*

Vase, H1, 5½"	*$15–$20*
Vase, H2, 5½"	*$15–$20*
Vase, H3, 5½"	*$18–$22*
Vase, H4, 6½"	*$20–$22*
Vase, H5, 6½"	*$20–$22*
Vase, H6, 6½"	*$20–$22*
Vase, H7, 6½"	*$20–$22*
Vase, H8, 8½"	*$35–$40*
Vase, H9, 8½"	*$35–$40*
Vase, H12, 10½"	*$40–$50*
Vase, H13, 10½"	*$40–$50*
Vase, H16, 12½"	*$60–$70*
Vase, H17, 12½"	*$60–$70*
Vase, H18, 12½"	*$60–$70*

Mardi Gras *(Also called Granada)*

Mardi Gras is a matte line that encompasses a variety of shapes—some plain and some with undecorated embossed flowers. Colors are: white, pink top/blue bottom, or peach/rose (on the floral pieces). Many of the vases and planters come in solid colors of pink and yellow.

Basket, 32, 8"	*$55–$65*
Basket, 65, 8"	*$45–$55*
Ewer, 31, 10"	*$50–$60*
Ewer, 66, 10"	*$45–$55*
Ewer, 63, 10½"	*$65–$85*
Planter, Madonna, 204	*$15–$20*
Vase, 47, 9"	*$18–$20*
Vase, 48, 9"	*$18–$20*
Vase, 49, 9"	*$18–$20*
Vase, 215, 9"	*$15–$20*
Vase, 216, 9"	*$15–$20*
Vase, 217, 9"	*$20–$25*
Vase, 218, 9"	*$20–$25*

Open Rose (Also called Camellia)

This is a diverse, matte-glazed line of multicolored open roses on pastel backgrounds of pink and blue or all white. Colored backgrounds are more desirable, but prices are the same as white. The 12″ vase is hard to find and the Mermaid planter is rare.

Basket, 142, 6¼″	$75–$90
Basket, 107, 8″	$100–$125
Basket, 140, 10½″	$250–$300
Basket, hanging, 132, 7″	$85–$100
Candleholders, Dove-shape, pair, 117, 6½″	$75–$90
Console bowl, 116, 12″	$110–$135
Cornucopia, 101, 8½″	$45–$55
Cornucopia, 141, 8½″	$50–$60
Creamer, 111, 5″	$25–$30
Ewer, 105, 7″	$65–$80
Ewer, 115, 8½″	$65–$85
Ewer, 106, 13¼″	$225–$300
Jardiniere, 114, 8¼″	$125–$150
Lamp base, no mark, 7¾″	$200–$250
Mermaid planter, 104, 10½″	$200–$300
Sugar, open, 112, 5″	$25–$30
Teapot, 110, 8½″	$100–$150
Vase, 127, 4¾″	$25–$30
Vase, 128, 4¾″	$25–$30
Vase, 130, 4¾″	$25–$30
Vase, 131, 4¾″	$25–$30
Vase, 113, 6¼″	$30–$40
Vase, 120, 6¼″	$35–$40
Vase, 121, 6¼″	$30–$35
Vase, 122, 6¼″	$35–$40
Vase, 133, 6¼″	$40–$50
Vase, 134, 6¼″	$30–$40
Vase, 135, 6¼″	$30–$35
Vase, 136, 6¼″	$35–$40
Vase, 137, 6¼″	$35–$40

Vase, 138, 6¼"	$35–$45
Vase, 123, 6½"	$40–$55
Vase, 102, 8½"	$50–$75
Vase, 103, 8½"	$50–$65
Vase, 108, 8½"	$50–$65
Vase, 119, 8½"	$45–$60
Vase, 143, 8½"	$50–$75
Vase, 124, 12"	$150–$200
Vase, bud, 129, 7"	$35–$45
Vase, hand, 126, 8½"	$110–$135
Vase, lamp shape, 139, 10½"	$175–$225
Vase, swan shape, 118, 6½"	$40–$50
Wall pocket, 125, 8½"	$150–$200

Orchid (1939)

Orchids decorate rose/cream, blue/rose, or all-blue matte-finished backgrounds. Pieces in this very collectible line have been increasingly difficult to locate lately, especially larger items such as the 9½" jardiniere.

Basket, 305, 7"	$150–$225
Bookends, pair, 316, 7"	$250–$300
Bowl, low, 312, 7"	$45–$55
Candleholders, 315, 4", pair	$60–$75
Console bowl, 314, 13"	$150–$175
Ewer, 311, 13"	$250–$300
Jardiniere, 317, 4¾"	$35–$45
Jardiniere, 310, 6"	$60–$80
Jardiniere, 310, 9½"	$200–$250
Lamp base, unmarked	$250–$300
Vase, 304, 4½"	$35–$40
Vase, 301, 4¾"	$35–$40
Vase, 302, 4¾"	$35–$40
Vase, 303, 4¾"	$35–$40
Vase, 307, 4¾"	$35–$45

Vase, 308, 4¾"	*$35–$40*
Vase, 301, 6"	*$40–$50*
Vase, 302, 6"	*$40–$50*
Vase, 303, 6"	*$40–$50*
Vase, 304, 6"	*$40–$50*
Vase, 300, 6½"	*$40–$50*
Vase, 307, 6½"	*$40–$50*
Vase, 308, 6½"	*$40–$50*
Vase, 301, 8"	*$60–$75*
Vase, 302, 8"	*$60–$75*
Vase, 303, 8"	*$60–$75*
Vase, 307, 8"	*$60–$75*
Vase, 308, 8"	*$60–$75*
Vase, 309, 8"	*$60–$75*
Vase, 304, 8½"	*$70–$85*
Vase, 301, 10"	*$125–$150*
Vase, 302, 10"	*$125–$150*
Vase, 303, 10"	*$125–$150*
Vase, 307, 10"	*$125–$150*
Vase, 304, 10¼"	*$125–$150*
Vase, 308, 10½"	*$125–$150*
Vase, bud, 306, 6¾"	*$40–$50*

Parchment and Pine

This line was decorated with pine cone sprays on glossy backgrounds of browns or greens. Larger pieces are getting scarce; cornucopias seem to be commonplace.

Ashtray, S14	*$70–$80*
Basket, S3, 6"	*$40–$50*
Basket, S8, 16"	*$70–$90*
Candleholder, pair, S10, 2¾"	*$30–$35*
Console bowl, S9, 16"	*$40–$50*
Cornucopia, S2, 8"	*$18–$22*
Cornucopia, S6, 12"	*$30–$40*
Creamer, S12	*$18–$20*
Ewer, S7, 13½"	*$80–$100*

Planter, S5	*$25–$35*
Sugar, S13	*$18–$20*
Teapot, S11	*$50–$60*
Teapot, tall, S15, 8″	*$80–$100*
Vase, S1, 6″	*$15–$20*
Vase, S4, 10″	*$50–$60*

Poppy

A matte line with hand-painted raised poppy flowers in pink and blue or pink and cream. Poppy has been getting more difficult to find and seems to be as popular as Bow-Knot. The large basket and ewer are rare.

Basket, 601, 9″	*$150–$200*
Basket, 601, 12″	*$350–$450*
Cornucopia, 604, 8″	*$75–$85*
Ewer, 610, 4¾″	*$40–$50*
Ewer, 610, 13½″	*$300–$450*
Jardiniere, 603, 4¾″	*$75–$85*
Jardiniere, 608, 4¾″	*$50–$65*
Lamp base, no mark	*$200–$250*
Planter/bowl, 602, 6½″	*$65–$85*
Vase, 605, 4¾″	*$35–$50*
Vase, 606, 4¾″	*$35–$50*
Vase, 607, 4¾″	*$35–$50*
Vase, 611, 4¾″	*$35–$50*
Vase, 612, 4¾″	*$35–$50*
Vase, 605, 6½″	*$50–$70*
Vase, 606, 6½″	*$50–$70*
Vase, 607, 6½″	*$50–$70*
Vase, 611, 6½″	*$50–$70*
Vase, 612, 6½″	*$50–$70*
Vase, 605, 8½″	*$75–$90*
Vase, 606, 8½″	*$75–$90*
Vase, 607, 8½″	*$75–$90*
Vase, 611, 8½″	*$75–$90*
Vase, 612, 8½″	*$75–$90*

Vase, 605, 10½″	*$125–$200*
Vase, 606, 10½″	*$125–$200*
Vase, 607, 10½″	*$125–$200*
Vase, 611, 10½″	*$125–$200*
Vase, 612, 10½″	*$125–$200*
Wall pocket, 609, 9″	*$150–$180*

Rosella

Rosella was decorated with glossy wild rose designs on either white or coral backgrounds. Flowers are found in either pink or white, with or without green painted leaves. One piece of R1 has been found in a matte finish. There are both left- and right-handed versions of R9 and R11; values are the same.

Basket, R12, 7″	*$75–$100*
Cornucopia, R13, 8½″	*$35–$45*
Creamer, R4, 5 12″	*$20–$25*
Ewer, R9, 6½″	*$30–$35*
Ewer, R11, 7″	*$40–$50*
Ewer, 9½″	*$125–$175*
Lamp base (from R2 vase)	*$100–$150*
Lamp base, L3, 11″	*$150–$250*
Lamp base, no mark, 10¾″	*$200–$275*
Sugar, open, R3, 5½″	*$20–$25*
Vase, R1, 5″	*$18–$22*
Vase, R2, 5″	*$18–$22*
Vase, R5, 6½″	*$20–$30*
Vase, R7, 6½″	*$20–$30*
Vase, R8, 6½″	*$35–$40*
Vase, R14, 8½″	*$40–$45*
Vase, R15, 8½″	*$40–$45*
Wall pocket, R10	*$40–$50*

Serenade

This line has birds on branches. Pieces are either pastel blue with yellow interior, pink with pearl-gray interior, or yellow with greenish interior.

Pricing

Add 10% for gold trim.

Ashtray, S23, 13″	*$40–$50*
Basket, bonbon, S5, 6¾″	*$30–$40*
Basket, S14, 12″	*$125–$190*
Bowl, ftd fruit, S15, 11½″	*$40–$60*
Candleholder, pair, S16, 6½″	*$30–$35*
Casserole, S20, 9″	*$40–$55*
Cornucopia, S10, 11″	*$25–$30*
Creamer, S18	*$15–$18*
Ewer, S8, 8½″	*$35–$45*
Ewer, S13, 13¼″	*$125–$200*
Mug, S22, 8 oz.	*$35–$45*
Pitcher, beverage, S21	*$50–$60*
Pitcher vase, S2, 6½″	*$25–$30*
Sugar, S19	*$15–$18*
Teapot, S17	*$50–$60*
Urn, no cover, S3, 5¾″	*$15–$20*
w/cover	*$30–$35*
Vase, S7, 8½″	*$25–$30*
Vase, S6, 8½″	*$25–$30*
Vase, S12, 14″	*$35–$50*
Vase, bud, S1, 6½″	*$20–$25*
Vase, hat, S4, 7¼″	*$25–$35*
Vase, rect, S11, 10½″	*$30–$35*
Window box, S9, 12½″	*$25–$30*

Sueno Tulip

Hand-painted tulips are featured on this popular matte-finish line in cream/blue, pink/blue, or all blue coloration.

Basket, 102–33, 6″	*$80–$100*
Ewer, 109, 8″	*$65–$85*
Ewer, 109–33, 13″	*$140–$185*
Flower pot/Saucer, 116–33, 4¾″	*$35–$45*
Flower pot/Saucer, 116–33, 6″	*$55–$75*

Jardiniere, 117–30, 5″	*$35–$45*
Jardiniere, 115–33, 7″	*$95–$125*
Vase, 100–33, 4″	*$30–$40*
Vase, 103–33, 6″	*$65–$85*
Vase, 104–33, 6″	*$35–$45*
Vase, 106–33, 6″	*$30–$40*
Vase, 107–33, 6″	*$30–$40*
Vase, 108–33, 6″	*$30–$40*
Vase, 110–33, 6″	*$30–$40*
Vase, 111–33, 6″	*$30–$40*
Vase, 100–33, 6½″	*$30–$40*
Vase, 101–33, 6½″	*$50–$75*
Vase, 100–33, 8″	*$50–$65*
Vase, 105–33, 8″	*$50–$75*
Vase, 107–33, 8″	*$50–$65*
Vase, 101–33, 9″	*$65–$85*
Vase, 100–33, 10″	*$80–$125*
Vase, 101–33, 10″	*$100–$125*

Sunglow

The line has pink or yellow high-gloss backgrounds with either pink or yellow flowers, and sometimes butterflies and bows. Some Bow-Knot molds were used for Sunglow pieces.

Basket, 84, 6½″	*$25–$30*
Bell, no mark	*$35–$40*
Bowl, 50, 5½″	*$10–$12*
Bowl, 50, 7½″	*$15–$18*
Bowl, 50, 9½″	*$20–$22*
Casserole, 51, 7½″	*$20–$25*
Cornucopia, 96, 8½″	*$30–$35*
Drip jar, 53	*$15–$20*
Ewer, 90, 5½″	*$15–$18*
Flower pot, 97, 5½″	*$15–$20*
Flower pot, 98, 7½″	*$20–$30*
Pitcher, 52, 24 oz	*$20–$24*

Pitcher, 55, 7½"	$40–$50
Planter, hanging, 99, 7"	$30–$40
Shaker, pair, 54	$8–$10
Vase, 88, 5½"	$10–$15
Vase, 89, 5½"	$10–$15
Vase, 92, 6½"	$15–$20
Vase, 93, 6½"	$15–$20
Vase, 100, 6½"	$25–$30
Vase, 94, 8"	$20–$25
Vase, 95, 8½"	$20–$25
Vase, flamingo, 85, 8¾"	$18–$24
Wall pocket, cup/saucer, 80	$25–$30
Wall pocket, iron	$28–$35
Wall pocket, pitcher, 81	$20–$26
Wall pocket, whisk broom, 82	$22–$28

Thistle

Embossed thistle flowers are featured on solid matte backgrounds of pink, blue, or turquoise.

Vase, 51, 6½"	$25–$35
Vase, 52, 6½"	$25–$35
Vase, 53, 6½"	$25–$35
Vase, 54, 6½"	$25–$35

Tokay (1958)

This line was renamed Tuscany in 1960. Names are used interchangeably. It was decorated with embossed grapes and leaves on high-gloss bodies of white and green or light green and pink. Tuscany is identical in color but some literature mentions solid pink with gray-green. We believe both lines are identical.

Pricing

Prices are the same for all colors, though pink and green seem to be more popular.

Basket, 6, 8"	*$30–$40*
Basket, 11, 10½"	*$35–$40*
Basket, 15, 12"	*$45–$65*
Bowl, fruit, 7, 9½"	*$60–$75*
Candy dish, covered, 9C, 8½"	*$30–$40*
Consolette, 14, 15¾"	*$55–$75*
Cornucopia, 1, 6½"	*$15–$20*
Cornucopia, 10, 11"	*$25–$30*
Creamer, 17	*$20–$25*
Ewer, 3, 8"	*$30–$35*
Ewer, 13, 12"	*$100–$150*
Ewer, 21, 16"	*$150–$200*
Leaf dish, 19, 15"	*$15–$18*
Planter, 9, 5½"	*$20–$25*
Sugar, 18	*$20–$25*
Teapot, 16	*$50–$75*
Urn, 5, 5½"	*$15–$20*
Vase, 2, 6"	*$15–$20*
Vase, 4, 8½"	*$20–$25*
Vase, 8, 10"	*$25–$30*
Vase, 12, 12"	*$25–$30*
Vase, floor, 20, 15"	*$50–$75*

Tropicana

This very rare and underpriced line consists of high-gloss Caribbean figures on a pure white background. Molds from the Continental line were used. The scarceness is partly due to Tropicana's issue in 1959–1960 during the Cuban crisis. It simply was not popular during this era and there is speculation that a lot of the product was destroyed because of the international situation.

Ashtray, 52, 10"	*$125–$175*
Basket, 55, 12¾"	*$250–$300*
Flower bowl, 51, 15½"	*$150–$200*
Pitcher, 56, 12½"	*$350–$450*
Planter vase, 57, 14½"	*$200–$250*

Vase, flat sided, 53, 8½"	*$125–$175*
Vase, 54, 12½"	*$150–$200*

Tuscany

See Tokay.

Water Lily

This line was decorated with bold water lilies on pastel backgrounds of either brown and peach or pink and turquoise; the latter is more popular.

Basket, L14, 10½"	*$125–$150*
Candleholder, pair, L22, 4½"	*$50–$55*
Console bowl, L21, 13½"	*$75–$90*
Cornucopia, L7, 6½"	*$35–$45*
Cornucopia, double, L27, 12"	*$70–$80*
Creamer, L19	*$25–$30*
Ewer, L3, 5½"	*$30–$35*
Ewer, L17, 13½"	*$160–$200*
Flower pot/Saucer, L25, 5½"	*$50–$60*
Jardiniere, L23, 5½"	*$40–$50*
Jardiniere, L24, 8½"	*$100–$135*
Lamp base, no mark, 7½"	*$100–$125*
Sugar, L20	*$25–$30*
Teapot, L18	*$80–$90*
Vase, LA, 8½"	*$60–$75*
Vase, L1, 5½"	*$25–$30*
Vase, L2, 5½"	*$25–$30*
Vase, L3, 5½"	*$30–$35*
Vase, L4, 6½"	*$30–$35*
Vase, L5, 6½"	*$25–$30*
Vase, L6, 6½"	*$25–$35*
Vase, L8, 8½"	*$50–$60*
Vase, L9, 8½"	*$50–$65*
Vase, L10, 9½"	*$50–$65*

Vase, L11, 9½"	*$50–$65*
Vase, L12, 10½"	*$65–$75*
Vase, L13, 10½"	*$70–$80*
Vase, L15, 12½"	*$125–$150*
Vase, L16, 12½"	*$100–$135*

Wildflower (Numbered, old series)

Wildflower sprays are featured in blue/pink or pink/brown colors. There are also a lot of yellow/blue pieces with gold trim. Larger items are quite scarce since their very ornate design renders them fragile. /* identifies pieces that are identical to regular Wildflower.

Basket, 65, 7"	*$125–$150*
Basket, 68, 10"	*$400–$500*
Candleholder, double, 69	*$40–$50*
Console bowl, 70, 12"	*$100–$125*
Cornucopia, 58, 6¼"	*$40–$55*
Creamer, 73	*$40–$50*
Ewer, 57, 4½"	*$60–$70*
Ewer, 55, 13½"/*	*$250–$300*
Jardiniere, 64, 4"	*$40–$50*
Sugar, open, 74	*$40–$50*
Teapot, 72	*$135–$200*
Vase, 56, 4½"	*$45–$55*
Vase, 52, 6¼"	*$40–$50*
Vase, 60, 6¼"	*$45–$55*
Vase, 62, 6¼"	*$45–$55*
Vase, 63, 6¼"	*$45–$55*
Vase, 51, 8½"	*$50–$65*
Vase, 53, 8½"/*	*$60–$75*
Vase, 61, 8½"	*$60–$75*
Vase, 67, 8½"	*$100–$135*
Vase, 76, 8½"	*$60–$75*
Vase, 75, 8½"	*$60–$75*
Vase, 78, 8½"	*$125–$150*
Vase, 59, 10½"	*$75–$90*
Vase, 71, 12"	*$200–$250*

Wildflower (Regular)

Pink/blue and yellow/rose combinations of hand-decorated wildflowers decorate this matte finish line. Flowers are often brighter than in the old series.

Basket, W16, 10½"	$100–$135
Candleholders, pair, no mark	$40–$50
Console bowl, W21, 12"	$60–$75
Cornucopia, W7, 7½"	$25–$30
Cornucopia, W10, 8½"	$30–$35
Ewer, W2, 5½"	$25–$35
Ewer, W11, 8½"	$55–$70
Ewer, W19, 13½"	$150–$200
Lamp base, W17, 12½"	$150–$200
Vase, W1, 5½"	$20–$22
Vase, W3, 5½"	$20–$25
Vase, W4, 6½"	$30–$35
Vase, W5, 6½"	$30–$35
Vase, W6, 7½"	$30–$35
Vase, W8, 7½"	$30–$40
Vase, W9, 8½"	$45–$60
Vase, W12, 9½"	$40–$55
Vase, W13, 9½"	$40–$50
Vase, W14, 10½"	$60–$70
Vase, W15, 10½"	$65–$75
Vase, W17, 12¼"	$75–$90
Vase, W18, 12½"	$75–$90
Vase, W20, 15½"	$200–$250

Woodland Matte (1949)

Pieces in this line were made before the 1950 fire. Matte-finish items have multicolored floral designs on background of yellow/green or rose/peach. Pink flowers are on both sides of the pieces. A number of all-white flossy pieces exist, some with gold trim; values are the same as the other pieces as these do not appeal to all collectors.

Basket, W9, 8¾"	$75–$85
Basket, W22, 10½"	$300–$400

Candleholder, pair, W30, 3½″	*$75–$85*
Console bowl, W29, 14″	*$80–$125*
Cornucopia, W2, 5½″	*$30–$35*
Cornucopia, W5, 6¼″	*$30–$40*
Cornucopia, W10, 11″	*$40–$55*
Cornucopia, double, W23, 14″	*$200–$300*
Creamer, W27	*$35–$45*
Ewer, W3, 5½″	*$35–$40*
Ewer, W6, 6½″	*$40–$50*
Ewer, W24, 13½″	*$300–$350*
Flower pot/Saucer, W11, 5¾″	*$60–$80*
Jardiniere, W7, 5½″	*$40–$50*
Jardiniere, hanging, W12, 7½″	*$200–$250*
Jardiniere, W21, 9½″	*$350–$450*
Planter, hanging, W31, 5¾″	*$80–$95*
Sugar, W28	*$35–$45*
Teapot, W26	*$175–$200*
Vase, W1, 5½″	*$30–$35*
Vase, W4, 6½″	*$30–$40*
Vase, W8, 7½″	*$35–$40*
Vase, W17, 7½″	*$70–$85*
Vase, W16, 8½″	*$50–$60*
Vase, W18, 10½″	*$90–$120*
Vase, W25, 12½″	*$225–$275*
Vase, double bud, W15, 8½″	*$50–$60*
Wall pocket, W13, 7½″	*$60–$75*
Window box, W14, 10″	*$40–$50*
Window box, W19, 10½″	*$50–$60*

Woodland Matte (1950)

These pieces were made after the fire (not every item in the original line was remade). They are similar to the previous line with the exception of the finish, which was of poorer quality, and the lack of fine detail. There is only a pink flower on the front side and leaves on the reverse. Post-fire pieces are more difficult to find than the earlier ones, but are not as desirable.

Basket, W9, 8¾"	*$75–$85*
Basket, W22, 10½"	*$300–$400*
Candleholder, pair, W30, 3½"	*$40–$60*
Console bowl, W29, 14"	*$65–$75*
Cornucopia, W2, 5½"	*$30–$35*
Cornucopia, W10, 11"	*$40–$55*
Creamer, W27	*$35–$45*
Ewer, W3, 5½"	*$35–$40*
Ewer, W6, 6½"	*$40–$50*
Ewer, W24, 13½"	*$300–$350*
Flower pot/Saucer, W11, 5¾"	*$60–$80*
Jardiniere, W7, 5½"	*$40–$50*
Sugar, W28	*$35–$45*
Teapot, W26	*$175–$200*
Vase, W4, 6½"	*$30–$40*
Vase, W8, 7½"	*$35–$40*
Vase, W16, 8½"	*$50–$60*
Vase, W18, 10½"	*$90–$120*
Vase, double bud, W15, 8½"	*$50–$60*
Wall pocket, W13, 7½"	*$60–$75*
Window box, W14, 10"	*$40–$50*

Woodland Glossy (1950)

This line is the same as the 1950 matte line, but it was decorated in glossy colors of peach/pink, chartreuse/rose, or blue/dark green. Pieces are easily found with gold trim.

Pricing

If you find white with gold, add 10%.

Basket, W9, 8¾"	*$40–$50*
Basket, W22, 10½"	*$90–$135*
Candleholder, pair, W30, 3½"	*$30–$35*
Console bowl, W29, 14"	*$40–$50*
Cornucopia, W2, 5½"	*$15–$20*
Cornucopia, W10, 11"	*$30–$35*

Creamer, W27	*$15–$20*
Ewer, W3, 5½″	*$20–$25*
Ewer, W6, 6½″	*$30–$35*
Ewer, W24, 13½″	*$120–$150*
Flower pot/Saucer, W11, 5¾″	*$35–$45*
Jardiniere, W7, 5½″	*$30–$35*
Lamp base, on pedestal, similar to teapot	*$600–$750*
Lamp base, similar to W24, 14¾″	*$300–$350*
Sugar, W28	*$15–$20*
Teapot, W26	*$45–$60*
Vase, W4, 6½″	*$20–$25*
Vase, W8, 7½″	*$25–$30*
Vase, W16, 8½″	*$35–$42*
Vase, W18, 10½″	*$40–$50*
Vase, double bud, W15, 8½″	*$30–$40*
Wall pocket, W13, 7½″	*$30–$40*
Window box, W14, 10″	*$30–$40*

KITCHENWARE

Not all of Hull's very early or late kitchenware is collectible. Some of the early ware, when unmarked, is not distinguishable from similar products made at the same time.

Cinderella (1948)

This line consists of two hand-painted, underglaze decorations on yellow or white backgrounds: (1) "Blossom"—a large yellow flower, or (2) "Bouquet"—three flowers: a yellow, blue, and pink.

Bowl, 20, 5½″	*$15–$20*
Bowl, 20, 7½″	*$25–$30*
Bowl, 20, 9½″	*$30–$35*
Casserole, 21, 7½″	*$25–$30*
Casserole, 22, 8½″	*$35–$40*
Cookie jar, 30, 10″	*$75–$90*
Creamer, 28	*$20–$25*

Grease jar, 24, 32 oz	*$30–$40*
Pitcher, 29, 16 oz	*$25–$30*
Pitcher, 29, 32 oz	*$30–$35*
Pitcher, ice lip, 22, 64 oz	*$60–$70*
Serving dish, sq, 9½″	*$40–$50*
Shaker, range, pair, 25	*$25–$30*
Sugar, 27	*$20–$25*
Teapot, 26	*$60–$75*

Early Utility

Issued in the 1920s, most pieces are either green or yellow, or have colored bands on solid-colored bodies, though many variations exist.

Bowl, green, 421, 7″	*$15–$20*
Bowl, fluted, 106, 5″	*$10–$15*
Canister, "Sugar," Wheat, 6½″	*$40–$50*
Casserole, 113, 7½″	*$30–$40*
Flower pot/Saucer, 538	*$15–$20*
Jar, "Mustard," Wheat, 3½″	*$30–$35*
Mug, "Chocolate Soldier," 3¾″	*$15–$20*
Mug, "Happy Days," 497	*$15–$20*
Pitcher, fluted, 107, 4¾″	*$15–$20*
Pretzel jar, 9½″	*$125–$175*
Same, hand-painted	*$225–$300*
Salt box, fluted, 111, 6″	*$65–$80*
Stein, 496, 6½″	*$25–$35*
Stein, 498, 6½″	*$25–$35*
Stein, 499, 6½″	*$15–$18*
Tankard, 492, 9½″	*$100–$150*

Little Red Riding Hood

This was a figural line featuring Red Riding Hood and the Wolf with hand-painted detail and floral decals (usually Poppy) on a gloss white background, with or without gold and red trim. Gold trim is fairly common. Some all-white pieces will be found; these are less popular.

The advertising plaque and baby dish are extremely rare. The water pitcher with the ruffled skirt may be unique. The 4 1/2 " mustard and shakers are hard-to-find sizes. Several types of mustard spoons exist, with and without floral decals. A wall bank with slot in top of head is too rare to price.

This line is not only popular among Hull collectors, but is sought by many others as well. For more on this subject, we refer you to Mark Supnick's *Collecting Hull Pottery's Little Red Riding Hood* (see Bibliography).

Note

Beware of Mexican cookie jars that closely resemble Hull's. Identification: they are slightly smaller in height and overall size.

Advertising plaque	*$3000+*
Baby dish	*$2000+*
Bank, standing, 7 "	*$200–$250*
Bank, wall, slot in basket	*$500–$600*
Butter dish	*$200–$250*
Canister, blank	*$300–$350*
Canister, cereal	*$325–$400*
Canister, coffee	*$300–$350*
Canister, flour	*$300–$350*
Canister, popcorn	*$600–$650*
Canister, potato chips	*$600–$650*
Canister, pretzels	*$600–$650*
Canister, salt	*$325–$400*
Canister, sugar	*$300–$350*
Canister, tea	*$300–$350*
Canister, tidbits	*$600–$650*
Casserole dish, red handle	*$550–$700*

ND = price is not determined; item too rare to price.
+ = worth at least sum indicated, but could be higher.

Cookie jar (dozens of floral variations)	*$80–$100*
Cookie jar (poinsettias)	*$150–$165*
Covered jar, basket in front, 8 ½ "	*$160–$200*
Covered jar, basket on side, 9 "	*$150–$185*
Creamer, side open	*$50–$60*
Creamer, spout on top of head	*$75–$85*
Creamer, ruffled skirt	*$100–$125*
Grease jar, Wolf	*$350–$450*
Jar, allspice	*$300–$350*
Jar, cinnamon	*$300–$350*
Jar, cloves	*$300–$350*
Jar, ginger	*$300–$350*
Jar, nutmeg	*$300–$350*
Jar, pepper	*$300–$350*
Jars, set of six	*$2000–$2300*
Jug, batter, 5 ½ "	*$80–$125*
Jug, milk, 8 "	*$125–$140*
Jug, water, ruffled skirt, 8 "	*$1000+*
Lamp	*$700–$800*
Match holder, 5 ¼ " (2 styles)	*$400–$450*
Mug, hot chocolate	*$400–$450*
Mustard jar, w/spoon, 5 ½ "	*$175–$195*
Without spoon, 5 ½ "	*$125–$135*
Mustard jar, 4 ½ "	*$200–$250*
Planter, basket on side	*$1200*
Shaker, pair, 3 ½ "	*$25–$30*
Shaker, pair, 4 ½ "	*$200*
Shaker, pair, 5 ½ "	*$50–$60*
Shaker, sugar (4 holes on top)	*$25–$40*
String holder, 9 "	*$700–$850*
Sugar, side open	*$50–$60*
Sugar, "creeping," hands on table	*$75–$90*
Sugar, ruffled skirt	*$100–$125*
Teapot	*$125–$150*
Wall pocket/planter	*$250–$325*

MISCELLANEOUS

Early Art Ware

Most of these pieces consist of multicolored banded vases and jardinieres predominantly in high-gloss red, blue, and green. Most have the circle "H" mark. Literally hundreds of pieces are known.

Flower pot/attached saucer	*$35–$45*
Jardiniere, 4"	*$20–$30*
Jardiniere, 6½"	*$40–$50*
Jardiniere, 546, 7"	*$40–$50*
Jardiniere, 550, 7"	*$40–$60*
Jardiniere, elephants around rim, 7½"	*$50–$70*
Pitcher, 27–30, 4"	*$50–$75*
Pitcher, 27, 6½"	*$80–$100*
Vase, 40, 7"	*$25–$30*
Vase, 32, 8"	*$20–$25*
Vase, 26, 8"	*$20–$25*
Vase, 39, 8"	*$25–$30*
Vase, rounded, 5½"	*$25–$30*

Novelties

Bank, Corky Pig, 1957/58 issue	*$20–$25*
Bank, "Dime Bank"	*$30–$40*
Bank, dinosaur (Sinclair)	*$60–$80*
Bank, pig, 14"	*$40–$50*
Candleholder, Bandanna Duck	*$12–$18*
Capri basket, 70, 6½"	*$15–$20*
Cornucopia, 64, 10"	*$10–$12*
Fiesta basket, 44	*$15–$20*
Fiesta cornucopia, 49, 8½"	*$20–$25*
Fiesta ewer, 48, 8¾"	*$20–$30*
Fiesta flower pot, 43, 6"	*$15–$20*
Fiesta strawberry vase, 44, 8½"	*$25–$28*
Fiesta vase, deer, 50	*$25–$30*

Figure, Bandanna Duck, 76	*$8–$10*
Figure, Bandanna Duck, 75	*$12–$15*
Figure, Bandanna Duck, 74	*$20–$25*
Figure, dachshund, 14″	*$50–$60*
Figure, love birds, 93	*$15–$20*
Figure, rabbit, 5½″	*$20–$25*
Figure, rooster, 951	*$20–$25*
Figure, swan, 69, 8½″	*$10–$15*
Figure, swing band, 5 different, each	*$30–$35*
Flower frog, 10½″	*$30–$45*
Imperial Madonna, F7	*$10–$12*
Imperial Madonna, 81	*$12–$15*
Imperial swan planter, 81, 10½″	*$20–$25*
Liquor bottle (Leeds)	*$15–$20*
Planter, angel face	*$30–$35*
Planter, baby, 92, 5½″	*$12–$15*
Planter, basket girl, 954	*$12–$15*
Planter, dancing girl, 955	*$22–$25*
Planter, dog w/yarn, 88	*$12–$15*
Planter, geese (pair), 95, 7¼″	*$20–$25*
Planter, giraffe, 115	*$15–$20*
Planter, girl pig	*$20–$25*
Planter, goose (long-neck), 411, 10½″	*$25–$30*
Planter, kitten w/thread, 89	*$12–$15*
Planter, kitten, 37	*$20–$25*
Planter, kitten	*$15–$20*
Planter, knight on horse, 55	*$25–$35*
Planter, lamb	*$20–$25*
Planter, little girl, 90, 5½″	*$10–$12*
Planter, llama	*$15–$20*
Planter, parrot, 60, 9½″	*$20–$25*
Planter, pheasant, 61	*$20–$22*
Planter, pig, 86	*$12–$15*
Planter, poodle, 38	*$20–$25*
Planter, poodle, 114	*$15–$20*
Planter, rooster	*$25–$30*

Planter, siamese cats, 93	*$30–$40*
Planter, telephone, 50, 9″	*$30–$35*
Planter, well, 101	*$12–$15*
Regal parrot planter, 313, 12½″	*$30–$40*
Vase, leaf, 100, 9″	*$10–$12*
Vase, suspension, 108	*$15–$20*
Vase, triple bulb, 107, 7″	*$10–$14*
Vase, Unicorn	*$30–$35*
Wall pocket, goose, 67	*$15–$20*

All prices given are for items in *mint* condition. In general, discoloration, crazing, chipping, and repairs will fetch lower prices.

THE IROQUOIS
CHINA COMPANY

Syracuse, New York

The Iroquois China Company produced hotel ware from 1905 until 1969. The company is best known to collectors today for its Russel Wright and Ben Seibel lines.

Marks

One of the stamps used on the Russel Wright line.

Casual China (1946)

Casual China was designed by Russel Wright. Several pieces were restyled including cup/saucer, gravy, teapot, sugar, creamer, butter dish, mug, water pitcher, and several other dishes. The old teapot is sometimes called a coffee pot. Hard-to-find pieces include: AD cup/saucer, butters, carafe, new gravy, mug, and party plate.

Colors found are Aqua, Avocado Yellow, Brick Red, Cantaloupe, Charcoal, Ice Blue, Lemon Yellow, Lettuce Green, Nutmeg Brown, Oyster Gray, Parsley (dark green), Pink Sherbet, Ripe Apricot, and

Sugar White. Around 1953–54, Iroquois added a mottled glaze effect to the line that it called Raindrop. Decorations, mostly floral, were added in 1959.

Pricing

For items that were restyled, the price is the same for old and new unless otherwise stated. Double prices for Aqua and Brick Red, and add 50% for Cantaloupe.

Dinnerware

Butter, old	$60–$70
Butter, new	$90–$100
Carafe	$85–$90
Casserole, 2 qt	$40–$45
Casserole, 4 qt	$60–$65
Coffee pot	$50–$55
Coffee pot, AD	$45–$50
Creamer, new	$10–$15
Creamer, stack	$10–$15
Cup	$8–$10
Cup, AD	$40–$45
Cup, coffee	$10–$12
Dish, small, all sizes	$7–$8
Gravy, w/lid/stand, new	$80–$90
Gravy, w/lid, old	$25–$28
Gravy stand, old	$10–$12
Mug	$50–$55
Party plate	$25–$28
Pitcher, w/lid, old	$65–$70
Pitcher, new	$65–$70
Plate, 6½"	$5–$6
Plate, 7½"	$7–$8
Plate, 9½"	$8–$9
Plate, 10"	$9–$10
Plate, chop, 14"	$30–$35
Platter, 12½"	$16–$18
Platter, 14½"	$20–$24
Salad bowl, 10"	$25–$30
Saucer	$2–$3
Saucer, AD	$15–$18

Casual China by Russel Wright: butter, creamer (old style) with bird decoration, carafe, sugar and creamer (new style).

Saucer, coffee	*$2–$3*
Shaker, stacking	*$10–$12*
Soup, 8½ "	*$18–$20*
Soup lid	*$10–$12*
Sugar, stack	*$15–$18*
Sugar, new	*$15–$18*
Teapot, old	*$40–$45*
Teapot, new	*$60–$65*
Vegetable, 8"	*$20–$22*
Vegetable, 10"	*$26–$28*
Vegetable, divided, w/lid	*$45–$50*

Cookware

Casserole, 3 qt	*$60–$65*
Casserole, 4 qt	*$60–$65*
Casserole, 6 qt	*$90–$100*
Dutch oven	*$90–$100*
Fry pan, w/lid	*$65–$70*
Percolator	*$100–$110*
Sauce pan, w/lid	*$60–$65*
Serving tray, electric	*$125*

Impromptu

Impromptu was designed by Ben Seibel. Some of the decorations are: Beige Rose, Blue Vinyard, Colonial Blue, Colonial Pink, Grapes, Harvest Time, and Old Orchard.

Butter, ¼ lb	*$15–$20*
Casserole, covered	*$20–$25*
Coffee pot	*$25–$30*
Compote	*$15–$20*
Creamer	*$4–$6*
Cup, low	*$4–$6*

Impromptu.

Cup, tall	$4–$6
Gravy faststand	$12–$15
Plate, B & B	$1–$2
Plate, dinner	$4–$5
Plate, salad	$3–$4
Platter, small	$5–$6
Platter, large	$6–$8
Relish tray	$5–$6
Saucer, low cup	$1–$2
Saucer, tall cup	$1–$2
Shaker, either size	$6–$8
Soup	$6–$7
Sugar	$8–$10
Vegetable	$8–$10
Vegetable, divided	$10–$12

Informal

Designed by Ben Seibel, this line's decorations include Blue Vineyard, Harvest Time, and Old Orchard.

Butter, ¼ lb	$15–$20
Casserole, 2 qt	$20–$25
Coffee pot	$25–$30
Creamer	$4–$6
Cup	$4–$6
Dish, fruit	$1–$2
Dutch oven, w/lid	$20–$25
Fry pan, w/lid	$20–$25
Gravy faststand	$12–$15
Plate, B & B	$1–$2
Plate, dinner	$4–$5
Plate, salad	$3–$4
Platter, 12″	$6–$8
Platter, 15″	$8–$10
Samovar	$25–$30

Informal.

Samovar stand	*$8–$10*
Sauce pan, w/lid	*$20–$25*
Saucer	*$1*
Shaker, either size	*$6–$8*
Soup, gumbo, open	*$6–$8*
Soup, gumbo, w/lid	*$12–$15*
Soup, lug	*$6–$8*
Sugar	*$8–$10*
Vegetable	*$8–$10*
Vegetable, divided	*$10–$12*

THE JAMES RIVER
POTTERIES

Hopewell, Virginia

Originally begun as the Hopewell China Company, it seems to have changed its name about 1940, possibly coinciding with the involvement of J. Palin Thorley who joined the pottery around that time.

Marks

Some pieces will be found with a backstamp, but usually pieces are unmarked or have this conjoint "JR" either impressed or stamped in a fuzzy blue.

Cascade (1935)

Designed by Simon Slobodkin.

Cookie jar	*$15–$20*
Creamer	*$4–$6*
Cup	*$4–$6*
Dish, 6"	*$1–$2*
Dish, lug, 6¼"	*$1–$2*
Pickle, 10¾"	*$4–$5*

Cascade: relish, sugar, creamer, and teapot.

Plate, 6¼″	$1–$2
Plate, 9½″	$4–$5
Platter, 13½″	$6–$7
Relish	$5–$7
Saucer	$1
Sugar	$8–$10
Teapot	$15–$20
Vegetable, rd, 8½″	$9–$10

KAY FINCH CERAMICS

Corona Del Mar, California

Kay Finch designed earthenware figures and dinnerware from 1935 until 1963 when the business closed.
    Her earthenware figures are the most collected.

Marks

Used a backstamp with a graphic element.

Figures

Angels, all styles, 4¼"	*$15–$18*
Cat, angry, 10¼"	*$75–$85*
Cat, contented, 6"	*$40–$45*
Cat, Persian, 10¾"	*$75–$85*
Cat, playful, 8½"	*$50–$60*
Chanticleer, 10½"	*$85–$100*
Cherub head, 2¾"	*$10–$12*
Chicken, Biddy, 8¼"	*$30–$35*
Chicken, Butch, 8¼"	*$30–$35*
Chinese girl, 7½"	*$20–$25*

Chanticleer, 10½", poly-chrome hand decoration. *(Photo courtesy of Jack Chipman)*

Chinese boy, 7½"	$20–$25
Court lady, arm raised, 10½"	$30–$35
Court lady, arms folded, 10½"	$30–$35
Dog, Coach, 17½"	$300–$350
Dog, Cocker, 11¾"	$75–$85
Dog, Pekinese, 14" long	$75–$85
Dog, Pomeranian, 10"	$75–$85
Dog, Yorkshire terrier, 11"	$75–$85
Dog, Yorky pup, 5½"	$20–$25
Dog, Yorky pup, 6"	$20–$25
Duck, 4"	$8–$10
Elephant, 5"	$20–$25
Elephant, trunk down, 6¾"	$40–$45

Elephant, trunk up, 8¾"	*$40–$45*
Elephant, trunk up, 17"	*$300–$350*
Godey Lady, 7½"	*$25–$30*
Godey Man, 7½"	*$25–$30*
Godey Lady, 9½"	*$30–$35*
Godey Man, 9½"	*$30–$35*
Godey Man/Lady w/cape & hats/each	*$35–$40*
Kitten, asleep, 3¼"	*$8–$10*
Kitten, at play, 3¼"	*$8–$10*
Lamb, kneeling, 2¾"	*$8–$10*
Lamb, prancing, 10½"	*$65–$75*
Mr. Bird, 4½"	*$18–$20*
Mrs. Bird, 3"	*$18–$20*
Owl, 3¾"	*$18–$20*
Owl, 8¾"	*$25–$30*
Peasant boy, 6¾"	*$25–$30*
Peasant girl, 6¾"	*$25–$30*
Pig, Grandpa, 10½" × 16"	*$65–$75*
Pig, Grumpy, 6"	*$25–$30*
Pig, Sassy, 3½"	*$20–$25*
Pig, Smiley, 6¾"	*$25–$30*
Pig, Winkie, 3¾"	*$20–$25*
Scandie Boy, 5¼"	*$20–$25*
Scandie Girl, 5¼"	*$20–$25*

Powder Jars

These jars will be found in the following decorations: Briar Rose, Cherry Blossom, Shaggy Daisy, and Zinnia.

Small, 2" × 3½"	*$20–$25*
Large, 3" × 3½"	*$25–$30*

Shakers

Pup, 6"	*$18–$20*
Puss, 6"	*$18–$20*

THE EDWIN M. KNOWLES
CHINA COMPANY

Chester and Newell, West Virginia

In 1900, six months after the announcement that Taylor, Smith and
Lee were building a pottery in Chester, Edwin M. Knowles, son of
the founder of Knowles, Taylor, Knowles, announced a second pottery for that town: the Knowles China Company. Ware was on the
market in 1901. Production was semi-porcelain: toilet ware, dinnerware, kitchenware, and specialties. In 1913, the company built additional facilities in Newell, West Virginia. The Chester plant was sold
to Harker in 1931 and the Newell plant ceased manufacturing in 1963.

E. M. Knowles did not have an outstanding sales success with any
one line, as did some of its competitors, but collectors today are
drawn to Deanna, a solid-colored ware with both bright and pastel
colors (as well as decals), Yorktown dinnerware for its art deco shape,
the Utility Ware kitchen line, and the Russel Wright dinnerware.

Marks

Knowles used a wide variety of backstamps, both general and specific
to lines. This urn is one of the commonly found general stamps.

Deanna (1938)

The easiest pieces to find are the sugar, creamer, and shakers. Casserole, butter, egg cup, and teapot are difficult.

Deanna was decorated in solid colors and decals. There were two lines of solid colors, bright colors that Knowles called "Festive," although this was not an official name: green, red, blue, and yellow. There was a pastel line, called Caribbean: peach, turquoise, lemon yellow, and powder blue. Pieces have also been found in russet, burgundy, and pink.

Bowl, 36s	*$4–$5*
Butter, open	*$10–$12*
Casserole	*$15–$20*
Chop dish	*$8–$10*
Coaster	*$8–$10*
Creamer	*$4–$6*
Cup	*$4–$6*
Cup, AD	*$4–$6*
Dish, 4"	*$1–$2*
Dish, 5"	*$1–$2*
Egg cup, double	*$5–$7*
Gravy boat	*$8–$10*
Pickle	*$3–$5*
Plate, 6"	*$1–$2*
Plate, 7"	*$2–$3*
Plate, 8"	*$2–$4*
Plate, 9"	*$4–$5*
Plate, 10"	*$4–$5*
Platter, 8"	*$4–$5*
Platter, 10"	*$5–$6*
Platter, 12"	*$6–$7*
Saucer	*$1*
Saucer, AD	*$1–$2*
Shaker	*$6–$8*
Soup, lug	*$4–$5*
Soup, coupe	*$4–$5*
Sugar	*$8–$10*

Teapot	$15–$20
Vegetable, rd, 7″	$7–$8
Vegetable, rd, 8″	$8–$9
Vegetable, oval, 7″	$7–$8

Esquire (1956–1962)

Designed by Russel Wright. There are six basic decorations (background colors in parentheses): Botanica (brown), Grass (blue), Seeds (yellow), Solar (white), Snow Flower (pink), and Queen Anne's Lace (white). Mayfair, a rose decal on a high-gloss white background, has also been found.

Compote	$32–$35
Creamer	$6–$8
Cup	$6–$8
Dish, cereal	$7–$9
Dish, fruit	$5–$7
Gravy	$12–$15
Jug, 2 qt	$18–$22
Plate, 6″	$5–$6
Plate, 7″	$7–$8
Plate, 10″	$8–$10
Platter, small	$15–$18
Platter, large	$18–$20
Saucer	$3–$4
Server, 22″	$28–$32
Shaker	$12–$15
Sugar	$18–$20
Teapot	$45–$50
Vegetable, divided	$28–$30
Vegetable, rd, w/lid	$35–$40
Vegetable, oval	$22–$25

Utility Ware

Batter jug	$20–$25
Butter, 1 lb	$15–$20

Casserole, 7 ½"	$15–$20
Casserole, 8 ½"	$15–$20
Casserole tray, 10"	$4–$6
Coffee pot (metal drip)	$15–$20
Cookie jar	$15–$20
Custard	$2–$3
Jug, refrigerator, no lid	$10–$15
Jug, water, w/lid	$20–$25
Leftover, 4" (also Drip)	$4–$5
Leftover, 5"	$6–$8
Leftover, 6"	$8–$10
Mixing bowl, 6"	$4–$5
Mixing bowl, 8"	$8–$10
Mixing bowl, 10"	$10–$15
Mug (tumbler)	$8–$10
Pie baker, 9 ½"	$6–$8
Salad bowl, 9"	$9–$10
Shaker, range	$6–$8
Shirred egg, 6 ¼"	$2–$4
Syrup jug	$20–$25
Teapot	$20–$25
Tray, batter set, lug, 11"	$10–$15

Yorktown (1936)

Sugar, creamer, and shakers are easy to find, candleholders are hard to find, and the cookie jar is rare.

Introduced with an ivory body, it was soon available in four colors: Cadet Blue, Russet, Yellow, and Burgundy. Other colors that have been found are: red (orange), green, pink, and Chinese red. The most readily found decal is Penthouse; Bar Harbor, Water Lily, Golden Wheat, and Green Wheat are others.

Bowl, coupe, 6"	$2–$3
Bowl, 36s	$4–$5
Butter, open	$10–$12
Candleholder	$12–$15
Casserole	$15–$20

Yorktown: Penthouse teapot, shaker, and Bar Harbor plate; Deanna teapot.

Coaster	*$6–$8*
Console fruit	*$12–$15*
Cookie jar	*$25–$30*
Creamer	*$4–$6*
Cup	*$4–$6*
Cup, AD	*$4–$6*
Custard cup	*$2–$3*
Dish, 6"	*$1–$2*
Gravy boat	*$10–$12*
Gravy, 2-handle	*$10–$12*
Oatmeal, 36s	*$3–$4*
Pickle	*$3–$4*
Plate, 6"	*$1–$2*
Plate, 7"	*$2–$3*
Plate, 8"	*$3–$4*
Plate, 9"	*$4–$5*
Plate, 10"	*$4–$5*
Plate, chop	*$6–$8*
Platter, 8"	*$4–$5*
Platter, 10"	*$5–$6*

Platter, 12″	*$6–$8*
Saucer	*$1*
Saucer, AD	*$1–$2*
Shaker	*$6–$8*
Soup, lug	*$4–$5*
Sugar	*$8–$10*
Teapot	*$20–$25*

All prices given are for items in *mint* condition. In general, discoloration, crazing, chipping, and repairs will fetch lower prices.

KNOWLES, TAYLOR
AND KNOWLES

East Liverpool, Ohio

In 1854, Isaac Knowles and Isaac Harvey began producing Rockingham and yellowware, the mainstays of the potteries in East Liverpool.
In the 1860s, Harvey withdrew and in 1870, Isaac Knowles' son Homer
Knowles, and his son-in-law John Taylor, joined the firm. In 1872,
they began to produce white ware and announced their intention to
build a china factory in 1887. Production of Belleek and art goods
began early in 1889 but the plant was destroyed by fire in November
of 1890. After it was rebuilt, a fine china body, but not Belleek, was
made and named Lotusware. By the end of 1897, KTK's interest in
Lotusware began to wane; it is likely that production stopped at this
time. It was too expensive to produce and the company was more
interested in semi-porcelain wares. In 1929, it joined the American
China Corporation but did not survive the dissolution of that ill-fated
venture.

 Marks

The two marks shown were used from about 1891 to 1897 and were
used on both factory-decorated pieces and undecorated white ware.

234

Lotusware

One of the features of Lotusware is the slip decoration, in the form of flowers, leaves and branches, or beading, that has been attributed to George Schmidt. These designs seem to have been applied free-hand to the green ware utilizing a squeeze-bag technique (like a baker decorating a cake). The floral decoration was done over Celadon, Olive, and blue bodies, as well as white. There is not a great deal of professionally decorated Lotusware. Most was either factory decorated or done by amateur decorators.

Bowl, 4 1/2 " high. Spherical body on a footed base with a ruffled, beaded rim. Hand-painted blossoms on bottom with applied lattice work on top that is highlighted in gold. Gilding on the rim and base. Factory decorated, mark 2. *$500–$700*

Bowl, 4 1/2 " high × 6 1/2 " wide. Oblong body with two applied, reticulated handles and a ruffled, beaded rim. Molded blossoms and leaves. Undecorated, mark 2. *$450–$650*

Bowl, 4 1/2 " high × 6 1/2 " wide. Oblong body with two applied, reticulated handles and a ruffled, beaded rim. Orange lustre glaze, mark 2. *$500–$700*

Bowl, 4 1/2 " high × 6 1/2 " wide. Oblong body with molded blossoms and leaves, two applied, reticulated handles and a ruffled, beaded rim. Flowers and leaves are highlighted in pink and green. Gilding on handles and rim, mark 2. *$1000–$1250*

Bowl, 6 1/2 high × 13 " wide. Round body with indented sides, ruffled rim and two twig handles. Decorated with gold paste designs and gilding. Factory decorated, mark 2. *$2800–$3500*

Bowl, 7 " high. Shaped like a ''Witches Pot.'' Round body with ruffled, beaded rim. Tripod-shaped twig handle, above the bowl, attaches to body at the rim. Molded blossoms and lattice work. Undecorated, mark 2. *$300–$350*

Chocolate Pot, 8 " high. Bulbous body with scalloped rim. Molded flowers and leaves on top and applied lattice work on bottom. Flowers and leaves are highlighted in pink and green. Lattice work is highlighted in gold. Gilding on handle and rim. Factory decorated, mark 2. *$650–$750*

Dish, 2 " high × 3 1/4 " wide. Molded in the shape of a shell with a curled edge. Inside is painted gold, outside has a pink lustre glaze. Amateur decoration, mark 2. *$160–$200*

Dish, 2½" high × 4" wide. Molded, shell-shaped body on three small feet. Pink lustre glaze, mark 1. *$160–$200*

Ewer, 10" high. Bulbous body with concave neck and curved handle. The neck has embossed, beaded designs. Hand-painted yellow flowers on the body, gold spray on the rim and handle. Factory decorated, mark 2. *$600–$800*

Jar, 7½" high. Spherical body on a pedestal base with lid. Very intricate, applied open work all over body, handles, lid, and finial. Factory decorated, mark 2. *$1500–$2000*

Pitcher, 6" high. Bulbous, high-waisted body with a small flared neck and a twisted, ear-shaped handle. Applied lattice work on bottom with tiny hand-painted purple violets on top. Factory decorated, mark 2. *$500–$700*

Vase, 6" high. Bulbous body with a flared neck and two "Art Nouveau" style, curved handles. Hand-painted pink roses on a green background. Gilding on handles. Amateur decoration, mark 1. *$250–$350*

Vase, 6½" high. Bulbous body with a flared neck and two curved handles. Hand-painted violets with gilding on handles and rim. Factory decorated, mark 2. *$1000–$1200*

Vase, 8" high. Bulbous body that tapers into a flared neck with two curved handles. Applied white flowers and leaves all over body and neck. Body is pale green. Factory decorated, mark 2. *$2400–$2800*

Vase, 10" high. Spherical body on a pedestal base with a concave neck and scalloped rim. Two long curved handles with embossed designs. There are two applied, reticulated medallions on the body and neck with additional applied and embossed beaded designs on the neck and base. Body has a dark green, matte finish. All the embossed designs and handles are gilded. Factory decorated, mark 2. *$1500–$2000*

Vase, 10½" high. Bulbous body that tapers into a narrow, concave neck with a scalloped rim. Two double ear-shaped handles. Hand-painted lilacs with gilding on handles, base, and rim. Factory decorated, mark 2. *$1100–$1500*

LEIGH POTTERS, INC.
Alliance, Ohio

Leigh was one of the Sebring family potteries that began life as the Crescent China Company. Its history was bound up with that of the Sebring China Company until 1943, when the joint company was bought by National Unit Distributors, which continued to manufacture pottery under the Leigh name.

Marks

Leigh used a number of backstamps.

Aristocrat

See Sebring.

Ultra (1929–1930)

Ultra is a square Art Deco shape released in 1930. A round Art Deco shape was released in 1929. This probably has a different name but until it is discovered, I have combined the two in this listing as they are both popular with collectors.

Butter dish, rd	$20–$25
Casserole, rd	$15–$20
Casserole, sq	$15–$20
Creamer, rd	$6–$8
Creamer, sq	$6–$8

Ultra: French Tulip square creamer, "Hyacinth" square sugar, "Deco Tulip" tidbit, round AD cup/saucer, and Green Wheat round casserole.

Cream soup, rd	$6–$8
Cup, rd	$4–$6
Cup, sq	$4–$6
Cup, AD, rd	$4–$6
Dish, 5″	$1–$2
Gravy, rd	$10–$12
Gravy faststand, rd	$12–$15
Plate, 7″	$2–$3
Plate, 8¼″	$3–$4
Plate, 9″	$4–$5
Platter, lug, 11½″	$5–$6
Saucer	$1
Saucer, AD	$1–$2
Sugar, rd	$10–$12
Sugar, sq	$10–$12
Teapot, rd	$25–$30
Teapot, sq	$25–$30
Tidbit, center handle	$10–$12

LENOX, INC.

Trenton, New Jersey

Lenox was founded in 1889 as the Ceramic Art Company by Jonathan Coxon, Sr. and Walter Scott Lenox. The partnership dissolved with Coxon's departure in 1896, and the company was renamed Lenox, Inc. in 1906. Lenox has manufactured giftwares and dinnerware in a china body exclusively. Belleek china was produced from 1889 to 1930, at which time the word "Belleek" was dropped due to a law suit by the Irish Belleek pottery. The body formula may have been changed a little. Later the body was changed to a cream-colored bone porcelain. Dinnerware production began in earnest after 1906. The company is still operating.

Marks

BELLEEK
Mark 1

BELLEEK
Mark 2

Mark 3

LENOX
Mark 4

LENOX
Mark 5

THE
CERAMIC ART CO
TRENTON, N.J.
POTTERS and DECORATORS
Mark 6

239

Mark 1 Usually called the C.A.C. palette mark. It was used for some time between 1889 and 1906, generally on dinner and utilitarian ware, as well as items decorated in standard factory patterns. It is commonly seen in the following colors:

a) Red: Almost always used for factory-decorated items

b) Lavender: Sometimes looks pink or purple. Usually found on professionally decorated and factory-decorated items, and occasionally on amateur-decorated ware. The theory is that this color was used on undecorated white ware sold to outside decorating firms that bought in large quantities. It may have also been used for factory-decorated items when red marked items were not in stock.

c) Green; Usually found on amateur-decorated items and some professionally decorated ware. The theory is that this color was used for undecorated white ware sold in small quantities to amateur artists or professionals who ran small decorating studios.

Mark 2 Usually called the Lenox Palette mark. The only difference between marks 1 and 2 is that the "CAC" is replaced by an "L" for Lenox. This mark was used from 1906 until 1924 and appears in green. It was put on all undecorated white ware sold to outside decorators and discontinued in 1924 when Lenox stopped making undecorated white ware.

Mark 3 Usually called the CAC wreath mark. It was used sometime between 1889 and 1900; exact dates are not known. It appears in lavender and green and mostly on better, more artistic factory-decorated items. The reason for the two colors is not known.

Mark 4 Usually called the Transitional mark. The same as mark 3 but has "LENOX" added underneath. Used from sometime in the 1890s until 1906, it is generally believed to indicate the period when Walter Lenox was taking over control of the company from Jonathan Coxon. It too appears in lavender and green and is generally seen on the better, more artistic factory-decorated items.

Mark 5 Usually called the Lenox wreath mark. It too is the same as Mark 3, except the "CAC" in the wreath is replaced with an "L." Used from 1906 until 1930 when Lenox stopped making Belleek-type ware. The mark was put on all factory-decorated items and used in conjunction with mark 2.

Mark 6 A less common mark usually seen in green. It seems to have been used for special order products and commemorative-type items until around 1906. One variation of this mark is the appearance of a second wreath, underneath the mark, with "1897 COMPETITION" added. It undoubtedly was used on white ware made for a china painting competition sponsored by the company in 1897.

Belleek (CAC & Lenox)

Bowl, 4½" high × 9½" wide. Round, wide body with a square pedestal base and angular handles. Hand-painted pink cabbage roses and green leaves on a blue and green background. Gilding on base, rim and handles. Professionally decorated, Lenox palette mark.

$175–$250

Bowl, 4½" high × 9½" wide. Electro-deposit, sterling silver overlay in Art Nouveau designs. Professionally decorated, Lenox palette mark.

$200–$275

Box, 1½" high × 3" wide. Embossed designs on lid and sides. Ribbon-shaped finial. Hand-painted pink flowers with gold sponge work. Gilding on finial. Professionally decorated, CAC palette mark.

$90–$125

Box, Trinket, 2½" high × 3¾" wide. Round shape with embossed designs on the body and the slightly domed lid. Tiny hand-painted red flowers, gold sponge work and gilding. Factory decorated, lavender CAC palette mark with "Davis and Callimore" added underneath.

$95–$125

Chocolate Pot, 9½" high. Edwardian shape with high-shouldered body on a square pedestal base with angular handle and long, curved spout. Lid has an urn-shaped finial. Hand-painted pink, orange, and white roses surrounded by gilded and gold paste designs. Artist signed, professionally decorated. Lenox palette mark.

$175–$225

Creamer, 4½" high. Bulbous body with footed base, ruffled rim, and scrolled handle. Gold paste floral designs on a matte finish with gilding. Factory decorated, red CAC palette mark.

$75–$110

Creamer/Sugar Set, creamer is 4½" high, sugar is 6½" wide. Bulbous body on creamer with ruffled rim, open sugar bowl is round with a ruffled rim. Gold paste floral designs on a matte finish. Factory decorated, red CAC palette mark.

$175–$225

Cup and Saucer, cup is 2¼" high, saucer is 5" wide. Hexagon shaped bodies with embossed fish scales. Gilding on handle and rims. Green CAC palette mark.

$30–$50

Cup and Saucer, cup is 2¼" high, saucer is 5" wide. Embossed fluted designs on bodies. Gold paste florals and gold sponge work. Factory decorated, red palette mark.

$75–$100

Cup and Saucer, cup is 2½" high, saucer is 5" wide. Molded ribs in a spiral pattern. Light pink color. Lavender CAC palette mark.

$65–$75

Cup and Saucer, cup is 2½" high, saucer is 5¼" wide. Ribbed body. Enameled tiny blue and pink flowers with green leaves. Gilding on handle and rims. Factory decorated, red CAC palette mark.

$95–$125

Dish, Candy, 2½" high × 6" long. Leaf-shaped body supported on four tiny feet. Hand-painted red flowers on the inside and colored from green to pink on the outside. Gilded highlights. Amateur decoration, green CAC palette mark.   *$65–$90*

Ewer, 11" high. Bulbous body with straight neck and twig handle. Hand-painted red flowers with gold paste vines and leaves on a matte finish. Factory decorated, red CAC palette mark.   *$250–$300*

Ink Well, 6" high. Bulbous body on a diamond-shaped base with embossed foliate designs. Hand-painted blue quill pen and gilding. Professionally decorated, lavender palette mark.   *$150–$200*

Jug, 5½" high. Narrow, octagon-sided body with small handle and spout at top. Hand-painted violets, leaves, and vines. Professionally decorated, Lenox palette mark.   *$100–$150*

Jug, 6" high. Indented rectangular body with handle and spout on top. Hand-painted peaches on a branch with leaves on varicolored background. Gilding inside of spout. Signed by George Morley, factory artist, lavender CAC/Lenox transitional mark.   *$400–$450*

Jug, 10" high. Teardrop-shaped body with stopper and two curved handles. Hand-painted foliage swags with various fruits and flowers. Gold plated trim and stopper. Signed by George Morley, factory artist, lavender CAC/Lenox transitional mark with "Tiffany and Co." added underneath.   *$450–$525*

Loving Cup, 6¾" high. Concave body with embossed designs on the base and three "C"-shaped handles. Hand-painted monk carrying a box in full color. Probably factory decorated, transitional mark in lavender.   *$200–$250*

Loving Cup, 8" high. Concave body with three "C"-shaped handles. Hand-painted monochrome green monk holding a barrel. Artist signed, professionally decorated, lavender CAC/Lenox transitional mark.

$250–$300

Loving Cup, 8" high. Long pedestal base with three angular handles on body. Hand-painted florals and gilding. Professionally decorated, green CAC palette mark.   *$175–$225*

Mug, 5½" high. Cylindrical body. Hand-painted monochrome brown monk seated. Professionally decorated, lavender CAC palette mark.

$100–$175

Mug, 5½″ high. Cylindrical body. Hand-painted portraits of a colonial man in cameo on one side and a colonial woman in a cameo on the other. Professionally decorated, lavender CAC palette mark.

$175–$250

Mug, 5½″ high.Tapered cylindrical body with a slight flare at the bottom and an ear-shaped handle. Hand-painted Indian in full color. Factory decorated, CAC wreath mark in green. *$225–$275*

Mug, 6″ high. Cylindrical body. Hand-painted berries on a vine. Artist signed, amateur decoration, green CAC palette mark.

$65–$100

Mug, 6″ high. Bulbous, high-waisted body with a slightly flared rim and base. Ear-shaped handle. Hand-painted cherries on a branch with leaves. Tan to brown background. Professionally decorated, lavender palette mark. *$100–$165*

Pitcher, Cider, 6″ high. Wide, low-waisted body with large angular handle that has embossed dots on the sides. Hand-painted colorful pansies on varicolored background from green to brown to yellow. Professionally decorated, lavender CAC palette mark. *$225–$275*

Pitcher, Cider, 6½″ high × 7″ wide. Low, bulbous, high-waisted body with a short, straight neck and ear-shaped handle. Hand-painted, highly stylized gold grapes and leaves, outlined in black, on a black and gold background. Artist signed, professionally decorated, lavender CAC palette mark with added Pickard Studio decorator's mark.

$275–$350

Planter, 7½″ high. Round, tilted shape with ruffled rim and large angular handle. Unglazed clay body is decorated with a carved shepherd and lamp. Unsigned, but unmistakably the work of Kate Sears, lavender CAC palette mark. Hairline crack. Note: Kate Sears was a talented young sculptor who worked at the Ceramic Art Company for a few years in the 1890s. She would carve the unfired wet clay using a pocket knife. Examples of her work are very rare and will sell for top dollar even if damaged. *$1500–$2000*

Plates, set of 5, 9″ in diameter. Each has a different hand-painted fish; Porgy, Sun Fish, Sea Bass, Yellow Perch, and Blue Fish. Gilded rims. Signed by William Morley, factory artist, Lenox wreath mark. Note: Usually these plates were sold in sets of 12. *$475–$500*

Plate, 10½″. Electro-deposit, sterling silver overlay in Edwardian-style patterns. Lenox palette mark. *$65–$85*

Salt, 2½″ wide. Round body. Tiny hand-painted red flower and gilding. Professionally decorated, green palette mark. *$20–$30*

Stein, 9½" high. Cylindrical shape with footed base and a copper lid. Decorated with a decal of a monk sitting in front of a large barrel. Dark brown background. Lid has hand-tooled designs. Green CAC palette mark. *$375–$450*

Tankard, 11" high. Cylindrical body with footed base and "C"-shaped handle. Decorated with a decal of a woman holding two birds in her hand. Brown tinting on top and bottom. Lavender CAC palette mark. *$275–$325*

Tankard, 14½" high. Cylindrical, slightly tapered body with embossed designs on the base and "C"-shaped handle. Hand-painted monochrome brown scene of a monk holding a mug surrounded by green floral and geometric designs. Professionally decorated, lavender CAC palette mark. *$450–$500*

Tankard, 14½" high. Cylindrical, slightly tapered body with embossed designs on the base and "C"-shaped handle. Hand-painted monochrome green monk sipping from a wine glass. Very nice artwork. Signed by William Clayton, factory artist, lavender CAC/Lenox transitional mark. *$700–$900*

Tankard, 15" high. Cylindrical, slightly tapered body with embossed designs on the base and "C"-shaped handle. Hand-painted raspberries on vines with leaves and butterflies. Artist signed, professionally decorated, green CAC palette mark. *$400–$500*

Teapot, 6¼" high. Low-waisted hexagon-shaped body. Hand-painted white and pink roses. Gilding on handle and lid finial. Professionally decorated, Lenox palette mark. *$150–$200*

Tea Set, teapot is 6½" high, covered sugar is 4¾" high, and creamer is 3¾" high. Round bodies with flared necks. Bodies and lids have heavily embossed flowers and ribs in the "Hawthorn" pattern. Handles also have embossed designs. Undecorated. Lenox palette mark. *$175–$225*

Tea Set, teapot is 9" high, covered sugar is 5" high, and creamer is 4½" high. Edwardian-styled with angular handles and square pedestal bases. Electro-deposit, sterling silver overlay designs. Professionally decorated, Lenox palette mark, hairline crack on base of teapot. *$175–$250*

Vase, 8" high. Ovoid body with small flared neck and footed base. Two hand-painted blue birds perched on a branch with red berries and leaves. Professionally decorated, Lenox palette mark. *$250–$300*

Vase, 8" high. Slightly ovoid body with small flared neck. Hand-painted scene of a young shepherdess leading a flock of sheep through a field. Professionally decorated, Lenox palette mark. *$500–$575*

Left: Tankard, 14 ½ " high. Hand-painted monochrome green monk. Signed by William Clayton, factory artist. Transitional mark. *Right:* Vase, 18 ½ " high. Hand-painted nymph. Gilding on neck, handles, and base. Artist signed, professional decoration. Green CAC palette mark. *(Photo courtesy of Richard Lewis)*

Vase, 8 ½ " high × 8 " across the rim. Cylindrical body flaring to a trumpet-shaped rim. Decorated with purple, white, blue, and orange chrysanthemums on a varicolored background, highlights on flowers are done in raised white enamel. Very creative. Professionally decorated, green CAC palette mark.   *$275–$350*

Vase, 8 ½ " high × 8 " across the rim. Cylindrical body flaring to a trumpet-shaped rim. Electro-deposit, sterling silver overlay in Edwardian patterns with tiny, hand-painted, pink flowers in a cameo. Lenox palette mark.   *$300–$400*

Vase, 10 " high. Bulbous body tapering into a narrow neck with a flared rim. Two curved handles. Hand-painted yellow roses and green leaves on the natural white background of the porcelain. Very nicely proportioned. Professionally decorated, lavender CAC palette mark.
          $250–$325

Vase, 10" high. Spherical body with tiny flared neck. Hand-painted portrait of a Gypsy woman on a green background. Signed by S. Wirkner, factory artist, lavender CAC/Lenox transitional mark.
$800–$1000

Vase, 10½" high. Bulbous body with a flared neck and applied scrolled handles. Decorated with a decal of a young woman on a swing with a green background. Gilding on handles, base, and rim. Lavender CAC palette mark. $175–$225

Vase, 11" high. Bulbous body with a long, wide cylindrical neck and round handles. Decorated with gold paste floral designs on a matte finish. Gilding on handles and rim. Factory decorated, red CAC palette mark. $200–$275

Vase, 11" high. Ovoid body with small flared neck. Hand-painted young black man playing a banjo on his knees. Tan background. Professionally decorated, lavender CAC palette mark. $375–$425

Vase, 12" high. Cylindrical shape. Hand-painted maiden in a springtime scene surrounded by apple blossoms. Professionally decorated, Lenox palette mark. $375–$450

Vase, 13½" high. Bulbous body with long thin, slightly flared neck. Hand-painted stylized red flowers on a bright background varying from red, to yellow, to blue and purple. Signed by Walter Marsh, factory artist, lavender CAC/Lenox transitional mark with words "Glen-Iris" underneath and part of mark. Note: There are few known examples marked "Glen-Iris." Most are signed by Marsh, and they all have bright background colors that are the primary decoration while the flowers are secondary. $700–$900

Vase, 15" high. Ovoid body, narrow neck, pedestal base, and interesting-shaped handles. Hand-painted red, orange, and white roses with green leaves, gilding on handles. Artist signed and dated 1903, amateur decoration, green CAC palette mark. $275–$350

Vase, 15" high. Classically shaped high-waisted body with flared neck. Hand-painted red, orange, and white poppies on a burnt orange to beige background, touched with blue. Outstanding artwork. Artist signed, professionally decorated, Lenox palette mark. $500–$575

Vase, 17" high. Ovoid body with small tapered neck. Hand-painted portrait of a woman in a cameo on a red background. Gold paste designs surround the cameo and are all over the vase. Very artistic and well executed. Signed by H. Nosek, factory artist, green CAC/Lenox transitional mark. $1200–$1500

Vase, 18" high. High-shouldered ovoid body with flared neck, pedestal base, and two handles with embossed designs. Hand-painted purple and white flowers on a varicolored background. Professionally decorated, lavender palette mark. $500–$600

Vase, 18″ high. Ovoid shaped, high-shouldered body with pedestal base and narrow trumpet-flared neck. Attached to the shoulder are two very elaborate Victorian handles. Decorated with hand-painted nymph sitting on a cloud playing a violin, on blue to gray background. Green neck and pedestal; gilding on neck, handles, and base. Artist signed, professionally decorated, green palette mark. *$1000–$1200*

All prices given are for items in *mint* condition. In general, discoloration, crazing, chipping, and repairs will fetch lower prices.

THE LIMOGES CHINA COMPANY

Sebring, Ohio

This pottery began life as the Sterling China Company, making porcelain dinnerware. This was not profitable and after a year and a half, production was changed over to semi-porcelain dinnerware. The name was changed to Limoges around 1903. Kitchenware was added in the thirties. In 1943 Limoges, and its sister company Sebring, were bought by National Unit Distributors. Around 1949, litigation brought by Limoges of France resulted in the name change to American Limoges. Operations ceased in 1955.

Viktor Schreckengost designed a number of interesting lines for Limoges but very little, besides Triumph and Casino, turns up today.

Note

Despite its name, Limoges made the same quality dinnerware as its competitors. Beware the dealer who charges high prices because they don't know better.

Marks

You will find a variety of stamped marks.

Casino diamond creamer/sugar, spade plate; Triumph sugar and creamer; "Square" teapot.

Casino (ca. 1954)

A short line in the shape of card suits, with matching decal decoration.

Ashtray, diamond	*$10–$12*
Creamer, diamond	*$6–$8*
Cup, club	*$6–$8*
Dish, diamond	*$3–$4*
Plate, spade	*$6–$8*
Platter, diamond	*$10–$12*
Saucer, heart	*$2–$3*
Sugar, diamond	*$12–$15*

"Square"

A square shape but with rounded corners, it is distinguished by its arrow-head finial.

Butter dish	*$15–$20*
Casserole	*$15–$20*
Creamer	*$4–$6*

Cup	*$4–$6*
Gravy	*$8–$10*
Plate, 6½"	*$1–$2*
Plate, 7"	*$2–$3*
Plate, 9"	*$4–$5*
Saucer	*$1*
Sugar	*$8–$10*
Teapot	*$20–$25*

Triumph (1937)

Triumph was designed by Viktor Schreckengost. Triumph, with its horizontal fluting, is an interesting variation on Salem's Victory, with vertical fluting, also designed by Schreckengost.

Casserole	*$15–$20*
Coffee pot	*$15–$20*
Creamer	*$4–$6*
Cup	*$4–$6*
Dish, 5½"	*$1–$2*
Gravy	*$8–$10*
Plate, 6½"	*$1–$2*
Plate, 10"	*$4–$5*
Plate, 11"	*$4–$5*
Plate, chop, 12½"	*$5–$6*
Platter, oval, 11¼"	*$5–$6*
Saucer	*$1*
Shaker	*$6–$8*
Soup, 8¼"	*$4–$5*
Sugar	*$8–$10*
Vegetable, rd, 8¾"	*$8–$10*

THE NELSON McCOY POTTERY COMPANY

Roseville, Ohio

Formed in 1910, the Nelson McCoy Pottery Company produced stoneware. In the mid-twenties, they began production of earthenware specialties, jardinieres, umbrella stands, and vases. The company was bought by Lancaster Colony in 1974.

Marks

Many of the cookie jars are either unmarked or have an impressed "USA" or shape number.

Cookie Jars

Animal Crackers	*$35–$45*
Apollo	*$250–$300*
Apple, yellow	*$25–$35*
Apples on Basket	*$35–$45*
Asparagus	*$25–$35*
Astronauts	*$250 –$300*
Bananas	*$45–$65*
Barnum's Animals	*$95–$125*
Baseball	*$35–$45*
Basket of Eggs	*$35–$45*
Basket of Fruit	*$55–$65*

Basket of Potatoes	$35–$45
Basket of Strawberries	$35–$45
Basket of Tomatoes	$35–$45
Betsy Baker	$95–$125
Black Cat	$125–$150
Black Lantern	$55–$65
Bobby Baker	$35–$45
Brown Bear	$35–$45
Brown Owl	$35–$45
Bugs Bunny	$75–$85
Burlap Bag	$25–$35
Burlap Bag w/Red Bird	$25–$35
Caboose	$125–$150
Cat on Basket	$35–$45
Cat on Coal Bucket	$75–$125
Chef's Head	$35–$45
Chiffonnier	$55–$65
Chipmunk	$125– $150
Christmas Tree	$175–$200
Churn	$25–$35
Circus Horse	$125–$150
Clown Head	$35–$45
Clown in Barrel	$55–$65
Clyde Dog	$55–$65
Coffee Mug	$25–$35
Coffee Grinder	$25–$35
Cookie Bank	$95–$125
Cookie Barrel, small	$25–$35
Cookie Barrel, large	$25–$35
Cookie Box	$25–$35
Cookie Boy	$95–$125
Cookie House	$95–$125
Cookie Pot	$45–$55
Cookie Sack	$25–$35
Cookstove	$25–$35
Covered Wagon	$35–$45

Cookie jars: Cookie House and Touring Car. *(Photo courtesy of Dave Pritchard)*

Davy Crockett	*$300+*
Dog in Basket	*$35–$45*
Dog in Doghouse	*$75–$85*
Drum	*$45–$55*
Duck	*$95–$125*
Duck on Basket	*$45–$55*
Dutch Boy	*$45–$55*
Dutch Girl	*$45–$55*
Dutch Treat Barn	*$45–$55*
Eagle Basket	*$35–$45*
Ear of Corn	*$95–$125*
Elephant	*$125–$150*
Elephant w/split trunk	*$150–$225*
Engine	*$95–$125*
Fat Pig	*$65–$75*
Fireplace	*$75–$85*
Football	*$35–$45*
Forbidden Fruit	*$55–$65*
Fortune Cookies	*$45–$55*
Friendship 7	*$75–$95*
Frontier Family	*$35–$45*
Gaytime Pitcher	*$35–$45*

ND = price is not determined; item too rare to price.
 + = worth at least sum indicated, but could be higher.

Globe	*$125–$150*
Grandfather Clock	*$55–$65*
Granny	*$55–$65*
Hamm's Bear	*$95–$125*
Hen on Nest	*$65–$75*
Hobby Horse	*$125–$150*
Hobnail	*$25–$35*
Hocus Rabbit	*$35–$45*
Honey Bear	*$45–$55*
Humpty Dumpty (nursery decal)	*$50–$60*
Indian Head	*$150–$225*
Jack-O-Lantern	*$150–$225*
Kangaroo I (blue)	*$95–$125*
Kangaroo II (tan)	*$200–$225*
Kissing Penguins	*$35–$45*
Koala Bear	*$45–$55*
Lamb on Basket	*$25–$35*
Lemon	*$35–$45*
Leprechaun	*$300+*
Liberty Bell	*$35–$45*
Little Bo-Peep (nursery decal)	*$50–$60*
Little Clown	*$45–$55*
Little Miss Muffet (nursery decal)	*$50–$60*
Log Cabin	*$65–$75*
Lollipops	*$45–$55*
Mac Dog	*$45–$55*
Mammy (ivory w/cold paint)	*$125–$150*
Mammy (aqua or yellow)	*$250+*
Mammy w/Cauliflowers	*$300+*
Mary Mary	*$50–$60*

Milk Can	$35–$45
Monk	$35–$45
Monkey on Stump	$30–$40
Mother Goose	$95–$125
Mouse	$25–$35
Mouse on Clock	$25–$35
Mr. and Mrs. Owl	$75–$85
Mushroom on Stump	$25
Nabisco Jar	$65–$75
Oaken Bucket	$25–$35
Orange	$25–$35
Pear, yellow	$55–$65
Pears on Basket	$35–$45
Penguin	$95–$125
Pepper	$25–$30
Picnic Basket	$55–$65
Pineapple	$35–$45
Pinecones on Basket	$25–$35
Pirates Chest	$55–$65
Polar Bear	$45–$50
Popeye	$95–$125
Pot-Bellied Stove	$25–$35
Puppy with Sign	$45–$55
Rabbit on Stump	$10–$25
Raggedy Ann	$35–$40
Red Apple	$15–$25
Rocking Chair Dalmatians	$150–$175
Rooster	$75 $85
Sad Clown	$45–$55
Safe	$45–$55
Snoopy	$150–$175
Snow Bear	$45–$50
Squirrel on Stump	$10–$25
Stagecoach	$300+
Strawberry, Old	$25–$35

Strawberry, New	$25–$35
Tepee	$150–$175
Thinking Puppy	$25–$35
Three Kittens on Yarn Ball	$65–$75
Tomato	$20–$25
Touring Car	$65–$75
Tureen	$25–$35
Turkey	$175–$195
Two Kittens in Basket	$200–$250
Upside-Down Bear	$45–$55
W. C. Fields	$125–$150
Wedding Jar	$55–$65
Windmill	$65–$75
Wishing Well	$15–$20
Woodsy Owl	$95–$125
Wren House	$95–$125
Yosemite Sam	$125–$150

Lotus Ware. Covered jar showing characteristic fish-net decoration. (*Photo courtesy of Larry Walton*)

California. Vernon Kilns Cottage Window chop plate (Gale Turnbull), Bauer Burgundy Ring water jug, Florence figurine (Claudia), Catalina Siesta ashtray (with original hand painting), and Bauer Yellow pastel kitchenware teapot.

Hand-painted Southern Potteries china pieces. "Verna" Fine Panel teapot, Charm House shakers, "Clinch Mountain Violets" four-part bonbon, Dancing Nude box, and Charm House pitcher. (*Photo courtesy of Tom Moore*).

Willets chalice, 11½" high. Hand-painted monk smoking a cigar, artist-signed. Mark 2 in brown. (*Photo courtesy of Richard Lewis*)

Teapots. *Clockwise from top*. Red Wing Cobalt blue Saturn, Harker Yellow Cameoware, Hall Chinese red Automobile, Universal black and white Upico, and Homer Laughlin Americana.

Cookie jars. Eeyore (California Originals), Mammy (Brayton), and Owl with gold (Shawnee). (*Photo courtesy of Dave Pritchard*)

Van Briggle bowl. (*Photo courtesy of Harry Rinker & Associates*)

Facing page. All that's red is not Fiesta.
Clockwise from top. Bauer Ring vase, Homer
Laughlin Tango plate, E. M. Knowles Deanna
plate, French-Saxon Zephyr creamer, Paden City
Caliente shaker, Stangl Colonial egg cup, E. M.
Knowles Yorktown shaker, Taylor, Smith and
Taylor Vistosa shaker, Salem Tricorne sugar, and
Universal canteen jug.

Kitchenware. *Clockwise from top.* E. M. Knowles red Utility Ware water jug, Harker Monterey Zephyr cookie jar, Paden Spinning Wheel carafe, Bennett Poppy bean pot, and Crooksville Petitpoint House refrigerator jug.

METLOX POTTERIES

Manhattan Beach, California

From 1927 to the present, Metlox Potteries has been making art ware, novelties, and Poppytrail dinnerware. They made solid-color ware in the thirties and decorated ware from the forties to the present.

Marks

Above is one of the Poppytrail backstamps used by the company.

California Ivy

Butter, ¼ lb	*$18–$20*
Coaster, 3¾"	*$4–$6*
Coffee pot	*$40–$45*
Creamer	*$6–$7*
Cup	*$5–$7*
Dish, 5¼"	*$3–$4*
Dish, 6¾"	*$6–$8*
Gravy	*$12–$15*
Jug, 2½ qt	*$20–$25*
Mug, 7 oz	*$8–$10*
Plate, 6⅜"	*$3–$4*

Plate, 8″	$5–$7
Plate, 10⅛″	$8–$10
Plate, chop, buffet server, 13⅛″	$12–$15
Platter, oval, 9″	$12–$15
Platter, oval, 11″	$15–$18
Platter, oval, 13″	$18–$20
Salad bowl, 11¼″	$12–$15
Saucer	$1
Shaker	$3–$4
Soup, 6¾″	$6–$8
Soup, ind, 5″	$3–$4
Sugar	$6–$7
Teapot	$40–$50
Tumbler, 13 oz	$15–$18
Vegetable, rd, 9″	$15–$18
Vegetable, rd, divided, 11″	$15–$18

Cookie Jars

Bandit	$35–$45
Bear	$35–$45
Clown	$35–$45
Drum	$35–$45
Mammy	$35–$40
Mouse Mobile	$35–$45
Pinecone, w/squirrel	$35–$45
Raggedy Andy	$35–$45
Raggedy Ann	$35–$45
Red Riding Hood	$125–$140
Rose	$35–$45
Topsy	$35–$40

Homestead Provincial

Homestead uses the same shapes as Rooster, and was decorated with Early American folk art themes in "deep red and rich green."

Ashtray, sq, 4 1/2 "	*$12–$15*
Ashtray, sq, 6 3/8 "	*$12–$15*
Ashtray, sq, 8 1/4 "	*$12–$15*
Bread server, rect, 9 1/2 "	*$20–$25*
Butter, rect	*$18–$20*
Canister set (four)	*$130–$150*
Canister, coffee	*$30–$35*
Canister, flour	*$30–$35*
Canister, sugar	*$30–$35*
Canister, tea	*$30–$35*
Casserole, hen lid, 1 1/4 qt	*$20–$25*
Casserole, kettle, 2 1/2 qt	*$30–$35*
Casserole, kettle, warmer base, metal	*$15–$18*
Coaster, 3 3/4 "	*$4–$6*
Coffee carafe, 44 oz	*$35–$40*
Coffee carafe warmer, metal	*$8–$10*
Coffee pot, 7 cup	*$40–$45*
Cookie jar	*$45–$50*
Creamer	*$6–$7*
Cruet	*$18–$20*
Cruet set, 2-piece	*$35–$40*
Cruet set, 5-piece	*$50–$60*
Cup	*$5–$7*
Dish, 6"	*$3–$4*
Dish, 7 1/4 "	*$6–$8*
Egg cup	*$8–$10*
Gravy	*$12–$15*
Jug, 1 1/2 pt	*$15–$20*
Jug, 1 qt	*$18–$20*
Jug, 2 1/4 qt	*$20–$25*
Lazy Susan set, 7-piece	*$130–$150*
Mug, 8 oz	*$8–$10*
Mug, tankard, 1pt	*$18–$20*
Mustard (cruet set)	*$20–$25*
Plate, 6 3/8 "	*$3–$4*
Plate, 7 1/2 "	*$7–$8*

Plate, 10″	*$8–$10*
Plate, chop/buffet server, 12¼″	*$12–$15*
Platter, oval, 11″	*$15–$18*
Platter, oval, 13½″	*$18–$20*
Platter, oval, 16″	*$20–$25*
Salad, 11⅛″	*$12–$15*
Saucer	*$1*
Shaker (cruet set)	*$4–$5*
Shaker, handled	*$3–$4*
Shaker, hen salt	*$12–$13*
Shaker, rooster pepper	*$4–$5*
Soup, 8″	*$6–$8*
Soup, ind, 5″	*$3–$4*
Sugar	*$6–$7*
Teapot	*$40–$50*
Tumbler, ftd, 11 oz	*$40–$50*
Vegetable, covered, 1 qt	*$20–$25*
Vegetable, rd, 7⅛″	*$12–$15*
Vegetable, rd, 10″	*$15–$18*
Vegetable, rd, divided, 12″	*$15–$18*
Vegetable, rect, 8⅛″	*$10–$12*

Red Rooster

Many of these shapes are based on old Tole ware (lacquered or enameled metalware) pieces—down to the "rivets" on the hollowware pieces.

Red Rooster Provincial is done in shades of deep red, straw yellow, and leaf green with a smoky effect on edges and handles. Some pieces were decorated only in solid red; these are indicated by an R following the item.

Ashtray, sq, 4½″/R	*$12–$15*
Ashtray, sq, 6⅜″/R	*$12–$15*
Ashtray, sq, 8¼″/R	*$12–$15*
Bread server, rect, 9½″/R	*$20–$25*
Butter, rect/R	*$18–$20*

Red Rooster-decorated dinner plate, solid red cup, and rooster-decorated saucer. *(Photo courtesy of Jack Chipman)*

Canister set (four)/R	*$130–$150*
Canister, coffee/R	*$30–$35*
Canister, flour/R	*$30–$35*
Canister, sugar/R	*$30–$35*
Canister, tea/R	*$30–$35*
Casserole, hen lid, 1 1/4 qt	*$20–$25*
Casserole, ind, Hen on lid	*$30–$35*
Casserole, kettle, 2 1/2 qt/R	*$30–$35*
Casserole, kettle, warmer base, metal	*$15–$18*
Coaster, 3 3/4 "/R	*$4–$6*
Coffee carafe, 44 oz/R	*$35–$40*
Coffee carafe warmer	*$8–$10*

Coffee pot, 6 cup/R	$40–$45
Cookie jar/R	$45–$50
Creamer/R	$6–$7
Cruet/R	$18–$20
Cruet set, 2-piece/R	$35–$40
Cruet set, 5-piece/R	$55–$60
Cup	$5–$7
Cup/R	$5–$7
Dish, 6″	$3–$4
Dish, 7¼″	$6–$8
Egg cup/R	$8–$10
Gravy/R	$12–$15
Jewelry box	$40–$45
Jug, 1½ pt/R	$15–$20
Jug, 1 qt/R	$18–$20
Jug, 2¼ qt/R	$20–$25
Lazy Susan set, 7-piece	$140–$150
Marmalade	$40–$45
Mug, 8 oz/R	$8–$10
Mug, tankard, 1pt/R	$15–$20
Mustard (cruet set)	$20–$25
Pepper mill/salt shaker, pair	$45–$50
Plate, 6⅜″	$3–$4
Plate, 7½″	$5–$7
Plate, 10″	$8–$10
Plate, chop/buffet server, 12¼″	$12–$15
Platter, oval, 9½″	$12–$15
Platter, oval, 11″	$15–$18
Platter, oval, 13½″	$18–$20
Platter, oval, 16″	$20–$25
Salad, 11⅛″/R	$12–$15
Salt box	$50–$55
Saucer	$1
Shaker, handled, small/R	$3–$4
Shaker, handled, large (cruet set)/R	$4–$5
Shaker, rooster pepper	$12–$13

Shaker, hen salt	*$4–$5*
Soup, 8"	*$6–$8*
Soup, ind, 5"/R	*$3–$4*
Sugar/R	*$6–$7*
Teapot/R	*$40–$50*
Tumbler, ftd, 11 oz/R	*$40–$50*
Tureen	*$150+*
Vegetable, covered, 1 qt	*$22–$25*
Vegetable, oval	*$10–$12*
Vegetable, rd, 7⅛"/R	*$12–$15*
Vegetable, rd, 10"	*$15–$18*
Vegetable, rd, divided, 7⅛"/R	*$20–$25*
Vegetable, rd, divided, 12"/R	*$15–$18*
Vegetable, rect, 8⅛"/R	*$10–$12*
Wall pocket	*$30–$35*
Watering can	*$20–$25*

MORTON
POTTERY COMPANY

Morton, Illinois

Morton was one of the six interrelated potteries in Morton. Begun in 1922 for the manufacture of utility items, the company began expanding into novelties in the late thirties, based on the successful marketing of political items. It closed in 1971.

Marks

An incised mark with "Morton" and "USA" or the shape number.

Banks

Bulldog, brown, 3¾" × 3"	*$20*
Cat, reclining, yellow, 4" × 6"	*$15*
Hen, white, 4" × 3"	*$18*
Pig, black, 5½" × 7"	*$25*
Uncle Sam, white, 4" × 2"	*$10*

Bookends

Priced per pair.

Atlas on book, globe on shoulders, white w/gold trim, 5"	*$20*
Eagles, golden brown, 6"	*$30*
Parrots, multicolored, 6"	*$25*

Turkey cookie jar. *(Photo courtesy of Burdell Hall)*

Cookie Jars

Basket of Fruit	*$22*
Hen w/chick finial on lid	*$50*
Panda	*$35*
Turkey w/chick finial on lid	*$65*

Figurines

Cat, reclining, gray, 4″ × 6″	*$10*
Davy Crockett, lamp base, 7½″	*$25*
John Kennedy, Jr., saluting, age three, buff and gray	*$25*
Man, in knickers, holding bouquet, pink, 7½″	*$12*
Oxen w/yoke, brown, pair, 3¼″	*$25*
Stork, multicolored, 7½″	*$12*
Woman in sunbonnet w/baskets of flowers, pink, 7¾″	*$12*

Figurines/Miniature

Bear, brown, 2″	*$5*
Blue Jay on stump, blue-gray, #596, 4″	*$7*

Blue Jay, natural, 2½"	$5
Deer, white, #595, 4½"	$7
Donkey, brown, "Kennedy," 2"	$25
Elephant, trunk up, gray or blue, "GOP/candidate's name" on side	$10–$15
Elephant, trunk up, pink, 2½"	$5
Fawn, blue, #542, 2½"	$5
Horse, green, #593, 2¾"	$5
Kangaroo, red, #602, 2¾"	$5
Lamb, yellow, #594, 2½"	$5
Rabbit, white, 3"	$5
Squirrel, brown, 2¼"	$5
Stork, green, #597, 4"	$7
Swordfish, pink, #598, 4"	$7
Turkey, natural, 2½"	$7
Wild Horse, white, #604, 2½"	$5

Miscellany

Incense burner, Church (Rockingham)	$20
Incense burner, Oriental figure, (Rockingham)	$35

Planters

All are in natural colors unless otherwise noted.

Cowboy & Cactus, 7"	$12
Fawn, #645, white, 6½"	$8
Lady, dancing, Deco, white, 8"	$18
Mrs. Claus, 9½"	$20
Santa Claus, 9½"	$25
Santa on Chimney, 7"	$15
Snowman, white w/black hat & green scarf, 9¾"	$18
Turkey, brown, 5"	$10

TV Lamps

Bird Dog w/pheasant, natural colors, 9″	*$38*
Black Panther, 28″	*$28*
Buffalo on rocky cliff, natural colors, 11″	*$50*
Horse w/colt, brown & tan, 9½″	*$35*
Leopard, natural colors, 14″	*$25*
Lioness on log, brown, 10″	*$30*

Woodland

Brown and green spatter on yellowware.

Casserole w/steel frame	*$75*
Coffee server, 8 cup	*$85*
Custard	*$30*
Grease jar, 4″	*$40*
Grease pitcher, 2¾″	*$35*
Jug, refrigerator, flat, 4″	*$70*
w/lid	*$85*
Jug, milk, w/advertising	*$80*
Jug, milk, double spout	*$55*
Jug, water, w/ice lip, 7″	*$90*
Mixing bowls, paneled, set of five, 3¾″–8″	*$150*
Pie baker, 9″.	*$100*
Shaker, pair	*$110*
Teapot, 4 cup	*$65*
Vase, bulbous, 10¾″	*$125*

THE MT. CLEMENS POTTERY COMPANY

Mt. Clemens, Michigan

The Mt. Clemens Pottery Company was founded in 1915 for the manufacture of semi-porcelain dinnerware. The company manufactured for S. S. Kresge, and continued in operation until 1987.

Marks

Much is unmarked or has a raised "USA" on it. One backstamp to be found is an intertwined "M. C. P. Co."

"Petal"

This line is most readily found in solid colors of burgundy, dark blue, medium green (most common), and yellow. Decals will also be found.

Bowl, 36s	*$4–$5*
Butter dish	*$10–$12*
Creamer	*$4–$6*
Cream soup	*$5–$6*
Cup	*$4–$6*
Dish, 5"	*$1–$2*
Dish, 6"	*$1–$2*
Gravy	*$8–$10*
Plate, 6"	*$1–$2*
Plate, 7½"	*$2–$3*
Plate, 9¼"	*$4–$5*

Platter, 11¼"	*$6-$7*
Platter, 13½"	*$7-$8*
Platter, lug, 15"	*$8-$10*
Saucer	*$1*
Soup, 8"	*$4-$5*
Sugar	*$8-$10*
Sugar, lug	*$8-$10*
Vegetable, rd, 7½"	*$7-$9*
Vegetable, rd, 8½".	*$7-$9*

Vogue

Has an embossed rim with birds, flowers, and urns. Decorated in solid colors and decals.

Butter dish	*$10-$12*
Creamer	*$4-$6*
Cup	*$4-$6*
Plate, 6¼"	*$1-$2*
Plate, 7"	*$2-$3*
Plate, 9¼"	*$4-$5*
Platter, 11¼"	*$6-$7*
Saucer	*$1*
Sugar	*$8-$10*

Vogue and "Petal" bread and butter plates.

OTT AND BREWER

Trenton, New Jersey

Founded in 1863, Ott & Brewer made a number of collectible lines including Parian, stoneware, and Belleek, the latter being produced from 1883 until the company closed in 1893.

Marks

Mark 1

Mark 2

Mark 3

Mark 4

Mark 5

Mark 6

Mark 7

MANUFACTURED BY
OTT&BREWER
TRENTON, N.J. USA

Mark 8

O&B
Mark 9

Although there are many marks for Ott and Brewer, it is not known if there was a specific purpose for any mark. All are stamped and usually in a reddish-brown color. Frequently, pieces have a combination of two marks.

Mark 1 Often called the crown mark; is considered to be the earliest Belleek mark.
Mark 2 Usually called the crescent mark.
Mark 3 Same as mark 2, but has "TRENTON, NJ" added.
Mark 4 Least common of the Belleek marks.
Marks 5–9 Were used for stoneware and semi-porcelain items. Again it is common for a piece to have two marks. Note the similarity between marks 1 and 9.

Note

Almost every piece of Ott and Brewer was factory decorated.

Belleek

Basket, 7½″ high × 9″ wide. Round body with molded cactus handle with applied pink flowers at the base. Hand-painted pink flowers with gold paste vines and leaves. Gilding on handle. Mark 1.

$900–$1100

Bowl, 7″ high. Round body with lid that has a cherub head finial. Applied flowers and gold paste florals on a matte finish. Repairs and regilding of some of the applied flowers. Mark 2. *$400–$500*

Bowl, 8¾″ high. Oblong body with twig handle and a deeply ruffled and scalloped rim. Off-center body has one side raised higher than the other. Gold paste thistle pattern on a matte finish with gold sponge work. Mark 1. *$800–$1000*

Creamer/covered sugar. Creamer is 3½″ high, has a bulbous body, footed base, ruffled rim, and angular handle. Sugar is 2″ high × 3¼″ wide, round with a ruffled rim. Decorated with red, blue, and pink enameled flowers, gilding on the rim, and creamer handle is painted a bronze color. Marks 1 and 2. *$350–$400*

Cup/saucer, cup is 2½″ high, saucer is 5″ wide. Red and pink enameled flowers with gold paste leaves and vines. Mark 1. *$125–$150*

Cup/saucer, cup is 2½″ high, saucer is 5″ wide. Small, with scalloped rims and indented rib designs on bodies. Gold paste thistle pattern with gold sponge work on the background. Mark 1. *$125–$150*

Cup/saucer, bouillon, 2¾″ high × 6″ wide. Very thin with Irish Tridacna designs on body. Two round handles on bowl. Gold paste florals with gilding and gold sponge work. Mark 1. *$150–$200*

Dish, 2¾″ high × 4″ wide. Shell shape supported on three shell-shaped feet. Blue luster finish. Mark 2. *$150–$200*

Pitcher, 6½″ high. Horn-shaped pitcher with twig handle. The bottom of the pitcher has an embossed bark design. The top has gold paste florals. There is gold spray on the handle and bark. Mark 1. *$600–$800*

Pitcher, 8″ high. Spherical body with footed base, scalloped rim, and angular handle. The front of the body is smooth with a gold paste thistle pattern. The rest of the body has embossed designs that are highlighted in gold. Gilding on the rim, base, and handle. Mark 1. *$400–$450*

All prices given are for items in *mint* condition. In general, discoloration, crazing, chipping, and repairs will fetch lower prices.

(*Photo courtesy of Richard Lewis*)

Pitcher, 8½" high. Bulbous, high-shouldered body with tapered sides and a slanted neck. Gilded handle is molded in the shape of a flower stem and has two applied pink flowers at the top. Other applied, gilded flowers on body. Two hand-painted pink flowers with gold paste leaves and vines on a matte finish. Mark 2. *$1000-$1500*

Pitcher, 8¾" high. Teardrop-shaped body with long thin neck, curved spout, and circular handle. Gold paste florals and gilding. Mark 2. *$500-$700*

Pitcher, 10" high. Bulbous body with neck open on one side. Ruffled rim with twig handle. Gold paste flowers on matte finish. Gilding on handle and rim. Mark 1. *$900-$1100*

Plate, 9" diameter. Scalloped rim. Hand-painted pink flowers with gold paste vines and leaves done in two shades of gold. Mark 1. *$225-$275*

Tea set, teapot is 5¾" high, sugar is 4" high, and creamer is 3" high. Spherical bodies with Irish Tridacna designs. Pink luster glaze with gilding on handles. Professionally repaired. Mark 1. *$500-$700*

Tray, 9" wide. Square shape with ruffled rim. Hand-painted King Fisher on a branch with a gold-sponged sun in the background. Mark 2. *$700-$900*

Vase, 3½" high × 5¼" long. Molded in the shape of a Ram's horn. Pink luster glaze with gilding on rim. Rare item. Mark 2. *$1500-$1750*

Vase, 4½" high. Bulbous body with straight neck and two handles that have applied masks. Gold paste thistle pattern with gilding and gold sponge work. Mark 1.   *$750–$900*

Vase, 6½" high. Round body with two indented sides. Double neck with two twig handles. Top of the vase has embossed bark design with some open work. Bottom has gold paste florals. The top and handles are painted a bronze color. Some small chips on rim. Mark 1.
                                                              $600–$800

Vase, 10" high. Bulbous body with straight neck. Two hand-painted pink flowers with gold paste vines and leaves. Marks 1 and 2.
                                                              $700–$900

Non-Belleek Pieces

Bust, Parian, 12" high. Bust of Abraham Lincoln. Signed by Isaac Broome and dated 1876. Small chip on shoulder and on eyebrow. Mark 8. Note: Isaac Broome was a famous ceramic artist that worked at Ott and Brewer before the Belleek period. His work is very rare and commands a high price.   *$1700–$2000*

Coffee pot, stoneware, 8" high. Low-waisted body with tapered neck and "C"-shaped handle. Transfer decorated blue and green flowers. Mark 7.   *$125–$150*

Cookie jar, stoneware, 10" high. Cylindrical body with lid and two handles with embossed designs. Transfer decorated blue, white, and green flowers. Gilding on handles and lid. Mark 7.   *$125–$150*

Tobacco jar, earthenware, 8" high. Slightly ovoid body with lid and two handles. Brown background with gold-sponged clouds and gilding on handles and lid. Hairline crack and gilding is very worn. Mark 7.
                                                                $50–$75

THE PADEN CITY
POTTERY COMPANY

Paden City, West Virginia

In 1914, Paden began manufacturing semi-porcelain dinnerware. Kitchenware was added in the thirties. The company closed in 1963.

Paden was one of the potteries that exhibited at the '38–'39 World's Fair. It manufactured a souvenir salad bowl. This and the Caliente line are most desired by collectors.

Marks

Paden used a number of backstamps, one of the best-known is this kiln graphic. It is usually found in black, but was used as a color decal for the World's Fair salad bowl. The Russel Wright mark bears the name of the distributor—Justin Tharaud.

Bak-Serve (1931)

Bak-Serve was distributed exclusively by the Great Northern Products Company of Chicago. Not much of this kitchenware line is found. It was decorated in solid Caliente colors as well as decals.

275

Carafe	$15–$20
Casserole underplate, sq	$4–$5
Casserole, lug handle	$15–$20
Casserole, open handle	$15–$20
Jug, ball	$12–$15
Teapot, Rose Marie	$15–$20

Blue Willow (1937)

Blue Willow was an interesting variation on a theme. Paden etched the Blue Willow design into the body of this short set (only seven different items were made) and glazed it in a deep blue in such a way that the design shows through.

Bowl, salad	$10–$12
Cup	$6–$7
Dish, cereal	$2–$3
Plate, 7″	$2–$3
Plate, 9″	$5–$6
Platter	$8–$10
Saucer	$1–$2

Elite/Shellcrest (1936)

The Elite shape has plain, round flatware and hollowware with shell-like handles, finials, and feet. In mid-1937, Paden took the hollowware, added flatware with a shell-like embossing at opposing edges, and called it their Shellcrest shape. Elite seems to have been phased out at this time.

The Caliente line, identified by bright colors on the Elite/Shellcrest shape, was introduced in mid-1936. The colors are Tangerine Red, Turquoise Green, Sapphire Blue, and Lemon Yellow. The shape was also glazed in pastels: Azure, Celadon, Cream, and Rose; shakers are the most easily found. Popular decals are Studio (pottery and flowers) and Patio (pottery and flowers next a doorway).

Candleholder	$12–$15
Casserole, no feet	$15–$20

Patio Shellcrest plate, Blue Willow plate, Morning Glory Shenandoah AD cup/saucer, and Paden Village Shellcrest teapot.

Casserole, ftd	*$15–$20*
Creamer	*$4–$6*
Cup	*$4–$6*
Dish, 5¼″	*$1–$2*
Dish, 6¼″	*$1–$2*
Gravy	*$8–$10*
Plate, 6¼″	*$1–$2*
Plate, 7½″	*$2–$3*
Plate, 9½″	*$4–$5*
Plate, 10½″	*$4–$5*
Platter, oval, 12″	*$5–$6*
Platter, oval, 14½″	*$8–$9*
Platter, oval, 16½″	*$10–$12*
Saucer	*$1*
Shaker	*$6–$8*
Soup	*$4–$5*
Sugar	*$8–$10*
Teapot	*$30–$35*
Vegetable, rd, 9″	*$8–$10*
Vegetable, oval, 10″	*$8–$10*

Highlight (1951–1953)

Highlight was designed by Russel Wright. It was made for a very short time, and there is some question as to whether a listed AD cup/ saucer, butter, divided vegetable, jug w/lid, mug, relish, and teapot were ever made.

The line was made in five colors: Blueberry, Citron, Nutmeg, Pepper, and White.

Creamer	$18–$20
Cup	$18–$20
Dish, small, all sizes	$15
Gravy	$32–$35
Plate, B & B	$8–$10
Plate, salad	$18–$20
Plate, dinner	$32–$35
Platter, oval, small	$22–$25
Platter, oval, large	$32–$35
Saucer	$8–$10
Shaker, both sizes	$22–$25
Sugar	$32–$35
Vegetable, oval	$35–$40
Vegetable, round	$40–$45

Shenandoah

This line was decorated with decals that are intended to resemble hand painting. Novice collectors sometimes mistake these for Blue Ridge. Seven decals are known: Cosmos, Jonquil, Miniver Rose, Morning Glory, Nasturtium, Poppy, and Strawberry.

Casserole	$15–$20
Creamer	$4–$6
Cup	$4–$6
Cup, AD	$4–$6
Pickle, 9″	$2–$3
Plate, 6¼″	$1–$2
Plate, 9″	$4–$5

Platter, oval, 13 ½ "	*$5–$6*
Platter, oval, 16 "	*$8–$10*
Saucer	*$1*
Saucer, AD	*$1–$2*
Shaker	*$6–$8*
Sugar	*$8–$10*

World's Fair

Salad Bowl	*$100–$125*

THE PFALTZGRAFF POTTERY COMPANY

York, Pennsylvania

Pfaltzgraff, the oldest family-owned pottery in continuous operation in America, is believed to have begun in 1811 for the manufacture of redware. A number of different potteries in various locations were operated by family members. The name changed to The Pfaltzgraff Pottery Company in 1896. Art pottery was manufactured from 1931 to 1937. Kitchenware was introduced in the thirties. The pottery is still in operation today.

Marks

The Keystone and the Castle marks are the most commonly found. They are usually embossed but can be stamped as well.

Cookie Jars

Some of these jars are in the Muggsy style but have not been attributed to the Jessops (see Muggsy).

Clown on Drum	*$45–$55*
Cookie Clock	*$35–$45*

Cookie Cop	*$65–$75*
Engine	*$20–$25*

Country-Time (1950s)

Country-Time was designed by Ben Seibel. Platters could be hung from the wall. Metal stands, with ceramic warmers, were available in copper, nickel or brass plating for the butter warmer, tureen, coffee pot, coffee samovar, gravy boat, and 2-quart and 3-part casserole.

Known colors are blue, Saffron Yellow, and Smoke Gray. Pieces were made in either solid color or in white. Two designs, a Sunburst and a Fruit/Leaf, decorated the lighter pieces.

Bar-B-Q plate (divided)	*$12–$15*
Butter warmer	*$25–$35*
Casserole, ind, 12 oz	*$15–$20*
Casserole, 2 qt	*$30–$35*
Casserole, 2-part, w/2 lids	*$65–$75*
Casserole, 3-part, w/3 lids, 21 ″	*$75–$90*
Coffee pot, 10 cup	*$35–$40*
Coffee samovar, 28 cup	*$55–$65*
Creamer	*$8–$10*
Cruet, oil	*$15–$20*
Cruet, vinegar	*$15–$20*
Cup	*$5–$7*
Gravy boat	*$20–$25*
Meat board and platter	*$20–$25*
Pitcher, 2 qt	*$20–$25*
Plate, 8½″	*$7–$8*
Plate, 10″	*$8–$10*
Plate, 11¼″	*$10–$12*
Platter, 11″	*$12–$15*
Platter, 12″	*$15–$18*
Platter, 13″	*$18–$20*
Relish and cheese tray, 16″	*$20–$25*
Salad fork, wood handle	*$15–$20*
Salad spoon, wood handle	*$15–$20*

Salad bowl, 10½″ $15–$20
Salad bowl, ind, 6″ $8–$10
Saucer $2–$3
Shaker $8–$10
Soup tureen, 6 qt $45–$55
Sugar $10–$12

Muggsy (ca. 1954)

This line was designed by Dorothy and Norman Jessop. The Cookie clock and Cookie cop are in the Muggsy style but have not been attributed to the Jessops. Decanter bottles to match the stoppers are very rare.

Myrtle the Sprinkler (metal sprinkler fits in back of head). *(Photo courtesy of Dave Pritchard)*

Ashtray	*$40–$50*
Canape Carri	*$50–$75*
Child's set (bowl, plate, and Ko-Ko the Clown mug)	*$15–$20*
Decanter stopper	*$10–$12*
Derby Dan cookie jar	*$35–$45*
Mugs, miniature	
Jigger	*$10–$15*
Rick	*$10–$15*
Mugs, regular set	
Cock-eyed Charlie	*$8–$15*
Flirty Gertie	*$8–$15*
Handsome Herman	*$8–$15*
Jerry the Jerk	*$8–$15*
Pickled Pete	*$8–$15*
Sleepy Sam	*$8–$15*
Mugs, sporting set	
Brawny Bertram	*$15–$20*
Diamond Dick	*$15–$20*
Fairway Freddie	*$15–$20*
Muscles Moo	*$40–$45*
Pigskin Pete	*$15–$20*
Rodney Reel	*$15–$20*
Tumblers	
Handsome Herman	*$8–$15*
Myrtle sprinkler	*$25–$75*
Pretzel Pete pretzel jar	*$45*

THE POPE-GOSSER
CHINA COMPANY

Coshocton, Ohio

This company was founded in 1902. Pope-Gosser was one of the potteries to join the ill-fated American China Corporation which went bankrupt in 1932. Pope-Gosser was reorganized and produced semi-porcelain dinnerware until 1958.

Marks

A variety of backstamps were used, including the one above.

Rosepoint (1934)

Rosepoint is distinguished by a raised design of trailing roses with a rose finial on the covered pieces. Introduced in plain white with no decoration, decals were added in 1935.

This is one of the more popular patterns in American tableware; there is also matching silverware and glassware.

Casserole	$15–$20
Cream soup	$5–$7

Rosepoint AD coffee pot.

Cream soup saucer	*$2–$3*
Creamer	*$4–$6*
Creamer, AD	*$4–$6*
Cup	*$4–$6*
Plate, 6"	*$1–$2*
Plate, 9"	*$4–$5*
Plate, 10"	*$4–$5*
Saucer	*$1*
Sugar	*$8–$10*
Sugar, AD	*$8–$10*
Teapot	*$15–$20*
Teapot, AD	*$15–$20*

PURINTON POTTERY

Shippenville, Pennsylvania

Bernard Purinton founded the company in 1936 in Wellsville, Ohio, and moved it to Shippenville in 1941. Dinnerware, kitchenware, and novelties were made. The primary product had a hand-painted slip decoration under the glaze. Some solid color ware was made as well. The plant closed in 1959.

Purinton's Apple decoration is the most collectible, perhaps due in part to the wide interest in "country" style.

Marks   *Purinton*
         SLIP WARE

Pieces are backstamped with the name "Purinton" in script, and sometimes with the words "Slip Ware" in block letters. Many pieces are not marked.

Decorations

Big Apple, Normandy Plaid (red), Heather Plaid (green), Intaglio (brown), Intaglio (green), Maywood, Pennsylvania Dutch, Fruit, Tea Rose, and Mountain Rose. A variety of other decorations, whose names are unknown, will be found.

Pricing

Prices are for Apple and Normandy Plaid. Add 20% for Heather Plaid and Intaglio. Add 50% for Maywood, Pennsylvania Dutch, and Tea Rose.

Dinnerware

The relishes will be found with and without ceramic handles and with metal handles. An old ad shows seahorse handles but these have not been seen.

Bean pot	*$18–$20*
Butter, ¼ lb	*$40–$45*
Casserole, 9″	*$25*
Chop plate, 12″	*$18–$20*
Coffee pot, 8 cup	*$35–$40*
Creamer	*$8*
Creamer, ind	*$6*
Cup	*$8*
Dish, cereal	*$6*
Dish, fruit	*$6*
Fruit, 12″	*$20*
Marmalade	*$14–$16*
Party plate, 8½″	*$12*
Pickle, 6″	*$6*
Plate, 6¾″	*$6*
Plate, 8½″	*$8*
Plate, 9¾″	*$12*
Platter, 11″	*$15*
Platter, 12″	*$18*
Relish, 3-part	*$20*
Salad, 11″	*$30*
Salad, ftd, 11″	*$25–$30*
Saucer	*$4*
Spaghetti bowl, 14½″ rect	*$45–$50*
Sugar	*$10*
Sugar, ind	*$6*
Teapot, 2 cup (matches 6-cup teapot)	*$12–$15*
Teapot, 2 cup (matches coffee pot)	*$12–$15*
Teapot, 6 cup	*$25–$30*
Tray, roll	*$22–$25*
Vegetable, 8½″	*$12–$15*
Vegetable, divided	*$20–$22*

Intaglio Shake and Pour shakers, Fruit tall canisters. *(Photo courtesy of Dave Pritchard)*

Kitchenware

The coffee pot and matching 2-cup pot on a platter were sold as a batter set.

Bottle, oil/vinegar, handled	*$14–$16*
Bottle, oil/vinegar, tall	*$15–$18*
Canister, bell shape	*$25–$30*
Canister, Lazy Susan, complete	*$45–$50*
Canister, sq, small	*$25*
Canister, sq, large	*$35*
Canister, tall	*$25*
Cookie jar	*$30*
Cookie jar, wide	*$40*
Cookie jar, sq, wooden lid	*$50–$60*
Dish, jam/jelly	*$25–$30*
Drip, bell shape	*$18–$20*
Drip, Shake & Pour shape	*$20–$22*
Dutch jug, 2 pt	*$12–$16*
Dutch jug, 5 pt	*$25–$30*
Kent jug, 1 pt	*$12–$14*
Mug, beer, 16 oz	*$40*
Mug, coffee, 8 oz	*$25*
Mug jug	*$15*

Oasis jug, leather handle	*$250*
Shaker, jug	*$6*
Shaker, range	*$10*
Shaker, Shake & Pour	*$12–$18*
Stack set	*$25*
Tumbler, 6 oz	*$10*
Tumbler, 12 oz	*$10*

Miscellany

You may find a Tom and Jerry bowl and mugs, a square tea tile, and small animals. These are rare. It is common to find the pieces listed here in "unidentified" decorations.

Bank, pig, small	*$25*
Bank, Uncle Sam	*$30*
Candleholder, Peasant Lady, pair	*$150*
Candy dish, double	*$25*
Cornucopia vase	*$10*
Honey pot/ivy planter	*$10*
Ivy jug	*$10*
Jug, Rebecca	*$18–$20*
Night bottle/vase	*$30*
Shaker, "Old Salt"	*$12–$15*
Shaker, "Pepper, His Wife"	*$12–$15*
Sprinkler (watering can)	*$15*
Vase, Shake & Pour shape	*$18–$20*
Wall pocket	*$20–$25*

RED WING POTTERIES, INC.

Red Wing, Minnesota

Begun in 1878 as the Red Wing Stoneware Company, the name was changed to Red Wing Union Stoneware Company in 1906 after a merger. It then became the Red Wing Potteries, Inc., in 1936 and it continued to manufacture under this name until its closing in 1967.

Early Red Wing stoneware is very collectible, as is the dinnerware manufactured from the thirties through 1967.

Marks

Most of the dinnerware is backstamped. A wing features prominently in many of the marks.

Bob White (1955)

This line was designed by Charles Murphy. The coffee mug, cruet, and lazy Susan are uncommon. The beverage server and large water pitcher are rare. The pepper mill, trivet, tumbler, and 2-gallon water jar are very rare.

Note

A few experimental Bob White plates have been found with all-white backgrounds rather than speckled. These are priced below.

Pricing

Bob White is the second most popular decoration after Round-Up. For Round-Up prices, add 40–50% to the prices below.

Bread tray, 24"	*$20–$30*
Beverage server, w/lid	*$100–$150*
Stand for above	*$15–$20*
Butter warmer, w/lid	*$15–$25*
Stand for above	*$15–$20*
Butter, ¼ lb	*$25–$30*
Casserole, 1 qt	*$15–$20*
Stand for above	*$15–$20*
Casserole, 2 qt	*$20–$25*
Stand for above	*$15–$20*
Double stand	*$20–$25*
Casserole, 4 qt	*$25–$35*
Stand for above	*$15–$20*
Cocktail tray	*$12–$20*
Coffee cup	*$8–$12*
Cookie jar	*$35–$50*
Creamer	*$15–$20*

Bobwhite tall shakers, butter, and creamer. *(Photo courtesy of Dave Pritchard)*

Cruet, w/stopper	*$50–$60*
Stand for above	*$15–$20*
Dish, cereal	*$10–$15*
Dish, fruit	*$8–$12*
Gravy boat, w/lid	*$15–$25*
Stand for above	*$15–$20*
Handled marmite, w/lid	*$10–$15*
Hors d'oeuvres holder	*$25–$45*
Lazy Susan	*$75–$100*
Mug	*$20–$25*
Nut bowl	*$15–$30*
Pepper mill, tall	*$150–$175*
Plate, 6½"	*$4–$7*
Experimental white	*$30–$40*
Plate, 7½"	*$5–$8*
Experimental white	*$30–$40*
Plate, 10½"	*$8–$10*
Experimental white	*$75–$100*
Platter, 13"	*$10–$15*
Platter, 20"	*$25–$35*
Stand for above	*$20–$25*
Relish dish, 3-part	*$15–$20*
Salad bowl, 12"	*$20–$25*
Saucer	*$5–$10*
Shaker, bird, pair	*$15–$25*
Shaker, tall, pair	*$20–$30*
Soup	*$10–$15*
Sugar	*$15–$25*
Teapot	*$20–$35*
Stand for above	*$15–$20*
Trivet	*$100–$125*
Tumbler	*$65–$75*
Vegetable	*$10–$15*
Vegetable, divided	*$15–$20*
Water jar, w/base, 2 gal	*$500–$650*
Water pitcher, small, 60 oz	*$20–$30*
Water pitcher, large, 112 oz	*$50–$75*

Cookie Jars

Cookie jars are commonly found in solid colors of blue, brown, and yellow. Green is a rare color.

Friar Tuck (Monk)	$45–$50
Green	$70–$75
Katrina (Dutch Girl)	$45–$50
Green	$70–$75
Pierre (Chef)	$45–$50
Green	$70–75

Fondoso (1939)

Fondoso was one of four shapes of Gypsy Trail hostess ware designed by Belle Kogan. The other three are Chevron, Reed, and Plain (will also be found in Ivory). Made in orange, powder blue, yellow, and turquoise, Fondoso was also made in pastel shades of green, blue, yellow, and pink. The bowls were made in russet.

Butter	$12–$14
Canister, coffee	$20–$25
Canister, flour	$20–$25
Canister, sugar	$20–$25
Casserole, 8½"	$25–$30
Coffee pot	$15–$20
Coffee server, wood handle	$12–$16
Console bowl	$10–$15
Cookie jar	$20–$25
Creamer, small	$6–$8
Creamer, large	$10–$12
Cup	$6–$8
Custard	$8–$10
Dessert cup, ftd, 4"	$4–$6
Dish, lug, cereal	$6–$8
Dish, 5½"	$8–$10
Jug, batter	$20–$25
Jug, syrup	$15–$20

All prices given are for items in *mint* condition. In general, discoloration, crazing, chipping, and repairs will fetch lower prices.

Marmite, French, w/lid	*$12–$14*
Marmite, low, w/lid	*$6–$8*
Mixing bowl, 5″	*$5–$8*
Mixing bowl, 6″	*$8–$10*
Mixing bowl, 7″	*$10–$12*
Mixing bowl, 8″	*$12–$15*
Mixing bowl, 9″	*$15–$20*
Pitcher, straight, 18 oz	*$14–$18*
Pitcher, straight, 32 oz	*$18–$22*
Pitcher, straight, 76 oz	*$22–$26*
Pitcher, tilt, 70 oz	*$25–$30*
Plate, 6½″	*$3–$5*
Plate, 8½″	*$4–$7*
Plate, 9½″	*$7–$10*
Plate, 12″	*$10–$12*
Plate, chop, 14″	*$10–$14*
Platter, oval, 12″	*$10–$12*
Relish dish	*$7–$10*
Relish tray	*$10–$15*
Salad bowl, 12″	*$12–$14*
Saucer	*$3–$4*
Shaker, small, pair	*$10–$12*
Shaker, large, pair	*$14–$16*
Shirred egg	*$10–$12*
Soup, 7½″	*$6–$8*
Sugar, small	*$6–$8*
Sugar, large	*$10–$12*
Teapot, 3 cup	*$15–$20*
Teapot, 6 cup	*$15–$20*
Tray, batter set	*$15–$20*

Tumbler (mug), 7 oz	*$8–$12*
Tumbler (mug) 10 oz	*$10–$14*
Vegetable, rd, 8 ″	*$8–$10*

Miscellany

Cowboy	*$100–$150*
Cowgirl	*$100–$150*
Saturn teapot	*$65–$85*

Town and Country (1947)

Designed by Eva Zeisel, with an informal, slightly eccentric design. The plates are coup shape, a little higher on one side. Glazes are glossy or half matte: Chalk white, Chartreuse, Coral, Dusk blue, Forest green, Gray, Metallic brown, Peach, Rust, and Sand.

Bean pot	*$100–$150*
Casserole, ind	*$20–$25*
Casserole	*$40–$55*
Coaster/ashtray	*$10–$12*
Creamer	*$8–$10*
Cruet w/lid	*$25–$30*
Cup	*$12–$15*
Dish, 5¾″	*$8–$12*
Fruit saucer	*$6–$10*
Ladle/wood handle	ND
Lazy Susan (7 relish trays on wood ring)	*$150–$175*
Mixing bowl	*$50–$75*
Mug	*$25–$40*
Mustard jar	*$30–$45*

> ND = price is not determined; item too rare to price.
> + = worth at least sum indicated, but could be higher.

Pitcher, small	*$25–$35*
Pitcher, medium	*$35–$45*
Pitcher, large	*$40–$60*
Plate, 6½″	*$4–$7*
Plate, 8″	*$6–$8*
Plate, 10½″	*$8–$12*
Platter, 9″	*$15–$18*
Platter, 10⅝″	*$18–$22*
Platter, 15″	*$25–$35*
Relish, 7″ × 5″	*$15–$18*
Salad bowl, 13″	*$25–$50*
Salad spoon/wood handle, left and right hand	*$50*
Saucer	*$3–$4*
Shaker, small	*$8–$10*
Shaker, large	*$12–$20*
Soup tureen	*ND*
Sugar	*$15–$18*
Syrup pitcher	*$35–$45*
Teapot	*$75–$90*
Vegetable, oval, 8″	*$20–$28*

REGAL CHINA CORPORATION

Antioch, Illinois

Founded ca. 1938, Regal was bought by Royal China and Novelty Company (no relation to Royal China) in the forties and has been used as the manufacturing arm of their contract and premium business ever since. Regal is the manufacturer of the Jim Beam bottles.

Cookie Jars

Alice in Wonderland (Disney)	$300+
Aunt Holly	$195–$225
Baby Pig	$95–$125
Davy Crockett	$125–$175
Dutch Girl	$125–$150
Goldilocks	$125–$150
Kraft Bear	$125–$150
Lion	$125–$150
Mr. Mistletoe	$125–$150
Old MacDonald's Barn	$95–$125
Quaker Oats	$75–$85
Salad Chef	$125–$150
Toby	$250–$300

Huggies (1948)

These shakers were designed by Ruth Van Tellingen Bendel. The official name is "Snuggle Hugs." Bunnies and bears are the easiest to find; pigs are the most elusive, especially the Pig Bank.

Color variations are not uncommon. Where the word "colors" appears in a listing, it refers to patches of different colors that can appear on a piece.

Marks

"c Van Tellingen" is embossed just below the tail or on the base of the item. Sometimes the name of the item or the words "Pat. Pend." is embossed as well. Fire destroyed the molds ca. 1958 and the new molds were embossed "Bendel."

Note

Be aware of Occupied Japan imitations. They weigh less than the Regal pieces.

Bear Hug Bear Hugs marked "Bendel" are worth *$50–$60*.

Brown w/black	*$12–$15*
Brown w/pink	*$12–$15*
Cream	*$12–$15*
Green	*$12–$15*
Green w/black tail, colors	*$12–$15*
Pink	*$12–$15*
Pink w/black tail	*$12–$15*
Pink w/black tail, colors	*$12–$15*
Pink w/brown and black	*$12–$15*
Tan (beige)	*$12–$15*
Tan w/brown	*$12–$15*
White w/pink and brown	*$12–$15*
Yellow	*$12–$15*
Yellow w/black tail	*$12–$15*
Yellow w/black tail, colors	*$12–$15*
Yellow w/gold	*$25–$30*

Boy/Dog Hug Boy's face can vary from light gray through dark gray to black, and from pink to tan. Variations in boy are listed. White dog w/brown goes with brown or pink/tan face, white dog w/black goes with gray to black face.

White	*$25–$30*
White w/brown face	*$25–$30*
White w/gray to black face	*$30–$40*
White w/pink/tan face	*$25–$30*

Bunny Hug Yellow or green bunnies with hand-painted underglaze clothes, and yellow bunnies with hand-painted overglaze roses, marked J. L. Stieff Art Studio, have also been found. Bunny Hugs marked "Bendel" are worth *$50–$60*.

Brown	*$12–$15*
Gray w/pink and dark gray	*$12–$15*
Green	*$12–$15*
Green w/black tail	*$12–$15*
Green w/black tail, colors	*$12–$15*
Green w/brown and black	*$12–$15*
Green w/painted clothes	*$30–$40*
White	*$12–$15*
White w/black tail	*$12–$15*
White w/black tail and spots	*$12–$15*
White w/black tail, colors	*$12–$15*
Yellow	*$12–$15*
Yellow w/black tail	*$12–$15*
Yellow w/black tail, colors	*$12–$15*
Yellow w/painted clothes	*$30–$40*

Duck Hug

Yellow	*$20–$25*
Yellow w/black	*$20–$25*
Yellow w/red	*$30–$35*

Dutch Boy/Girl Hug Boy is white w/red hair, rosy cheeks, yellow shoes and marks on trousers. Girl is white w/rosy cheeks and blue on cap and apron.

White	*$20–$25*
White w/color	*$20–$25*

Love Bug Hug, small Large variation in gray/green coloring

Gray/Green	*$30–$35*
Maroon	*$35–$40*
Pink w/black spots	*$70–$80*

Love Bug Hug, large

Maroon	*$75–$85*

Mary/Lamb Hug Listings reflect variations in lamb only; Mary is white w/red/brown hair, green on scarf and orange on skirt.

Black lamb	*$22–$25*
Gray lamb	*$22–$25*

Gray lamb w/black tail	*$22–$25*
Gray lamb w/black tail and ears	*$22–$25*
White	*$22–$25*
White lamb w/black tail	*$22–$25*
White lamb w/black tail and ears	*$22–$25*
Yellow lamb	*$22–$25*
Yellow lamb w/black tail	*$22–$25*
Yellow lamb w/black tail and ears	*$22–$25*

Mermaid/Sailor Hug Mermaid is tan w/red-brown hair and green tail. Sailor is white w/rosy cheeks, black shoes, and blue trim.

Tan mermaid/White sailor	*$65–$75*
Painted mermaid and sailor	*$75–$85*

Pig Hug, small Too rare to price.
Pink
Pink w/colors
Yellow

Pig Hugs, large

White w/black spots	*$100–$125*
White w/gray and black	*$100–$125*
White w/gray and black/BANK	*$125–$150*

Peek-A-Boos

These bears in pajamas were designed by Ruth Van Tellingen Bendel. A complete shaker set has each bear covering alternate eyes. There was limited production on the cookie jar.

Peek-a-Boo cookie jar, large and small shakers. *(Photo courtesy of Tony Oge)*

Cookie jar
    White w/red   *$300–$350*

Shaker, small
    White w/red   *$40–$50*
    White w/peach   *$50–$60*

Shaker, large
    White w/red   *$100–$125*
    White w/gold   *$100–$125*

THE
ROBINSON-RANSBOTTOM
POTTERY COMPANY

Roseville, Ohio

In the fall of 1900, the four Ransbottom brothers acquired the Oval Ware and Brick Company in Beem City (one mile north of Roseville) and, early in 1901, began producing stoneware jardinieres, cuspidors, and red flower pots as The Ransbottom Brothers Pottery. They soon became the world's largest producer of stoneware jars. In 1908, they incorporated as The Ransbottom Brothers Pottery Company. In 1920, with the market for stoneware declining, they merged with The Robinson Clay Product Company, a manufacturer of tile and brick products. In the early twenties, production shifted to gardenware: bird baths, planting tubs, jardinieres with pedestals, large vases, urns, and strawberry jars. Kitchenware was added in the thirties.

Marks

Two impressed marks are generally found. One is a crown, and the other is the inscription "RRPCo, Roseville, Ohio" (sometimes just "RRPCo"). Note: some dealers mistake this mark for Roseville Pottery.

Cookie Jars

Brownie	$65–$85
Captain	$65–$85
Chef	$45–$55
Cow Over Moon	$95–$125
w/gold	$125–$150
Firechief	$65–$85
Girl Head	$65–$85
Jocko	$125–$150
Old King Cole	$195–$225
Oscar	$55–$65
Peter, Peter, Pumpkin Eater, w/gold or w/o gold	$125–$150
Preacher	$65–$85
Rings w/Tiger finial	$45–$55
Rooster	$45–$55
Sheriff Pig	$85–$95
Snow Man	$125–$175
Whale	$250–$325
Wise Bird	$35–$45
WW I soldier	$65–$85
WW II soldier	$85–$95
WW II sailor	$85–$95

Hobnail (1937–1943)

Hobnail was made in ivory, blue, turquoise, pink, and yellow.

Bakers, covered, 4 sizes	$10–$20
Bowl, 5 sizes	$5–$15
Custard	$2–$3
Pitcher, 3 1/4 pt	$10–$12
Pitcher, ice lip, 4 pt	$10–$12
Pitcher, 2 1/4 pt	$8–$10
Pitcher, 1 1/4 pt	$6–$8

Kitchenette (1938 to early '50s)

Kitchenette was made in blue, pink, turquoise, yellow, and brown.

Bowls, 5 sizes	*$5–$15*
Casserole, 2 sizes	*$15–$20*
Custard cup	*$2–$3*
Mustard, covered	*$10–$12*
Nappies, 5″, 6″, 7″, and 8″	*$3–$8*
Pie plate	*$6–$6*
Pitcher, covered, 2 sizes	*$15–$20*
Pitcher, plain, 5 sizes	*$5–$12*
Pitcher, ice lip, 2 sizes	*$10–$12*
Refrigerator jar, covered, 2 sizes	*$15–$20*
Sugar	*$8–$10*

Zephyrus (1946)

Zephyrus was made in turquoise, pink, yellow, ivory, and Robin's egg blue; look for a hand-tinted version in turquoise, pink, and blue on an ivory body.

Zephyrus jug and Kitchenette jug.

Baker, 5½″, 6½″, 7¼″, and 8¼″   *$5–$12*
Bowl, 5″, 6″, 7″, 8″, and 9″   *$5–$15*
Casserole, covered, 8¼″   *$15–$20*
Pitcher, 1½ pt   *$5–$6*
Pitcher, 3½ pt   *$6–$8*
Pitcher, 2½ pt   *$8–$10*

THE ROYAL
CHINA COMPANY

Sebring, Ohio

Royal began in 1933 on the site of the old E. H. Sebring Pottery. They made semi-porcelain dinnerware, as well as cookware and premiums. In 1969, the company was purchased by the Jeannette Glass Corporation and changed ownership several times after that. Operations ceased in 1986.

Marks

This is one of the general backstamps you will commonly find.

Regal (1937)

This shape is distinguished by thin fluting. On the flatware pieces, the fluting extends from the rim over the verge and slightly into the well.

Creamer	*$4–$6*
Cup	*$4–$6*
Plate, 6¼″	*$1–$2*
Plate, lug, 11½″	*$5–$6*
Plate, 7¼″	*$2–$4*

Saucer	*$1*
Shaker, tall	*$6–$8*
Sugar	*$8–$10*
Teapot	*$15–$20*
Vegetable, rd, 8¾"	*$7–$8*

Royalty (1936)

A band of spider web embossing distinguishes this shape. So far only decal decorations have been seen; no solid colors.

Casserole	*$15–$20*
Creamer	*$4–$6*
Cup	*$4–$6*
Dish, 5"	*$1–$2*
Gravy	*$8–$10*
Pickle, 8¼"	*$2–$3*
Plate, 6¼"	*$1–$2*
Plate, 7¼"	*$2–$3*
Plate, 9¼"	*$4–$5*
Saucer	*$1*
Shaker, tall	*$6–$8*
Sugar	*$8–$10*
Teapot	*$15–$20*

Swirl

Casserole	*$15–$20*
Creamer	*$4–$6*
Cup	*$4–$6*
Cup, AD	*$4–$6*
Gravy	*$8–$10*
Plate, 6¼"	*$1–$2*
Plate, 10½"	*$4–$5*
Saucer	*$1*
Saucer, AD	*$1–$2*

Shaker	*$6–$8*
Soup, 8"	*$4–$5*
Sugar	*$8–$10*
Teapot	*$15–$20*

Windsor

Windsor is distinguished by a square, Art Deco-like shape. The cup has a square foot and the saucer a square cup ring.

Cake plate, lug, 11"	*$4–$5*
Casserole	*$15–$20*
Casserole, rd	*$15–$20*
Coffee pot	*$15–$20*
Creamer	*$4–$6*
Cup	*$4–$6*
Dish , 5"	*$1–$2*
Dish, 6"	*$1–$2*
Gravy	*$8–$10*
Plate, 6¼"	*$1–$2*
Plate, 7¼"	*$2–$3*

Windsor coffee pot, Royalty creamer and sugar, and Swirl teapot.

Plate, 9 ¼ "	*$4–$5*
Platter, oval, 8 ¼ "	*$4–$5*
Platter, oval, 11 ¼ "	*$5–$6*
Saucer	*$1*
Shaker	*$6–$8*
Soup, 7 ¾ "	*$4–$5*
Sugar	*$8–$10*

All prices given are for items in *mint* condition. In general, discoloration, crazing, chipping, and repairs will fetch lower prices.

THE SALEM
CHINA COMPANY

Salem, Ohio

The Salem China Company was founded in 1898 and purchased by the Sebrings in 1918. Salem made semi-porcelain dinnerware. Most of the shapes and many of the decorations marketed in the thirties and forties were designed by Viktor Schreckengost. Manufacturing ceased in 1967, and Salem is now operating as a distributor.

Marks

Salem used a wide variety of backstamps, many designed for the particular shapes.

Briar Rose (ca. 1930)

Briar Rose was designed by J. Palin Thorley for the American China Corporation and was bought by Salem when ACC went bankrupt.

Butter dish, open	$10–$12
Cake plate, 10″	$4–$5
Casserole	$15–$20
Creamer	$4–$6
Cup	$4–$6
Dish, fruit	$1–$2
Dish, cereal	$1–$2
Gravy	$8–$10

Pickle	*$3–$4*
Plate, 6″	*$1–$2*
Plate, 7″	*$2–$3*
Plate, 9″	*$4–$5*
Plate, bread, 10″	*$4–$5*
Platter, 11″	*$5–$6*
Platter, 13″	*$6–$7*
Saucer	*$1*
Soup, coupe, 7″	*$4–$5*
Sugar	*$8–$10*
Vegetable, rd, 8″	*$8–$10*
Vegetable, oval, 9″	*$8–$10*

Tricorne (1934)

Distinguished by its triangular flatware and angular handles, Tricorne was designed to attract attention. It was introduced initially in Mandarin, a bright red art glaze, and the first brightly colored dinnerware made by an Ohio pottery. Later decorations are colored concentric bands: Coral Red, Royal Blue, and Platinum, and decals: Polo (pony and rider in black outlined in gray and coral red), Sailing (sailboats), Dutch Petitpoint (boy and girl), and a Bridge Set with card suits. Mandarin is the most easily found.

Candleholder	*$18–$20*
Casserole	*$20–$25*
Compote/cream soup	*$12–$15*
Creamer	*$6–$8*
Cup	*$6–$8*
Cup, AD	*$6–$8*
Dish, 5¼″	*$2–$3*
Nut dish, 3¾″	*$4–$5*
Plate, 5½″	*$2–$3*
Plate, 6¼″	*$3–$4*
Plate, 9″	*$6–$8*
Plate, party, 9″	*$8–$10*
Plate, sandwich, 11½″	*$8–$10*

Tricorne: advertising nut dish and Sailing teapot. Victory: Mary Had a Little Lamb AD coffee pot and Petitpoint Basket coffee pot.

Saucer	*$2–$3*
Saucer, AD	*$2–$3*
Sugar	*$12–$15*
Teapot	*$25–$35*

Victory (1938)

Victory was designed by Viktor Schreckengost. The mustache cup is a hard-to-find novelty. You will find a wide variety of decals including Godey Ladies, Indian Tree, Basket Petitpoint, and Parkway (red berries and black leaves).

A Little Lady Party Set for children was assembled from the AD pieces and the lug plate. It was decal-decorated with Basket Petitpoint or Mary Had a Little Lamb.

Ashtray	*$6–$8*
Bowl, 6¼″	*$2–$3*
Bow, lug, 6¾″	*$2–$3*
Cake plate, 10″	*$4–$5*
Casserole	*$15–$20*

Candleholder	*$12–$15*
Coffee pot	*$20–$25*
Coffee pot, AD	*$15–$20*
Cream soup	*$5–$6*
Cream soup saucer	*$2–$3*
Creamer	*$4–$6*
Creamer, AD	*$4–$6*
Cup	*$4–$6*
Cup, AD	*$4–$6*
Dish, 5½"	*$1–$2*
Dish, 7¼"	*$2–$3*
Gravy	*$8–$10*
Mustache cup	*$12–$15*
Plate, 6"	*$1–$2*
Plate, 7"	*$2–$3*
Plate, 10"	*$4–$5*
Plate, lug, 7¼"	*$2–$3*
Platter, oval, 11"	*$5–$6*
Platter, oval, 13"	*$6–$7*
Saucer	*$1*
Saucer, AD	*$1–$2*
Shaker, small	*$6–$8*
Shaker, tall	*$6–$8*
Soup, 8¼"	*$4–$5*
Sugar	*$8–$10*
Sugar, AD	*$8–$10*
Vegetable, rd, *8"*	*$8–$10*

THE SEBRING
POTTERY COMPANY

Sebring, Ohio

The Sebring family established its first pottery in East Liverpool in 1887. In 1899, after having opened several other potteries, the Sebrings decided to consolidate their interests, bought land in Mahoning county, Ohio, and established the town of Sebring. The second pottery to be built there was named the Sebring Pottery. It produced semi-porcelain dinnerware, toilet ware, and specialties. Some art ware and kitchenware was made in the thirties. Sebring and its sister company Limoges (q.v.) were bought in 1943 by National Unit Distributors, and the name Sebring disappeared; only the Limoges name was used in advertisements.

Note

From the introduction of semi-porcelain ca. 1890, dinnerware had been produced in a white body. In 1923, Sebring broke with convention and brought out its Ivory Porcelain, a semi-porcelain dinnerware with an ivory body. E. M. Knowles followed in kind two years later, and by the end of the twenties, the white body had virtually disappeared from dinnerware production, not to be seen again until the late forties.

Marks

Sebring used a few general backstamps that identified the glaze more often than the shape.

Aristocrat (1932)

Introduced by Sebring, you will find a lot of Aristocrat also made by (and marked) Leigh. You will find a lot of solid colors with band treatments as well as decals.

Casserole	*$15–$20*
Coffee pot	*$15–$20*
Creamer	*$4–$6*
Cup	*$4–$6*
Plate, 6½"	*$1–$2*
Plate, 7¼"	*$2–$3*
Plate, 9"	*$4 $5*
Platter, 13"	*$7–$8*
Saucer	*$1*
Shaker	*$6–$8*
Soup, 7⅜"	*$4–$5*
Sugar	*$8–$10*
Teapot	*$15–$20*

Doric (1930)

This line is distinguished by a square shape that has wide ribs and scalloped edges, and a shell finial. It was originally introduced in solid colors of ivory, rose, green, and yellow, as well as a number of decal decorations.

Creamer	*$4–$6*
Creamer, AD	*$4–$6*
Cup	*$4–$6*
Cup, AD	*$4–$6*
Dish, 5"	*$1–$2*
Dish, 5½"	*$1–$2*
Gravy	*$8–$10*
Jug, batter	*$20–$25*
Plate, 6"	*$1–$2*
Plate, 7"	*$2–$3*

Plate, 9"	*$4–$5*
Platter, rect, *11"*	*$5–$6*
Platter, rect, *13"*	*$6–$7*
Saucer	*$1*
Saucer, AD	*$1–$2*
Soup, 8"	*$4–$5*
Soup, coupe, *7½"*	*$4–$5*
Sugar	*$8–$10*
Sugar, AD	*$8–$10*
Vegetable, 8"	*$7–$9*

"Gadroon"

Distinguished by a gadroon edge shape, this line is most often found in the Golden Maize glaze. Decals, especially The Poppy and Jonquil, are common. You will also find solid colors with line treatments.

Casserole, oval	*$15–$20*
Creamer	*$4–$6*

Aristocrat coffee pot, Poppy "Gadroon" teapot, and Doric batter jug.

Cup	*$4–$6*
Dish, 5 1/4"	*$1–$2*
Dish, 6 1/4"	*$1–$2*
Domed cover	*$15–$20*
Plate, 6 1/4"	*$1–$2*
Plate, 9"	*$4–$5*
Plate, lug, 7 1/2"	*$2–$3*
Plate, sq, 9"	*$4–$5*
Platter, oval, 11 1/2"	*$5–$6*
Saucer	*$1*
Soup, 8"	*$4–$5*
Sugar	*$8–$10*
Teapot, 4 cup	*$15–$20*
Teapot, 6 cup	*$15–$20*

Trojan

A round version of Doric.

Casserole	*$15–$20*
Coffee pot	*$15–$20*
Creamer	*$4–$6*
Cup	*$4–$6*
Dish, 5 1/4	*$1–$2*
Egg cup	*$5–$7*
Gravy	*$8–$10*
Plate, 6"	*$1–$2*
Plate, 7"	*$2–$3*
Plate, 9"	*$4–$5*
Plate, lug, 11 1/4"	*$5–$6*
Plate, sq	*$4–$5*
Saucer	*$1*
Sugar	*$8–$10*
Vegetable, oval, 9"	*$8–$9*

THE SHAWNEE
POTTERY COMPANY

Zanesville, Ohio

Shawnee began operations in 1937, stating their intention to produce art pottery, brightly colored dinnerware and kitchenware, among other products, in an earthenware body. The company closed in 1961.

Shawnee is best known for (1) the Rudy Ganz designs of Smiley Pig, Puss-N-Boots, Mugsey, and other whimsical characters, and (2) Corn King, the most popular of the Corn line dinnerware.

Marks

You will find a shape number, "USA" or "Shawnee," or a combination of two of these, embossed on the bottom of pieces. Some of the character pieces will have names on them. Some pieces are unmarked. Shape numbers have been included in the listings where known.

Cookie Jars

The Dutch Boy and Dutch Girl are marked "Great Northern."

Pricing

Add 30–50% for cookie jars with gold trim.

Basket of Fruit, short	$45–$55
Basket of Fruit, tall	$45–$55

Clown, w/seal	$125–$150
Drummer Boy (10)	$75–$85
Dutch Girl (1026)	$100–$120
Dutch Boy (1025)	$100–$120
Elephant (60)	$30–$45
Jug (75)	$70–$80
Lucky Elephant	$50–$60
Mugsey the Dog	$100–$120
Octagon	$20–$25
Owl	$80–$90
Puss-N-Boots	$50–$60
Smiley the Pig	$50–$70
Winnie the Pig	$50–$70

Corn King

The utility jar doubled as sugar, with small jug as creamer, and was also a drip jar making a range set with the large shakers.

Casserole, ind	$30–$35
Casserole, 1½ qt	$45–$50
Cookie jar	$75–$100
Cup	$18–$20
Dish, 6″	$5–$7
Jug, 1 qt	$40–$50
Mixing bowl, 5″	$20–$22
Mixing bowl, 6½″	$20–$25
Mixing bowl, 8″	$30–$35
Mug	$25–$30
Plate, 10″	$25 $30
Platter, 12″	$30–$40
Relish tray	$20–$22
Shaker, small, pair	$10–$12
Shaker, large, pair	$18–$20
Soup/cereal bowl	$25–$30
Teapot, 30 oz	$40–$50
Utility jar	$25–$30

Creamers

Elephant	*$14–$16*
Puss-N-Boots (85)	*$18–$20*
Smiley the Pig (86)	*$20–$22*

Figurines

Gazelle (614)	*$35–$40*
Oriental (602)	*$4–$5*
Oriental w/parasol (601)	*$5–$6*
Pekingese	*$20–$22*
Puppy	*$20–$22*
Rabbit	*$20–$22*
Teddy bear	*$20–$22*
Tumbling bear	*$20–$22*

Pitchers

Little Bo Peep (47)	*$30–$35*
Little Boy Blue (46)	*$40–$45*
Smiley Pig	*$40–$45*

Planters

Boy w/chicken (645)	*$10–$12*
Boy w/dog (582)	*$2–$4*
Boy w/wheelbarrow (750)	*$10–$12*
Boy at fence	*$4–$6*
Boy at stump (532)	*$3–$5*
Boy at stump, leaning (533)	*$3–$5*
Bridge (756)	*$6–$8*
Buddha (524)	*$12–$14*
Bull (668)	*$12–$14*
Bull w/leaf	*$35–$40*

Smiley Pig pitcher and Tom Tom teapot. *(Photo courtesy of Dave Pritchard)*

Butterfly (524)	*$3–$5*
Canopy bed (734)	*$28–$30*
Cat playing saxophone (729)	*$18–$20*
Chick w/cart (720)	*$10–$12*
Circus cage	*$16–$18*
Donkey w/basket, head up (722)	*$12–$14*
Donkey w/basket, head down (671)	*$12–$14*
Donkey w/cart, small (538)	*$3–$5*
Donkey w/cart, large (709)	*$12–$14*
Duck (720)	*$12–$14*
Duck w/cart (752)	*$10–$12*
Dutch kids at well (710)	*$10–$12*
Elephant and leaf	*$35–$40*
Elephant, small (759)	*$4–$5*
Elf shoe (765)	*$6–$8*
Four birds on perch (502)	*$30–$35*
High chair (727)	*$30–$35*
Tractor trailer cab (680)	*$25–$30*

Tractor trailer (681)	*$25–$30*
Train set, caboose (553), box car (552), coal car, locomotive (550)	*$85–$100*

Shakers

Priced per pair.

Bo-Peep	*$6–$8*
Chanticleer, small	*$12–$14*
Duck	*$18–$20*
Dutch boy	*$14–$16*
Dutch girl	*$14–$16*
Dutch kids	*$16–$18*
Flower pots	*$8–$10*
Milk can	*$6–$8*
Mugsey, large	*$18–$20*
Owl	*$6–$8*
Puss-N-Boots	*$6–$8*
Sailor Boy	*$6–$8*
Smiley Pig, large	*$20–$25*
Swiss kids	*$20–$22*
Watering can	*$8–$10*
Wheelbarrow	*$8–$10*
Winnie Pig, large	*$20–$25*

Teapots

Elephant	*$60–$70*
Tom Tom (44)	*$25–$35*

Vases

Bow-knot (819)	*$12–$14*
Cornucopia (835)	*$6–$8*
Doe in shadowbox (850)	*$14–$16*

Doves (829)	*$16–$18*
Gazelle w/baby (841)	*$50–$60*
Leaf (821)	*$16–$18*
Leaf (823)	*$18–$20*
Swan (806)	*$10–$12*

Wall Pockets

Bird house (830)	*$12–$14*
Bow	*$6–$8*
Girl w/rag doll (810)	*$14–$16*
Little Jack Horner (585)	*$14–$16*
Mantel clock (530)	*$14 $16*
Telephone (529)	*$14–$16*

Miscellany

Bank, bull dog	*$45–$50*
Bookends, flying geese (4000)	*$24–$26*
Candlestick holder (3026)	*$12–$14*
Darner, woman	*$18–$20*
Winnie cookie jar bank (61)	*$125–$135*

SOUTHERN POTTERIES, INC.

Erwin, Tennessee

Established in 1917 as Clinchfield Pottery (after the Carolina, Clinchfield and Ohio Railroad that sold them land), it was chartered on April 8, 1920 as Southern Potteries, Inc. In the early years, they produced decal-decorated hotel ware and dinnerware. Collectors interested in this period focus primarily on advertising pieces: plates, bowls, and ashtrays.

Underglaze hand painting gradually became the major type of decoration and in the mid-thirties, the name Blue Ridge was introduced for these wares. By the early fifties, they were averaging 24 million pieces of pottery per year, and had produced over 4100 patterns. In 1942, a line of china specialties was added. Hand painting is labor intensive; escalating labor costs as well as cheap imports led to the closing of the pottery in 1957.

The most desirable decorations are people, animals, holiday themes, indoor scenes, outdoor structures, Victory edge trim (repeated border trim of three dots and a dash, which is Morse code for ''V''), and anything else that isn't floral or fruit.

Marks

Backstamps in script indicating ''Underglaze, hand painted, Southern Potteries.'' The words ''Blue Ridge'' were added ca. 1935.

Note

Southern made ware for a number of distributors, also called jobbers, who bought from several different potteries. Finding one of these jobber's marks on a piece of pottery does not necessarily mean that it was made by Southern.

Pricing

Blue Ridge prices are fluctuating. In some instances, there is a wide range listed here. That reflects the wide range around the country. Prices are highest in the southeast.

Character Jugs/Artist-Signed Pieces

All the jugs were made in china and the plates and platters in earthenware.

Note

Unauthorized reproductions of the jugs, plates, and platters are currently being made and are marked with a Blue Ridge stamp. Here's what you need to know to recognize these: (1) the new jugs are earthenware, not china, (2) jug handles are cast in the mold, not applied as were the originals, (3) impressed names found on the original jugs (except Indian) are missing, and (4) scenes other than the ones listed below are used on the plates and platters.

Daniel Boone	*$375–$475*
Indian	*$350–$450*
Paul Revere	*$350–$450*
Pioneer Woman	*$225–$325*
Plate, "Flower Cabin," 10½"	*$200–$400*
Plate, "Gold Cabin," 10½"	*$200–$400*
Plate, "Green Mill," 10½"	*$200–$400*
Plate, Tom Turkey, "Turkey Gobbler," 10½"	*$300+*
Plate, "White Mill," 10½"	*$200–$400*
Plate, "Quail," 11¾"	*$200–$400*
Platter, Tom Turkey, "Turkey Gobbler," 17½"	*$350–$500*
Platter, Wild Turkey, "Turkey Hen," 17½"	*$300–$450*

China/Specialties

Called Classic Specialties in some old ads, these pieces began to be introduced in 1942. Most were made in the new china body. Many were decorated to match the dinnerware lines. The hard-to-find pieces are the advertising plates, counter sign, chocolate tray, AD pot with matching flared sugar and creamer, Duck, Lily and Nude boxes, carafe, Watauga jug, and small-size jugs. If there is a specific Southern name, it is included in the listing. Note: Alice and Antique are the same shape but different sizes.

Pricing

Most specialties were produced in china only, some in earthenware only, and some in either body. This is indicated by a C or E following the item. For items made in both bodies, there are two listings.

If an item has the Good Housekeeping or Charm House mark, add 50%. For the desirable decorations mentioned above add 50% to 100%.

Advertising counter plate, all variations/E	*$150–$250*
Ashtray	
Round/E	*$10–$25*
Round w/RR advertising/E	*$45–$75*
Square/E	*$8–$12*
Ashtray w/rests/E	*$5–$13*
Bonbon, 4-part, top-handle/C	*$45–$65*
Bonbon, deep shell (Shell Bonbon)/C	*$35–$40*
Bonbon, deep shell (Shell Bonbon)/E	*$25–$30*
Bonbon, flat shell (Dorothy)/C	*$30–$48*
Bonbon, flat shell (Dorothy)/E	*$20–$38*
Box, Duck/C	*$225–$350*
Box, Lily/C	*$350–$550*
Box, Nude/C	*$225–$350*
Box, Shell/C	*$60–$90*
Box, tiered, "Rose"/C	*$60–$90*
Box, tiered, "Rose"/E	*$40–$70*
Candy box, rd, 6″/C	*$60–$85*
Carafe, w/lid/E	*$75–$95*
w/o lid	*$50–$60*

Celery leaf/C	$20–$35
Celery leaf/E	$10–$18
Child's bowl/E	$25–$35
Child's deep bowl/E	$25–$40
Child's grill plate/E	$35–$60
Child's mug/E	$15–$30
Child's plate/E	$25–$40
Chocolate pot, pedestal/C	$90–$140
Cigarette box, square/E	$45–$65
Cigarette box w/4 ashtrays/E	$70–$85
Coffee pot, AD, flared/C	ND
Counter sign/C	$100–$175
Creamer, AD, flared/C	$40–$45
Creamer, pedestal/C	$25–$35
Cup, AD/C	$15–$20
Pitchers	
Abby/C	$70–$85
Abby/E	$25–$35
Alice/C	$90–$110
Alice/E	$65–$85
Antique, 3½"/C	$65–$85
Antique, 5"/C	$40–$55
Antique, 5"/E	$40–$45
Betsy/C	$90–$125
Betsy/E	$65–$85
Charm House/C	$100–$175
Chick/C	$55–$75
Chick/E	$25–$45
Clara (Paneled)/C	$55–$65
Clara (Paneled)/E	$20–$35
Grace/C	$45–$65
Grace/E	$35–$55
Helen/C	$65–$80
Jane/C	$65–$90
Martha (Grace Scroll)/C	$70–$95
Martha (Grace Scroll)/E	$35–$55
Milady/C	$80–$100
Raised Fruit (Petite), 6½"/C	$45–$65
Raised Fruit, 7"/C	$45–$65

Raised Fruit (DeLuxe), 7½″/C	*$45–$65*
Rebecca/C	*$85–$105*
Sally/C	*$70–$95*
Skyline/E	*$30–$40*
Spiral, 4″/C	*$65–$90*
Spiral, 7″/C	*$45–$60*
Virginia, 3¾″/C	*$65–$90*
Virginia, 6½″/C	*$45–$60*
Watauga (Eunice), 5¼″/C	*$125–$150*
Watauga (Eunice), 5″/E	*ND*
Watauga (Eunice), 6¼″/E	*ND*
Powder box, rd/C	*$65–$90*
Relish, Charm House, 2 styles/C	*$150+*
Relish, heart/C	*$45–$60*
Relish, leaf, T-handle/C	*$40–$55*
Relish, leaf, 3-part, (Martha Snack Tray)/C	*$60–$85*
Relish, loop handle/C	*$40–$60*
Relish, Maple leaf	
(Maple Leaf cake tray)/C	*$25–$40*
(Maple Leaf cake tray)/E	*$15–$30*
Saucer, AD/C	*$10–$15*
Shaker, apple, small, pair/E	*$10–$20*
Shaker, apple, large, pair/E	*$15–$25*
Shaker, blossom top, pair/E	*$25–$30*
Shaker, bud top, pair/E	*$25–$30*
Shaker, Charm House, pair/C	*$80–$100*
Shaker, chicken, pair/E	*$75–$95*
Shaker, duck/E	*$100–$150*
Shaker, Good Housekeeping, pair/C	*$50–$80*
Shaker, tall, pair/C	*$20–$40*
Sugar, AD, flared/C	*$40–$45*

ND = price is not determined; item too rare to price.
+ = worth at least sum indicated, but could be higher.

Sugar, pedestal/C	*$25–$35*
Tea tile, rd, all sizes/E	*$25–$40*
Tea tile, sq, all sizes/E	*$25–$40*
Teapots	
Charm House/C	*$100–$175*
Chevron Handle/C	*$70–$90*
Fine Panel/C	*$65–$80*
Good Housekeeping/C	*$80–$100*
Snub Nose/C	*$75–$90*
Good Housekeeping, "Mini-Ball"/C	*$65–$90*
Tray, chocolate pot/C	*$225–$350*
Vase, boot, 8"/C	*$40–$55*
Vase, bud/C	*$55–$80*
Vase, handled/C	*$45–$65*
Vase, handled/E	*$25–$35*
Vase, rd/C	*$50–$70*
Vase, ruffled/C	*$50–$70*
Vase, tapered/C	*$60–$85*

Dinnerware

These lines were made in earthenware only. The round cake plate comes in two versions. One is the regular 10½" Colonial plate and the other is flatter with a bit of a rim. This is harder to find. The Chop plate is the same as the Salad bowl underplate. The French casseroles (stick handle) are also called ramekins by collectors. The rare pieces are the AD tray, butter dish, covered vegetable, fork and spoon. The hard-to-find pieces are the AD creamer and sugar, butter pat, egg cup, sherbet, toast lid, and 12" square cake plate.

Shapes

A number of official shape names have turned up. In addition to the ones listed here (unofficial names in quotes) with date of introduction, there is also the Bristol, Richmond, Dixie, and LeComte shapes, which were all introduced pre-1935. One of these is probably the official name for Trellis. Note that some Skyline hollowware was re-styled in 1953 and 1955.

Palisades shape. *(Drawing courtesy of Jean Rettmer)*

Skyline shape (original cup plus two restyled versions). *(Drawing courtesy of Jean Rettmer)*

Known shapes: Astor (early '40s?), Candlewick (1939), Clinchfield (pre-1935), Colonial (1939), Monticello ["Waffle"] (pre-1939), Palisades ["Moderne"] (1955–1956), Piecrust (1948), Skyline (1950), Trailway ["Rope Handle"] (1953), "Trellis" (pre-1935), Woodcrest (1953).

Pricing

Dinnerware prices are relatively the same for most shapes except Trellis (double prices) and Woodcrest (add 30%) which are harder to find and therefore more desirable. Interest in Monticello is rising due to its elusiveness; add 50%. Astor prices may start to rise as it is proving hard to find.

Prices are for most of the decorations you will find; pay double for desirable decorations mentioned above.

Butter pat, rd, 4″	*$15–$20*
Butter, ¼ lb	*$15–$30*
Cake plate, rd, 10½″	*$12–$20*
Cake plate, rd, flat rim, 10½″	*$18–$25*
Cake plate, sq, 12″	*$22–$35*
Cake server	*$15–$25*
Celery tray	*$10–$20*
Chop plate, 11″–12″	*$15–$25*
Coffee pot	*$65–$85*
Coffee pot, AD	*$45–$75*
Covered toast	*$70–$90*
lid only	*$40–$60*
Creamer	*$8–$10*
Creamer, AD	*$10–$20*
Cup	*$5–$10*
Cup, AD	*$6–$12*
Cup, jumbo	*$12–$18*
Dish, 5¼″	*$3–$5*
Dish, 6″	*$4–$7*
Dish, lug	*$4–$7*
Egg cup	*$15–$25*
Fork	*$20–$30*
French casserole, 7″	*$20–$35*
French casserole, ind, 5″	*$15–$25*
Gravy boat	*$8–$18*
Grill plate	*$18–$30*
Party plate, 8½″	*$12–$20*
Pickle/gravy tray	*$10–$15*

French Peasant. *(Photo courtesy of Tom Moore)*

French Peasant Variant. *(Photo courtesy of Tom Moore)*

Language of Flowers. *(Photo courtesy of Tom Moore)*

Still Life. *(Photo courtesy of Tom Moore)*

Kitchen Shelf. *(Photo courtesy of Tom Moore)*

Ham 'n' Eggs. *(Photo courtesy of Tom Moore)*

Cock O' the Morn. *(Photo courtesy of Tom Moore)*

Rooster. *(Photo courtesy of Tom Moore)*

Cock O' the Walk. *(Photo courtesy of Tom Moore)*

Thanksgiving Turkey. *(Photo courtesy of Tom Moore)*

Weathervane. *(Photo courtesy of Tom Moore)*

Christmas Tree (mistletoe variation). *(Photo courtesy of Tom Moore)*

Plate, 6″	$2–$4
Plate, 7″	$4–$7
Plate, 8″	$5–$9
Plate, 9″ or 10″	$6–$15
Plate, sq	$5–$15
Platter, oval, 9″	$10–$12
Platter, oval, 11″	$12–$15
Platter, oval, 13″	$15–$18
Platter, oval, 15″	$18–$25
Relish, Palisades, triangular	ND
Salad bowl, large	$25–$45
Saucer	$2–$5
Saucer, AD	$5–$10
Saucer, jumbo	$5–$10
Shaker, all shapes, pair	$8–$20
Sherbet	$10–$20
Soup, 8″	$8–$12
Spoon	$15–$25
Sugar	$8–$10
Sugar, AD	$10–$20
Teapots	
Ball	$45–$60
Colonial	$45–$85
Palisades	ND
Piecrust	$50–$75
Skyline	$40–$60
Square Round	$45–$70
Trailway (''Rope Handle'')	$40–$65
Woodcrest	$70–$100
Tidbit, 1, 2 & 3 tier	$15–$25
Tray, AD (rect or oval)	$40–$70
Vegetable, oval	$10–$15
Vegetable, oval, divided	$15–$22

All prices given are for items in *mint* condition. In general, discoloration, crazing, chipping, and repairs will fetch lower prices.

Vegetable, rd	*$8–$18*
Vegetable, rd, divided	*$15–$18*
Vegetable, covered	*$35–$60*

Dinnerware Sets

High on collectors' want lists are the 13-piece Breakfast Set (AD pot/ lid, AD sugar and creamer, cup/saucer, covered toast/lid, egg cup, butter pat, cereal, 8˝ plate and 6˝ plate, always on the Astor shape), the 16-piece Child's Tea Set (AD pot/lid, AD sugar and creamer, four AD cups and saucers and four 6˝ plates), and the 8-piece Salad Plate Set (eight 8˝ salad plates, with different but related decoration, e.g., eight different birds on same shape with same border trim).

Pricing

These prices are for *complete* sets; individual pieces are priced above. Child's Set prices are dropping as it is easy to assemble these piece by piece. Breakfast Sets are hard to assemble, especially the flatware.

Breakfast Set	
Everyday patterns	*$175–$200*
Interesting patterns	*$225–$300*
Fruit patterns	*$250–$325*
People/Desirable patterns	*$325–$500*
Child's Tea Set	*$150–$250*
Salad Plate Set	
Everyday patterns	*$100*
Interesting patterns	*$100–$150*
Desirable patterns	
Birds (45–60 each)	*$300–$400*
Sowing Seeds (50–60 each)	*$300–$400*
Language of Flowers (40–50 each)	*$300–$400*
Square Dancers (40–50 each)	*$300–$400*

Kitchenware

Rare pieces are the Batter Set trays, the Batter and Syrup jug lids, and the leftovers.

Leaf decorations are the most common; anything else is considered desirable.

Pricing

Leaves are the common decoration; use the low end of the range. Add 30% for the desirable decorations.

Baking dish, 8″ × 13″	*$20–$25*
Baking dish, 5-part, 8″ × 13″	*$20–$25*
Bowl, utility, all sizes	*$20–$35*
Casserole, deep lid	*$30–$40*
Casserole, knob lid	*$30–$40*
Custard	*$10–$15*
Jug, batter w/lid	*$55–$85*
Jug, syrup w/lid	*$65–$80*
Leftover, small	*$10–$15*
Leftover, medium	*$15–$25*
Leftover, large	*$25–$35*
Mixing bowl, 5″	*$10–$15*
Mixing bowl, 6″	*$10–$15*
Mixing bowl, 7½″	*$15–$20*
Mixing bowl, 8½″	*$15–$20*
Mixing bowl, 9½″	*$20–$25*
Mixing bowl, 10½″	*$20–$25*
Mixing bowl, 11¼″	*$25–$30*
Pie baker	*$15–$25*
Range shaker, pair	*$20–$30*
Tray, batter set, 7½″ × 11½″	*$100–$150*
Tray, batter set, 9½″ × 13½″	*$100–$150*

STANGL POTTERY

Flemington and Trenton, New Jersey

John Martin Stangl joined the Fulper Pottery Company in 1910 as a chemist and plant superintendent. He left in 1914 to work for Haeger and returned in 1919. He became president of Fulper in 1926, at which time he bought a share of the company. In the same year, the company bought the Anchor Pottery Company of Trenton and began manufacturing operations there. J. M. Stangl died in 1972, and his estate ran the company until it was bought in 1973 by the Wheaton Glass Company. It closed in 1978 when the Susquehanna Broadcasting Company bought it for its real estate.

Birds

In 1940 Stangl introduced a line of pottery birds which they expanded greatly in 1942 when WW II cut off Japanese imports. The return of foreign competition in 1947 resulted in curtailed production, with sporadic reissues until 1977.

Note

Birds which were also made in an early limited porcelain edition are marked with /P. It is a seller's market on these very rare pieces.

Birds continued in production until 1978. These later birds are either (1) hand painted but have a date, or (2) are all white.

> Because we felt collectors would like to know which birds were made but hard to find, we listed them with an ND which indicates that price is Not Determined.

3250 A Standing Duck	$30–$40
3250 B Preening Duck	$30–$40
3250 C Feeding Duck	$30–$40
3250 D Gazing Duck	$30–$40
3250 E Drinking Duck •	$30–$40
3250 F Quacking Duck	$30–$40
3273 Rooster	$60
3274 Penguin	$250–$350
3275 Turkey	$300–$350
3276 S Bluebird	$60–$80
3276 D Bluebird, double	$100–$150
3281 Duck	ND
3285 Rooster, shaker	$25–$35
3286 Hen, shaker	$25–$35
3285 Rooster	$20–$25
3286 Hen	$20–$25
3400 Lovebird, single	$40–$60
3401 S Wren	$35–$50
3401 D Wren, pair	$60–$75
3402 S Oriole	$50–$60
3402 D Oriole, pair	$90–$110
3404 D Lovebirds, pair	$95–$100
3405 S Cockatoo	$45–$60
3405 D Cockatoo, pair	$75–$100
3406 S King Fisher	$50–$75
3406 D King Fisher, pair	$100–$125
3407 Owl	$185–$200
3408 Bird of Paradise	$60–$80
3430 Duck	ND
3431 Standing Duck	$300–$400
3432 Running Duck	$300–$400
3443 Flying Duck	$250–$350
3444 Cardinal	
Pink	$65
Red matte	$85–$90
3445 Rooster	$125–$150
3446 Hen	$125–$150

ND = price is not determined; item too rare to price.
+ = worth at least sum indicated, but could be higher.

3447	*Prothonatary Warbler*	$65–$80
3448	*Blue-headed Vireo*	$55–$65
3449	*Paraquet*	$150
3450	*Passenger Pigeon*	$600–$650
3451	*Willow Ptarmigan*	ND
3452	*Painted Bunting*	$75–$100
3453	*Mountain Bluebird*	ND
3454	*Key West Quail Dove*	$250–$275
3455	*Shoveler*	ND
3456	*Cerulean Warbler*	$55–$65
3457	*Pheasant*, large	$500–$550
3458	*Quail*, large	ND
3459	*Fish Hawk* (Falcon)	$1500
3490 D	*Redstarts*, pair	$125–$150
3491	*Hen Pheasant*	$200–$225
3492	*Cock Pheasant*	$200–$225
3518	*White-headed Pigeon*	ND
3518 D	*White-headed Pigeon*, double	$450–$500
3580	*Cockatoo*, medium	$100–$125
3581	*Chickadees*, group	$175–$200
3582	*Parakeets*, pair (green/blue)	$165–$185
3583	*Parula Warbler*	$50–$60
3584	*Cockatoo*, large	$175–$200
3585	*Rufous Hummingbird*	$45–$50
3589	*Indigo Bunting*	$55–$65
3590	*Chat* (Carolina wren)	$60–$65
3591	*Brewer's Blackbird*	$60–$80
3592	*Titmouse*	$40–$45
3593	*Nuthatch*	$40–$50
3594	*Red-faced Warbler*	$50–$60
3595	*Bobolink*	$100–$125
3596	*Gray Cardinal*	$60–$70

3597	*Wilson Warbler*	*$45*
3598	*Kentucky Warbler*	*$40–$50*
3599	*Hummingbirds*, pair	*$200–$250*
3625	*Bird of Paradise*	*$500–$600*
3626	*Broadtail Hummingbird*	*$100–$125*
3627	*Rivoli Hummingbird*, pink or blue flower	*$80–$90*
3628	*Rieffers Hummingbird*	*$100–$125*
3629	*Broadbill Hummingbird*	*$100–$125*
3634	*Allen Hummingbird*	*$50–$60*
3635	*Goldfinches*, group	*$200–$225*
3715	*Blue Jay* (peanut)	*$500–$550*
3716	*Blue Jay* (leaf)	*$500–$550*
3717	*Blue Jay*, pair	*$500–$600*
3722	*European Finch*	*$100–$125*
3726	*Crossbill/P*	*ND*
3727	*Crossbill*, pair, /P	
	Pink glossy	*$145–$200*
	Red matte	*$150–$200*
3728	*Scissor-tail Flycatcher/P*	*$400–$500*
3738	*Magpie-Jay/P*	*$500–$550*
3739	*Audubon Warbler/P*	*$85–$95*
3740	*Audubon Warbler*, pair/P	*ND*
3741	*Robin/P*	*ND*
3742	*Robin, pair/P*	*ND*
3746	*Canary right*, rose flower	*$150–$175*
3747	*Canary left*, blue flower	*$150–$175*
3749 S	*Scarlet Tanager*, pink	*$150–$165*
3749 S	*Western Tanager*, red	*$150–$165*
3750 D	*Scarlet Tanager*, pink, pair	*$275–$350*
3750 D	*Western Tanager*, red, pair	*$275–$350*
3751 S	*Red-headed Woodpecker*	
	Pink glossy	*$75*
	Red matte	*$100*
3752 D	*Red-headed Woodpecker*, pair	
	Pink glossy	*$150*
	Red matte	*$175*
3754 S	*White-wing Crossbill*	*ND*

3754 D	White-wing Crossbill, pair	$200–$250
3755 S	Audubon Warbler	$150–$200
3756 D	Audubon Warbler, pair	ND
3757	Scissor-tail Flycatcher	$350–$400
3758	Magpie-Jay	$500
3810	Blackpoll Warbler	ND
3811	Chestnut-backed Chickadee	$65–$75
3812	Chestnut-sided Warbler	$65–$75
3813	Evening Grosbeak	$90–$110
3814	Black-throated Green Warbler	$75
3815	Western Blue Bird	$95
3848	Golden-crowned Kinglet	$75
3849	Goldfinch	$45–$50
3850	Yellow Warbler	$50–$65
3851	Red-breasted Nuthatch	$55–$65
3852	Cliff Swallow	$65–$75
3853	Kinglets, group	ND
3868	Summer Tanager	$80–$90
3921	Yellow-headed Verdum	$125–$150
3924	Yellow-throated Warbler	$50
3925	Magnolia Warbler	$350–$400

Colonial Dinnerware

This line with a fluted shape is most easily identified by its shape number 1388 inscribed on the bottoms of pieces. It is decorated in solid colors: Colonial Blue, Persian Yellow, Tangerine, and Silver Green are the basic four. Others are Aqua Blue, Rust, Satin Brown, Satin White, Rainbow, and Mauve.

Hand-painted decorations will be found. For Harvest (fruits) and Newport (sailing ship) add 50% to plates. For Ranger (cowboy) double plate prices and add 50% to other pieces.

Ashtray, 3½"	$12–$15
Baking shell	$8–$10
Bean pot	$25–$30
Bean pot, ind	$15–$18

Bowl, lug soup, 4 1/2 ″	*$6–$8*
Bowl, lug soup w/lid, 5 ″	*$12–$15*
Butter chip	*$4–$5*
Candleholder, single	*$8–$10*
Candleholder, triple	*$20–$25*
Carafe, w/china stopper, wood handle	*$25–$30*
Casserole, 5 ″	*$12–$15*
Casserole, 8 ″	*$25–$30*
Cigarette box, 4 1/2 ″ × 8 1/2 ″	*$15–$20*
Coaster	*$5–$7*
Coffee pot, AD	*$25–$35*
Compote, 7 ″	*$12–$15*
Console bowl, 12 ″	*$20–$25*
Creamer	*$6–$8*
Creamer, AD	*$8–$10*
Creamer, ind, 2 1/2 ″ high	*$6–$8*
Custard cup, 3 1/2 ″	*$5–$6*
Cup	*$6–$8*
Cup, AD	*$6–$8*
Dish, 6 ″	*$6–$8*
Egg cup	*$6–$8*
Gravy	*$12–$15*
Hors d'oeuvres, 5 compartments, 12 ″	*$15–$20*
Hors d'oeuvres, rd, 9 ″	*$15–$20*
Jug, ball	*$25–$30*
Jug, syrup	*$15–$20*
Jug, waffle, 2 qts, w/lid	*$25–$30*
Mixing bowl, 5 ″	*$12–$15*
Mixing bowl, 7 1/2 ″	*$15–$18*
Mixing bowl, 9 ″	*$18–$20*
Mixing bowl, 14 ″	*$20–$25*
Mug, coffee	*$6–$8*
Pie baker	*$15–$20*
Pitcher, 3 1/2 ″	*$10–$12*
Pitcher, 4 1/2 ″	*$12–$15*
Pitcher, 5 1/2 ″	*$15–$18*

Plate, 6"	$1–$2
Plate, 7"	$2–$3
Plate, 8"	$4–$5
Plate, 9"	$6–$7
Plate, 10"	$8–$10
Plate, chop, 12"	$15–$18
Plate, chop, 14"	$20–$22
Plate, grill, 10"	$10–$12
Platter, oval, 12"	$8–$10
Platter, oval, 14"	$10–$12
Ramekin, 4"	$6–$8
Refrigerator bottle, w/stopper	$25–$35
Relish dish, 2 comp, 6½" × 7"	$8–$10
Salad bowl, lug, 8"	$12–$15
Salad bowl, lug, 10"	$15–$20
Saucer	$1–$2
Saucer, AD	$2–$3
Shaker	$4–$6
Shirred egg, 8" × 6"	$8–$10
Sugar	$10–$12
Sugar, AD	$10–$12
Sugar, ind, 2½" high, open	$6–$8
Tea cup	$6–$8
Teapot, 6 cup	$25–$35
Teapot, ind	$15–$20
Tray/shakers	$5–$8
Tray, sugar & creamer, ind, 8 × 4"	$8–$10
Vegetable, oval, 10"	$10–$12

Hand-Painted Dinnerware

Stangl first began hand painting dinnerware on their Colonial shape ca. 1936. In 1942, Stangl switched from a white body to a red body and began introducing new shapes as well as new decorations. In the fifties some patterns were made on a white body again, in limited production.

Apple Delight

Blueberry

Country Garden

Fruit

Fruit and Flowers

Golden Blossom

Thistle

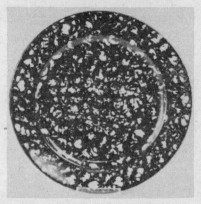

Town & Country

Tulip

Wild Rose

Very Very Popular Patterns: Blue Town and Country, Country Garden, Fruit, Fruit and Flowers.

Very Popular Patterns: Blueberry, Country Life, Father Christmas, Garden Flower, Holly, Jewelled Christmas Tree, Thistle.

Popular Patterns: Amber Glo, Apple Delight, Blue Daisy, Bitter Sweet, Blue Caughley, Chicory, Colonial, Festival, Golden Blossom, Golden Harvest, Grape, Magnolia, Mediterranean, Orchard Song, Rooster, Sculptured Fruit, Star Flower, Terra Rose, Yellow Tulip, White Dogwood, Wild Rose.

Average Interest Patterns: Bachelor's Button, Blossom Ring, Blue Tulip, Colonial Rose, First Love, Flora, Florette, Garland, Golden Grape, Harvest, Lyric, Mountain Laurel, Newport, Petite Flowers, Prelude, Provincial, Ranger, Rustic Garden, Sun Pebbles, Tiger Lily, Town and Country (all colors except blue).

Some Interest Patterns: Americana, Belle Rosa, Carnival, Colonial Dogwood, Cranberry, Dahlia, Daisy, Delmar, Diana, Fairlawn, Field Daisy, Florentine, Frosted Fruit, Green Caughley, Inspiration, Jonquil, Kumquat, Lime, Maple Whirl, Morning Blue, Paisley, Pie Crust, Pink Cosmos, Pink Dogwood, Pink Lily, Posies, Red Ivy, Ringles, Roxane, Rustic, Sesame, Sierra, Spun Gold, Stardust, Sunshine, Susan, Treasured, Trinidad, Water Lily, White Grape, Wildwood, Windfall, Wood Rose, Yellow Caughley, Yellow Flower.

Pricing

White backstamp indicated seconds, however most of these are in good condition. And it is condition, not the mark, that determines price. Prices in column 1 are for very, very popular patterns, column 2 for very popular and column 3 for popular. For average interest patterns deduct 25% from column 3 and for some interest patterns deduct 50%.

	1	*2*	*3*
Bowl, 8″	$30	$25	$20
Bowl, 10″	$40	$35	$25
Bowl, 12″	$50	$50	$35
Bread tray	$35	$30	$20
Butter, ¼ lb	$35	$25	$20
Candle			
warmer	$20	$18	$15

	1	2	3
Casserole, covered	$45	$35	$30
Casserole, ind	$20	$15	$10
Casserole, handled, 6″	$25	$20	$15
Casserole, handled, 8″	$30	$25	$20
Coaster/ ashtray	$15	$10	
Coffee pot, 8 cup	$50	$40	$25
Coffee pot, AD			$15
Condiment tray		$25	$20
Creamer	$12	$8	$7
Creamer, AD		$8	
Cruet	$35	$30	$25
Cup	$12	$10	$8
Dish, cereal 5⅝″ (1¼″ H)	$15	$12	$10
Dish, fruit, 5⅝″ (1⅞″ H)	$12	$10	$10
Egg cup	$8	$7	$6
Gravy boat	$18	$15	$10
Gravy boat stand	$12	$10	$9
Mug, coffee, low	$15	$15	$15
Mug, coffee, 2 cup	$25	$25	$25
Pickle dish, 10⅜″	$18	$16	$15
Pitcher, 6 oz	$15	$12	$12
Pitcher, ½ pt	$15	$15	$15
Pitcher, 1 pt	$20	$20	$20
Pitcher, 1 qt	$25	$25	$25
Pitcher, 2 qt	$40	$35	$35
Plate, 6″	$6	$6	$4
Plate, 8″	$12	$10	$10
Plate, 10″	$15	$13	$12

	1	2	3
Plate, chop, 12½"	$30	$25	$25
Plate, chop, 14½"	$35	$30	$30
Plate, party	$8	$6	$5
Platter, oval, 15"	$35	$35	$30
Platter, casual, 13½"	$45	$35	$25
Relish, 11⅜"	$28	$25	$18
Saucer	$6	$5	$4
Shaker	$10	$8	$6
Soup, lug, 5¼"	$15	$12	$10
Soup, coupe, 7¾"	$18	$15	$12
Sugar	$18	$15	$12
Sugar, AD	$12	$10	$8
Teapot	$45	$35	$35
Vegetable, divided	$35	$30	$28
Warmer/trivet	$15	$12	$10

Kiddieware (mid-1940s)

There are a variety of decorations; early sets were hand carved and hand painted.

Pricing

All decorations are equally desirable.

Bowl	$20–$25
Cup	$20–$25
Divided dish	$30–$35
Plate	$35–$40

Rainbow Ware

This is an art ware line. Pieces are glazed in a combination of red, bronze, turquoise, and green.

Pricing

Occasionally a piece with yellow in the glaze will be found; add 25%.

Bowl, 6″	$20–$25
Bowl, 10½″	$35–$45
Flower frog, rd, 2¾″	$20–$25
Flower pot, 7¾″	$25–$35
Horse handle candy	$35–$45
Planter, fish, 9″	$50–$75
Planter, pig, 5¼″	$35–$50
Sand jar, 2 loop handles, 18″	$150–$200
Vase, 3 twist handles, 7″	$45–$65
Vase, wide, 3 handles, 9″	$40–$60
Vase, low, squat, 2 handle, 5″	$35–$45
Vase, 2 long handles, 11″	$65–$75
Vase, narrow, 3 handles, 9½″	$50–$65

Sportsmen's Giftware (mid-1940s)

The square ashtray was made with either a round well or a square well. Cigarette boxes were sold individually or with two ashtrays, either the small round ones or coasters, which doubled as trays.

Decorations include a variety of wild birds, ducks, and fish. There is also a golf course and a deer.

Pricing

All decorations are equally desirable.

Ashtray, boomerang	$20–$25
Ashtray, oval, 10⅝″	$35–$45
Ashtray, rd, 8¼″	$30–$35
Ashtray, sq, 9″	$35–$45
Cigarette box, 3¾″ × 4½″	$20–$25
Cigarette box, 3½″ × 7¼″	$20–$25
Coaster, 5″	$10–$12
Mug	$30–$35
Plate, 11″	$35–$45
Plate, 14½″	$35–$45

Stoby mugs. *Left to Right. Top:* Chief, Batch, Cry Baby, and Parson. *Bottom:* Sport, Grand, Henpeck, and Archie. *(Photo courtesy of Lou Kovi, Jr.)*

Stoby Mugs (1936)

Stoby Mugs were designed by Tony Sarg. The hat (lid) serves as an ashtray.

Pricing

Prices are for mugs with *correct* hat. Expect to pay less if it is a marriage. For the reissues in solid colors of chartreuse, yellow, and brown with black, pay 50% of the prices below.

Archie	*$100–$125*
Batch	*$100–$150*
Chief	*$100–$150*
Cry Baby (Depression)	*$100–$150*
Grand	*$100–$150*
Henpeck	*$100–$150*
Parson	*$100–$150*
Sport	*$100–$150*

THE STERLING
CHINA COMPANY

Wellsville, Ohio

The company began in 1911, making vitreous hotel ware. One of the major manufacturers in the United States, Sterling bought the Scammell China Company of Trenton, NJ, in 1954, taking over the manufacture of Lamberton ware. For business purposes, the company used an East Liverpool address.

There is much to interest hotel ware collectors in this company's lines, but for other collectors, only the Russel Wright line attracts.

Marks

The Russel Wright pieces will be found with "Casual China by Russel Wright," either raised or impressed.

Russel Wright (1948)

Wright chose colors that would provide attractive backgrounds for food: Ivy green, Straw yellow, Suede gray, and Cedar brown. Decals on white will also be found: Add 15–20% for Polynesian. Others are not found in enough abundance to make them more desirable.

Ashtray	*$60–$70*
Bouillon	*$8–$10*
Celery, 11″	*$12–$15*
Coffee bottle, 2 cup	*$70–$80*
Coffee pot	*$70–$80*

Russel Wright: Polynesian teapot (special design), Palm Tree ashtray, coffee bottle, and ball jug.

Creamer	*$5–$7*
Creamer, ind, 1 oz	*$5–$7*
Creamer, ind, 3 oz	*$7–$9*
Cup	*$8–$9*
Cup, AD	*$12–$15*
Fruit	*$5–$6*
Jug, ball	*$80–$90*
Onion soup, covered	*$18–$20*
Plate, 6¼″	*$5–$6*
Plate, 7½″	*$6–$7*
Plate, 9″	*$7–$8*
Plate, 10¼″	*$8–$9*
Plate, 11½″	*$12–$15*
Platter, oval, 7⅛″	*$8–$10*
Platter, oval, 10½″	*$10–$12*
Platter, oval, 11¾″	*$12–$14*
Platter, oval, 13⅝″	*$16–$18*
Relish, oval, 4-compartment, 16½″	*$32–$35*
Salad, 7½″	*$6–$7*
Sauce boat	*$8–$10*
Saucer	*$3–$4*
Saucer, AD	*$12–$15*

Soup bowl, 6½"	*$10–$12*
Sugar	*$8–$10*
Teapot, 10 oz	*$55–$65*
Teapot, large	*$55–$65*
Water pitcher, 2 qt	*$80–$90*

All prices given are for items in *mint* condition. In general, discoloration, crazing, chipping, and repairs will fetch lower prices.

THE STETSON
CHINA COMPANY

Lincoln, Illinois

Stetson began as a decorating firm. In 1946 they acquired the Illinois China Company for purposes of manufacturing. The firm closed in 1966.

Marks

The shield backstamp is one of the more common marks.

Airflow (1936)

Covered onion soup	*$10–$12*
Creamer	*$4–$6*
Creamer, small	*$4–$6*
Cup	*$4–$6*
Plate, 6¼"	*$1–$2*
Plate, 9"	*$4–$5*
Platter, 11¼"	*$5–$6*
Saucer	*$1*

Airflow bread and butter and "Mexican" small creamer.

Sugar	*$8–$10*
Sugar, small	*$6–$8*
Vegetable, 8½ ″	*$7–$9*

THE STEUBENVILLE
POTTERY COMPANY

Steubenville, Ohio

Begun in 1879, Steubenville made white granite and semi-vitreous ware typical of the period that included dinnerware and toilet ware. Its most famous product was American Modern dinnerware designed by Russel Wright. In its time, it was the most popular dinnerware in America; by the mid-fifties, over 125 million pieces had been sold. The company closed in 1959 but molds were bought by the Canonsburg Pottery and they continued to produce some pieces.

American Modern is by far the most popular Steubenville line, but there is also a lot of interest in Woodfield because of the similarity of glazes.

Marks

Steubenville used a wide variety of backstamps.

Adam (Antique) (1932)

Ashtray	*$6–$8*
Cereal, lug, 5 ½ "	*$2–$3*
Coffee pot	*$15–$20*
Coffee pot, AD	*$15–$20*
Covered muffin	*$15–$20*
Cream soup	*$5–$6*
Cream soup saucer	*$2–$3*
Creamer	*$4–$6*

Creamer, AD	*$4–$6*
Cup	*$4–$6*
Cup, AD	*$4–$6*
Egg cup	*$5–$7*
Gravy	*$8–$10*
Gravy faststand	*$10–$12*
Hot water pot	*$15–$20*
Jug, 1 qt	*$10–$12*
Jug, 2 qt	*$12–$15*
Pickle	*$3–$4*
Plate, 6″	*$1–$2*
Plate, 7″	*$2–$3*
Plate, 8″	*$3–$4*
Plate, 9″	*$4–$5*
Plate, 10″	*$4–$5*
Plate, 11″	*$4–$5*
Plate, sq, 8″	*$3–$4*
Platter, 11″	*$5–$6*
Saucer	*$1*
Saucer, AD	*$1–$2*
Shaker	*$6–$8*
Sugar	*$8–$10*
Sugar, AD	*$8–$10*
Teapot	*$35–$40*

American Modern (1939–1959)

This shape was designed by Russel Wright. Hard-to-find pieces include the butter, carafe, hors d'oeuvre tray, handled relish, lidded jug, party plate, ramekin, refrigerator dish, stack set, and tumbler. The fork and the spoon were made for the Woodfield shape but are collected as part of American Modern, due to similarity of glaze.

The line was decorated in the following solid colors: Bean Brown, Chartreuse Curry, Coral, Granite Gray, Seafoam Blue (a deep turquoise), and white were the original colors; during WW II Black Chutney replaced Bean Brown and Cedar Green was added. Cantaloupe and Glacier Blue were added in the fifties.

Pricing

Chartreuse Curry is at the low end of the range. Add 25% for Bean Brown, Cantaloupe, Glacier Blue, and white.

Ashtray/coaster	$12–$15
Bowl, rect	$18–$20
Bowl, sq	$45–$55
Butter	$140–$150
Carafe (small jug)	$80–$90
Casserole, stick handle	$45–$50
Celery	$22–$25
Child's bowl	$20–$25
Child's mug	$25–$30
Child's plate	$20–$25
Coffee cup cover	$75–$100
Coffee pot	$110–$125
Coffee pot, AD	$60–$65
Creamer	$8–$10
Cup	$8–$10
Cup, AD	$12–$15
Dishes, small, all sizes	$8–$10
Dishes, lug, all sizes	$8–$10
Fork	$25–$30
Gravy	$15–$18
Hors d'oeuvre tray	$140–$150
Jug, tall	$50–$60
Jug, w/lid	$90–$100
Pickle tray	$12–$15
Plate, 6¼″	$4–$5
Plate, 8″	$10–$12
Plate, 10″	$9–$11
Plate, party	$30–$35
Platter, divided	$50–$60
Platter, rect	$22–$25
Platter, sq	$28–$30
Ramekin, w/lid	$100–$110

Woodfield butter and teapot, American Modern butter and coffee pot.

Refrigerator dish, w/lid	*$140–$150*
Relish, w/handle	*$110–$120*
Saucer	*$3–$4*
Saucer, AD	*$8–$10*
Shaker	*$4–$5*
Spoon	*$20–$25*
Stack set	*$120–$130*
Sugar	*$15–$18*
Teapot	*$60–$70*
Tumbler	*$40–$50*
Vegetable, w/lid	*$45–$50*

Woodfield

Woodfield is distinguished by the leaf pattern on the body and the leaf finials on the covered pieces. It comes in solid colors of Salmon Pink, Tropic, Dove Gray, Rust, and Golden Fawn.

Ashtray, 4 1/2 "	*$6–$8*
Butter, 1/4 lb	*$15–$20*
Creamer, rd	*$4–$6*
Creamer, large	*$5–$7*
Cup	*$4–$6*

Dip bowl, 6¾"	$3–$4
Dip bowl tray, 10¼"	$8–$10
Gravy	$8–$10
Plate, 6¾"	$1–$2
Plate, 9"	$4–$5
Plate, 10½"	$4–$5
Plate, party, 9"	$4–$5
Platter, 13½"	$6–$7
Relish, divided, 9½"	$8–$10
Saucer	$1
Shaker	$6–$8
Sugar, rd	$8–$10
Sugar, large	$10–$12
Teapot	$20–$25
Vegetable, rd, 11"	$9–$10

THE TAYLOR, SMITH
AND TAYLOR COMPANY

Chester, West Virginia

In 1899 John Taylor, Charles and William Smith, and Joseph Lee announced the formation of the Taylor, Smith and Lee Company to be located in Chester, West Virginia (an East Liverpool, Ohio, postal address was used for business purposes). Construction began in January of 1900 and ware was on the market a year later. In 1901, Joseph Lee left the company and the name changed to Taylor, Smith and Taylor. The company may have manufactured white granite in the early years, but most of the company's production was in semi-porcelain toilet ware, dinnerware, kitchenware, and specialties. In 1972, the company was sold to Anchor Hocking and production continued until 1981.

Collectors have the most interest in Luray, the pastel solid-colored dinnerware. Vistosa, the bright solid-colored dinnerware, would be more interesting to collectors if the line was more extensive.

Marks

The wreath backstamp is a common mark. Luray bears the backstamp above or just "USA."

Note

The Luray line is based on two earlier shapes, Empire and Laurel. Because some collectors like these "Luray shapes with decals" and because many are confused, I have included these lines.

Laurel (1933)

This is T, S & T's first thin-rim shape. The flatware had an embossed tab handle. It was used as the flatware in the Empire shape and the Luray line.

Bowl, 36s	*$5–$8*
Butter dish	*$12–$15*
Cake plate, rd, 10¾"	*$8–$10*
Casserole	*$15–$18*
Cream soup	*$8–$10*
Cream soup saucer	*$3–$4*
Creamer	*$3–$4*
Cup	*$3–$5*
Gravy	*$5–$8*
Pickle tray, 9½"	*$5–$8*

Empire teapot, Vogue teapot, Taverne Laurel sugar and creamer, Southern Belle Vogue plate.

Plate, 6½″	*$1–$2*
Plate, 7¼″	*$3–$6*
Plate, 8½″	*$5–$8*
Plate, 9¼″	*$2–$4*
Plate, 10″	*$4–$7*
Platter, oval, 7⅛″	*$4–$7*
Platter, oval, 11½″	*$4–$7*
Platter, oval, 13½″	*$5–$8*
Saucer	*$1–$2*
Sugar	*$4–$5*
Teapot	*$15–$20*
Vegetable, oval, 9¼″	*$5 $8*
Vegetable, oval, 10¼″	*$5–$8*

Empire (1936)

The hollowware in this shape was used for the Luray line, as well as the flatware that it shared with Laurel. Any sighting of ''Luray in Ivory with decals'' is Empire.

Bowl, 36s	*$5–$8*
Butter dish	*$12–$15*
Casserole	*$15–$18*
Creamer	*$3–$5*
Cup	*$3–$5*
Dish, 5⅜″	*$1–$2*
Dish, lug, 5⅞″	*$2–$4*
Drip jar	*$12–$15*
Gravy	*$5–$8*
Pickle tray, 9½″	*$5–$8*
Plate, 6½″	*$1–$2*
Plate, 7¼″	*$3–$6*
Plate, 8½″	*$5–$8*
Plate, 9¼″	*$2–$4*
Plate, 10″	*$4–$7*
Platter, oval, 7⅛″	*$4–$7*
Platter, oval, 11½″	*$4–$7*

Platter, oval, 13½"	*$5–$8*
Saucer	*$1–$2*
Soup, 7¾"	*$5–$8*
Sugar	*$4–$6*
Teapot	*$15–$20*
Vegetable, oval, 9¼"	*$5–$8*
Vegetable, oval, 10¼"	*$5–$8*

Luray (mid-1938)

This line was named after the Lu-Ray Caverns. Some T,S & T ads refer to their "Luray shape," but actually Luray is an amalgam of two shapes and several pick-up pieces. The hollowware is Empire (except for the Laurel cream soup) and the flatware is Laurel/Empire (see above). The tea cup and the AD cup belong to neither line, having been designed specifically for Luray. In the listing below, I have marked E or L next to the hollowware to indicate the shape; unmarked hollowware items are pick-up pieces (see "Background on Dinnerware").

Luray came in Windsor Blue, Surf Green, Persian Cream (yellow), and Sharon Pink. Chatham Grey was added in 1948. Decals were used on the colored pieces as early as 1938. These pieces are elusive. Decaled ivory pieces, marked Luray, occasionally turn up; these seem to be from the late forties. Matching silverware and tumblers (three sizes) were also available.

Coral-Craft, a line that looks like pink Luray with a white decoration, was introduced in 1939. There were five decorations: Maple Leaf, Tulip, Floral Border, Laurel Wreath, and Chinese Temple. Use mid-range Luray prices for these pieces.

Pricing

No one color of the original four seems to be more desirable. Though gray is hard to find, not that many collectors are actively seeking it; add 20% when pricing gray.

AD coffee pot (E)	*$75–$85*
Ad creamer (E)	*$18–$25*
AD cup	*$8–$10*
AD saucer	*$5–$7*

Luray bud vase, urn vase, and epergne.

AD sugar (E)	*$20–$30*
Bowl, 36s	*$28–$30*
Bud urn	*$100–$125*
Bud vase	*$100–$125*
Butter (E), ¼ lb	*$30–$35*
Cake plate, lug, 11″	*$25–$30*
Casserole (E), 8″	*$70–$75*
Chocolate creamer	*$40–$50*
Chocolate cup	*$35–$45*
Chocolate pot	*$125–$150*
Chocolate saucer	*$10–$15*
Chocolate sugar	*$45–$65*
Chop plate, 14″–15″	*$20–$25*
Coaster	*$25–$30*
Cream soup (L)	*$25–$35*
Cream soup saucer, 6½″	*$8–$10*
Creamer (E)	*$3–$5*
Cup	*$3–$5*
Dish, 5″	*$2–$3*

Dish, lug, 6¼"	*$10–$12*
Egg cup	*$12–$15*
Epergne	*$60–$80*
Gravy (E)	*$15–$18*
Gravy faststand (E)	*$15–$20*
Grill plate, 10"	*$15–$18*
Jug, juice (E), 38 oz	*$60–$75*
Jug, water, flat (E), 76 oz	*$35–$40*
Jug, water, ftd (E), 76 oz	*$40–$50*
Mixing bowl, 5½"	*$45–$50*
Mixing bowl, 6¾"	*$50–$60*
Mixing bowl, 8¾"	*$50–$60*
Mixing bowl, 10"	*$60–$75*
Muffin cover (E)	*$65–$75*
Nut dish, 4½"	*$20–$30*
Pickle tray, 9½"	*$15–$18*
Plate, 6½"	*$1–$3*
Plate, 7¼"	*$4–$6*
Plate, 8½"	*$10–$15*
Plate, 9¼"	*$5–$6*
Plate, 10"	*$10–$12*
Platter, 11½"	*$10–$12*
Platter, 13½"	*$12–$14*
Relish, 4-part	*$75–$85*
Salad bowl, 9¾"	*$30–$40*
Saucer, 6"	*$1–$2*
Shaker (E)	*$4–$6*
Soup, 7¾"	*$8–$10*
Sugar (E)	*$6–$8*
Teapot w/curved spout (E)	*$45–$50*
Teapot w/flat spout (E)	*$55–$65*
Tumbler, juice, 5 oz	*$20–$25*
Tumbler, water, 9 oz	*$40–$45*
Vegetable, rd, 9"	*$10–$12*
Vegetable, oval, 10½"	*$8–$10*

Vistosa.

Vistosa (1938)

Vistosa was colored green, blue, yellow, and red. Egg cups have turned up in matte white.

Chop plate, 11"	*$15–$20*
Chop plate, 14"	*$20–$25*
Creamer	*$10–$12*
Cup	*$10–$12*
Cup, AD	*$12–$15*
Dish, 5"	*$8–$10*
Egg cup	*$25–$30*

Gravy boat	*$125–$150*
Jug, ball	*$40–$50*
Plate, 6″	*$3–$4*
Plate, 7″	*$5–$7*
Plate, 9″	*$8–$10*
Plate, 10″	*$10–$12*
Salad bowl, ftd	*$125–$150*
Saucer	*$3–$5*
Saucer, AD	*$5–$7*
Shaker	*$7–$9*
Soup, lug, 6½″	*$25–$30*
Soup, 7½″	*$15–$18*
Sugar	*$15–$18*
Teapot	*$100–$125*
Vegetable bowl, rd, 8½″	*$90–$100*

Vogue (1934)

Some pieces of Vogue will be found in Luray colors.

Casserole	*$15–$20*
Creamer	*$4–$6*
Cup	*$4–$6*
Gravy	*$8–$10*
Plate, 6¼″	*$1–$2*
Plate, 7¼″	*$2–$3*
Plate, 9¼″	*$4–$5*
Plate, 10″	*$4–$5*
Saucer	*$1*
Sugar	*$8–$10*
Teapot	*$15–$20*

THE UNIVERSAL POTTERIES, INC.

Cambridge, Ohio

In early 1934, the Oxford Pottery Company, which was the successor to the Atlas-Globe China Company, reorganized and took the name The Universal Potteries. It continued to manufacture semi-vitreous dinnerware, kitchenware, and specialty ware. It ceased producing these wares in 1954 and turned to tile manufacturing.

Its most famous shape is Ballerina; Upico, Mt. Vernon, and much of its kitchenware will be easily found as well. It is best known for its Cattail decal which will be found on many pieces.

Marks

Universal used only one general backstamp for both its dinnerware and much of its kitchenware. It did use a number of special marks for specific shapes and decorations.

Ballerina

Ballerina platters were called Utility Trays. Ballerina will be found in a variety of decorations as well as the following solid colors: Periwinkle Blue, Jade Green, Jonquil Yellow, Dove Gray, Forest Green, Chartreuse, Burgundy, Pink, and Charcoal.

Bowl, 36s	*$4–$5*
Butter, ¼ lb	*$12–$15*

Casserole	$15–$20
Casserole, French, open	$6–$8
Coaster	$6–$8
Coffee pot	$15–$20
Coffee pot, AD	$15–$20
Creamer	$4–$6
Cream soup, lug, 6⅞″	$4–$5
Cup	$4–$6
Cup, AD	$4–$6
Dish, 5¼″	$1–$2
Dish, 6″	$1–$2
Dish, 7¾″	$2–$3
Egg cup	$5–$7
French casserole	$15–$20
Gravy	$8–$10
Jug, ice lip	$12–$15
Mug	$10–$12
Pickle	$3–$4
Plate, 6¼″	$1–$2
Plate, 7⅜″	$2–$3
Plate, 9⅛″	$4–$5
Plate, 10″	$4–$5
Plate, sq, 7¼″	$3–$4
Platter, rd, lug, 10¼″	$4–$5
Platter, rd, lug, 11½″	$5–$6
Platter, rd, lug, 13¼″	$6–$7
Saucer	$1
Saucer, AD	$1–$2
Shaker	$6–$8
Soup, coupe, 7¾″	$4–$5
Sugar	$8–$10
Teapot	$15–$20
Tumbler	$8–$10
Vegetable, rd, 7¾″	$7–$8
Vegetable, rd, 9″	$8–$10

Kitchenware

Universal has a very extensive kitchenware line. You will find many of the items listed here in the Mt. Vernon and Upico shapes, as well as others for which we have no names.

Note

A number of pieces of kitchenware with the impressed mark "Oxford Ware" will be found. This is a Universal line. Originally designed with a "waterfall" shape (see photo), it was redesigned in 1939 as a smooth shape.

Bean pot, America shape, lug handle	*$15–$20*
Bean pot, America shape, open handle	*$15–$20*
Butter, ¼ lb	*$12–$15*
Butter, 1 lb	*$12–$15*
Cake server	*$12–$15*
Cake plate	*$4–$5*
Cookie jar, America shape	*$15–$20*
Cookie jar, barrel	*$15–$20*
Fork, long	*$25–$30*
Fork, short	*$25–$30*

Chrysanthemums tall canteen jug, Old Curiosity Shop regular canteen jug, Calico Fruit tilt-top Canteen jug, and Cattail wide canteen jug.

Cattail America bean pot (open handle), Cattail America cookie jar, Hollyhock America bean pot (tab handle), and Cattail barrel cookie jar.

Jug, ball	*$12–$15*
Jug, ball, cork-tipped	*$15–$20*
Jug, barrel	*$12–$15*
Jug, batter	*$20–$25*
Jug, batter, chrome top	*$25–$30*
Jug, canteen	*$15–$20*
Jug, canteen, tall	*$15–$20*
Jug, canteen, tilt-top	*$15–$20*
Jug, canteen, wide	*$15–$20*
Jug, "Puffin"	*$15–$20*
Jug, "Puffin," tilt-top	*$15–$20*
Jug, syrup	*$20–$25*
Jug, syrup, chrome top	*$25–$30*
Leftover, rd, small	*$4–$5*
Leftover, rd, medium	*$6–$8*
Leftover, rd, large	*$8–$10*
Leftover, rect	*$8–$10*
Mug	*$8–$10*

"Stendahl Poppy" Puffin tilt-top jug, Texas Under Six Flags stoppered ball jug, and "Rose Bouquet" Puffin jug.

Pie baker	*$6–$8*
Salad bowl	*$10–$12*
Spoon, long	*$20–$25*
Spoon, short	*$20–$25*
Tumbler	*$8–$10*
Tumbler, handled	*$10–$12*

Mt. Vernon (1934)

Mt. Vernon dinnerware was added in 1935. Drip coffee is the teapot with a handled china drip; the drip is not in the Mt. Vernon shape. In most dinnerware lines, the creamer and sugar are easier to find than the teapot. In this line, the teapot is easy to find; the creamer and sugar difficult.

Baker, rd, 5″	*$2–$3*
Baker, rd, 5¾″	*$2–$3*
Casserole, 7½″	*$15–$20*
Creamer	*$6–$8*
Cup	*$4–$6*
Custard	*$2–$3*

Drip coffee	*$35–$45*
Jug, syrup	*$20–$25*
Leftover, 4⅛"	*$4–$5*
Leftover, 5⅛"	*$6–$8*
Leftover, 6⅛"	*$8–$10*
Mixing bowl, 5¼"	*$4–$5*
Mixing bowl, 6½"	*$5–$8*
Mixing bowl, 7½"	*$8–$10*
Mixing bowl, 9"	*$10–$15*
Plate, chop, 11¼"	*$5–$6*
Plate, rd, 6⅛"	*$1–$2*
Plate, sq, 10"	*$4–$5*
Platter, oval, 13½"	*$6–$7*
Saucer	*$1*
Shaker	*$6–$8*
Sugar	*$12–$15*
Teapot	*$15–$20*

Upico (1937)

Upico was designed by Walter Karl Titze. The name apparently stands for *U*niversal *P*otteries *I*nc., *C*ambridge, *O*hio. This is one of the most extensive of Universal's shapes, including both dinnerware and kitchenware. The easy-to-find pieces are pitchers, leftovers, casseroles, and plates. Hard-to-find pieces are the teapot, Tom and Jerry bowl and mugs, and baby dish.

Decorations include both solid colors, decals, and combinations of both. The solid colors were put on the lower, banded portions of the ware. The easiest color to find is Eleanor blue. Red, black, and yellow are scarce. Gold and Orange sunset are mentioned in the trade papers but have not been seen.

The most common decal found is Circus, almost always with Eleanor blue except on the flatware. Cattail is also easily found.

Pricing

Prices are for decal-decorated or Eleanor blue pieces. Add 50% for red, black, or yellow pieces.

Brown Oxford teapot w/Snowflower decoration, Circus Oxford teapot, Upico teapot, and Poppy Mt. Vernon teapot.

Baby feeder	$15–$20
Ball jug	$12–$15
Ball jug, ind	$8–$10
Bean pot	$15–$20
Bowl, nested, 5 1/8 ″	$4–$5
Bowl, nested, 8 3/4 ″	$8–$10
Butter, 1/4 lb	$12–$15
Butter, 1 lb	$12–$15
Casserole, lug, 8 1/2 ″	$15–$20
Creamer	$4–$6
Cup	$4–$6
Custard	$2–$3
Gravy boat	$8–$10
Leftover, rect, pinch knob, 7 1/4 ″	$8–$10
Leftover, rect, tab knob, 7 3/4 ″	$8–$10
Leftover, rd, 4 3/4 ″	$4–$5
Leftover, rd, 5 1/2 ″ (plain lid)	$5–$6
Mixing bowl, 5 1/4 ″	$4–$5
Mixing bowl, 6 1/2 ″	$5–$8

Mixing bowl, 7 ½"	*$8–$10*
Mixing bowl, 9"	*$10–$15*
Mug	*$8–$10*
Plate, 6 ¼"	*$1–$2*
Plate, 8 ⅛"	*$2–$3*
Plate, 9 ¼"	*$4–$5*
Plate, 10 ¼"	*$4–$5*
Platter, rd, lug, *11 ½"*	*$5–$6*
Salad bowl, 9 ¼"	*$9–$10*
Saucer	*$1*
Shaker	*$6–$8*
Sugar	*$8–$10*
Teapot	*$15–$20*
Tom and Jerry bowl, 10"	*$12–$15*
Tumbler	*$8–$10*

All prices given are for items in *mint* condition. In general, discoloration, crazing, chipping, and repairs will fetch lower prices.

THE VAN BRIGGLE POTTERY

Colorado Springs, Colorado

This company was founded in 1901 by Artus Van Briggle, who had worked as a decorator at Rookwood, and his wife, Anne. Artus moved to Colorado for his health but died in 1904. His widow continued the business for a few years, and then it passed into other hands. It is still in operation. See "Traveler's Directory."

Artus Van Briggle is known for his dead matte glaze, which he worked for several years to perfect, and for his use of modeling and colored glazes, as opposed to hand painting, to achieve his effects. Pre-1920 pieces are the most desirable to collectors.

Marks

The common elements of a Van Briggle mark are the conjoint A and the name "Van Briggle." Pieces were dated until 1920. For a detailed chronology, see "Nelson" in the Bibliography.

Pricing

Each entry is followed by the shape number (reference "Nelson" in Bibliography). Prices are chronological, with the date or period included in each listing.

Bookends, owl, teens period, pair, 6″
    Dark blue $175
    Dark brown $250

Bowl, plain design, 5″ diameter
    Maroon, signed "Schlegel"/1922   *$125*
    Turquoise, marked "Original"/1940s   *$25*

Bowl, #22, styled leaves, 8″ diameter
    Turquoise/1902   *$650*
    Yellow w/green on leaves/1903   *$1200*
    Grayish blue w/brown clay showing on leaves/1907   *$475*
    Bronzed/1907–1912   *$950*

Bowl, #762, pine cone and branches, 10″ diameter
    Medium green/1907–1912   *$750*
    Turquoise/1970s (75th Anniversary)   *$275*

Conch shell/1940s
    Turquoise, 8″   *$35*
    Turquoise, 12″   *$60*

Jug, "Firewater" w/stopper, #12, 7″
    Mustard/1901   *$7500*
    Curdled brown/1907–1912 period   *$2250*

Lamp, Rebecca at the Well, 14″
    Maroon/1940s   *$275*

Mug, #28B, plain, 5½″
    Medium blue/1902   *$475*
    Dark green/1906   *$450*
    Lavender/1907–1912   *$375*

Paperweight, rabbit, 2½″
    Turquoise/teens   *$75*

Plaque, Indian head, 2½″ × 4″
    Maroon & dark blue, fine mold/teens   *$275*
    Turquoise/1920s   *$75*
    Turquoise/1970s   *$35*

Plate, #20, stylized poppy, 8″ diameter
    Green, brown, and white/1902   *$1500*
    Dark and light blue/1907–1912   *$275*

Tile/1907–1912, 6″
    White water lilies, green leaves on turquoise ground,
    marked "VBP Co."   *$675*
    Art Nouveau floral design, rose, green, yellow,
    and blue, unmarked   *$275*

Vase, #645, violets & leaves, 4½″
    White w/green buds/1907–1912   *$375*
    Light and dark green/1915   *$150*

Light and dark blue/1920s (USA)	*$35*
Dark brown w/green/1930s	*$35*

Vase, #833, stylized flowers, 5½"
Light blue stippled glaze w/pink flowers/1907–1912	*$875*
Curdled green/1917	*$375*
Maroon & dark blue, poor mold/1920s	*$25*
High-glaze orange/1920s	*$275*
Blue & turquoise/1940s	*$20*

Vase, #132, flowers, 6"
Purple w/white flowers/1903	*$2250*
Light green/1903	*$950*
Black w/experimental marks/1904	*$1500*
Rose w/curdled green on flowers/1905	*$850*
Bronzed/1907–1912	*$1500*

Vase, floral design, 8"
Turquoise matte/1960s	*$25*
Moonglo matte white/1970s	*$25*
High-glaze brown w/green drip, marked ''Anna Van''	*$20*
Black matte/1980s	*$35*
Cobalt blue/1986	*$25*
Tawny yellow/1989	*$20*

Vase, Lorelei, #17, 10"
Charcoal green, dead matte glaze/1902	*$25000*
White/1906	*$7500*
Dark Maroon/1917	*$750*
Brown w/green/1930s	*$450*
Turquoise & Blue/1970s	*$75*

Vase, #240, plain, ribbed w/two handles, 10½"
Black matte/1904	*$950*
Medium green/1906	*$675*
Dark maroon/1920s	*$175*

Vase, Three-Headed Indian, 12"
Brown/1915	*$1500*
Maroon/1920s	*$250*

Vase, #139, closed Yucca, 14"
Yellow/1903	*$2000*
Yellow w/red flowers/1903	*$3750*
Maroon, 1904	*$1250*
Blue w/green leaves, white flowers/1907–1912	*$2500*

VERNON POTTERIES, LTD./ VERNON KILNS

Vernon and Los Angeles, California

In 1931, Faye Bennison bought the Poxon China Company and renamed it Vernon Kilns. At first Vernon used Poxon molds, but soon developed its own distinctive dinnerware shapes. Specialties and some art ware were also produced, all in an earthenware body. In 1958, the pottery was sold to Metlox (q.v.) and they continued to produce a few lines in their Vernonware division.

Vernon has the largest variety of collectible lines of any California pottery: its specialty ware depicting cities, states, famous people and more; its bright and pastel-colored dinnerware; its lines by famous designers such as Rockwell Kent (Salamina, Moby Dick, and Our America) and Don Blanding (floral lines); and Walt Disney figurines and Fantasia dinnerware.

Marks

Vernon used a wide variety of marks, all specific to the lines they appear on.

Bits Series

There were eight lines: Bits of Old New England, Bits of the Middle West, Bits of the Old Northwest, Bits of the Old South, Bits of the Old Southwest, Bits of the Old West, Bits of Old England, and California Missions. Note: (1) No chop plate for Northwest Bits; (2) Northern California Mission plates are scarcer and would be in the upper range.

Chop plate, 14″	$45–$55
Plate, 8½″	$25–$35

Disney Figurines (1941)

Disney figurines were available for one and a half years. Figurines 1–36 are from Fantasia, 37 from The Reluctant Dragon, and 38–42 from Dumbo.

Pricing

These figurines will bring higher prices at auction.

1. Satyr	$135
2. Satyr	$135
3. Satyr	$135
4. Satyr	$135
5. Satyr	$135
6. Satyr	$135
7. Sprite	$135
8. Sprite, reclining	$135
9. Sprite	$135
10. Winged Sprite	$135
11. Sprite	$135
12. Sprite	$135
13. Unicorn	$250–$350
14. Sitting Unicorn	$250–$350
15. Rearing Unicorn	$250–$350
16. Donkey Unicorn	$250–$350
17. Centaurette	$300–$400
18. Centaurette	$300–$400
19. Baby Black Pegasus	$175–$225
20. Pegasus	$300–$350
21. Pegasus	$300–$350
22. Centaurette	$300–$400
23. Nubian Centaurette	$300–$400
24. Nubian Centaurette	$300–$400
25. Elephant	$250–$350

26.	Elephant	$250–$350
27.	Elephant	$250–$350
28.	Ostrich Ballerina	$600–$700
29.	Ostrich Ballerina	$600–$700
30.	Ostrich	$600–$700
31.	Centaur	$600–$650
32.	Hippo in Tutu	$250–$350
33.	Hippo	$250–$350
34.	Hippo	$250–$350
35. & 36.	Hop Low Mushroom, shakers, pair	$95–$125
37.	Baby Weems	$200–$300
38.	Timothy Mouse	$175–$200
39.	Mr. Crow	$650–$800
40.	Dumbo	$95–$125
41.	Dumbo	$95–$125
42.	Mr. Stork	$650–$800

Disney Bowls and Vases

These were available either in solid colors (pink, blue, turquoise, and white) or hand painted.

		Solid	Hand Painted
120.	Bowl, mushroom	$95	$150
121.	Bowl, goldfish	$150	$250
122.	Bowl, winged nymph	$125	$175
123.	Vase, winged nymph	$150	$225
124.	Bowl, satyr	$95	$125
125.	Bowl, sprite	$125	$175
126.	Vase, goddess	$275	$350
127.	Vase, winged Pegasus	$250	$350

Montecito

Montecito was decorated in solid colors and hand-painted patterns. The colors are the bright Early California colors of brown, dark blue, green, ivory, light blue, maroon, orange, peach, pink, turquoise, and yellow, and the soft pastel Modern California colors of Azure Blue, Beige, Gray, Pistachio Green, Straw Yellow, and Orchid.

The desirable hand-painted patterns are by Gale Turnbull, and include Native American (scenes of California in old Mission days), Coastline (maps), Brown-Eyed Susan, and a wide variety of Plaids. Also collectible are patterns designed by Harry Bird, and Winchester '73 (later called Frontier Days), a print and paint design signed by Paul Davidson. There is hard-to-find barware by Heisey with a matching Winchester '73 etching.

Note

Please remember that pieces were added and dropped from the line and all patterns were not produced over the life of the line. This means that you will not find every piece in every pattern. To help in understanding this, /* follows early pieces and /** follows late pieces.

Pricing

Prices are for solid colors. In general, add 10% for Brown-Eyed Susan, 20% for Coastline, and 30% for Winchester '73. Organdie is the most common of the Plaids; do not overpay.

Ashtray, rd, 5½"/*	$6
Ashtray, sq, 3"/*	$4
Ashtray/coaster, rd, 4"/**	$5
Butter, ¼ lb	$20
Butter pat/**	$5
Candle holder	$15
Carafe, w/stopper	$20
Casserole, 8"	$22
Casserole, ind, 4"/**	$12
Casserole, stick handle, 4"/**	$12
Coffee pot, AD	$35
Compote, 9½"/*	$35
Creamer, AD	$8
Creamer, covered	$10
Creamer, open	$7
Custard, 3"/**	$12
Cup, Tea	$6

Cup, AD	*$10*
Cup, jumbo/**	*$10*
Cup, colossal/**	*$35*
Dish, 5 1/2 "	*$4*
Dish, 1 pt	*$8*
Dish, lug, covered, 6 "	*$12*
Dish, lug, open, 6 "	*$7*
Egg cup	*$7*
Flower pot, 3 "/**	*$10*
Flower pot, 4 "/**	*$12*
Flower pot, 5 "/**	*$15*
Gravy boat	*$10*
Gravy faststand	*$12*
*Grill plate/**	*$8*
Jug, bulb bottom, 1 pt	*$8*
Jug, bulb bottom, 1 qt	*$12*
*Lapel pin/***	*$10*
Marmalade, 5 "/*	*$30*
Mixing bowl, 5 "	*$7*
Mixing bowl, 6 "	*$9*
Mixing bowl, 7 "	*$11*
Mixing bowl, 8 "	*$13*
Mixing bowl, 9 "	*$15*
Muffin cover/tray	*$35*
Mug, clip handle, 8 oz/*	*$10*
Mug, handle, 8 oz	*$12*
Mug, 9 oz	*$12*
*Pepper mill/***	*$20*
Pitcher, disk/*	*$20*
Pitcher, 1/4 pt/**	*$8*
Pitcher, 1/2 pt/**	*$10*
Pitcher, 1 pt/**	*$12*
Pitcher, 1 qt/**	*$14*
Pitcher, 2 qt/**	*$18*
Plate, 6 1/2 "	*$2*
Plate, 7 1/2 "	*$4*

Plate, 9½"	*$5*
Plate, 10½"	*$6*
Plate, chop, 12"	*$10*
Plate, chop, 13"	*$12*
Plate, chop, 14"	*$12*
Plate, chop, 17"	*$20*
Platter, 8½"	*$8*
Platter, 9½"	*$8*
Platter, 10½"	*$10*
Platter, 12"	*$12*
Platter, 14"	*$15*
Platter, 16"	*$18*
Salad, 10½"/**	*$18*
Saucer	*$2*
Saucer, AD	*$3*
Saucer, jumbo/**	*$4*
Saucer, colossal/**	*$10*
Saucer, 3" FP/**	*$5*
Saucer, 4" FP/**	*$5*
Saucer, 5" FP/**	*$5*
Server, center handle, 6"/*	*$12*
Server, 2-tier	*$10*
Server, 3-tier	*$15*
Shaker	*$4*
Shaker, large/**	*$6*
Soup, 8½"	*$8*
*Spoon holder/**	*$10*
Sugar	*$8*
Sugar, AD	*$10*
*Syrup/**	*$25*
Tankard/	*$20*
Teapot, 6 cup/*	*$20*
Teapot, 8 cup	*$15*
Tumbler, all styles	*$12*
Vegetable, divided	*$12*
Vegetable, oval, 10"	*$10*

Vegetable, rd, 7½″	*$7*
Vegetable, rd, 8½″	*$9*
Vegetable, rd or oval, 9″	*$10*

State/City Plates *(Also other commemoratives)*

Prices for these plates range from $10–$35. The plentiful, plain print plates go for $10–$12. Multicolor (hand-tinted) plates bring $12–$15. World War II, airplane, and train plates go for up to $35.

Ultra *(1937)*

Ultra was decorated in solid colors, hand-painted designs, and transfer prints. The colors are Astor Blue, Buttercup Yellow, Carnation Pink, Gardenia Ivory, Ice Green, and Maroon.

The most desirable transfer prints are: (1) Our America (1940), designed by Rockwell Kent. There are over thirty one-color scenes from around the United States in walnut brown, dark blue, maroon, or green. Brown is the most common color, green the scarcest. (2) Moby Dick (1939), designed by Rockwell Kent. Based on his illustrations of the novel, there are one-color scenes in walnut brown, light orange, maroon, and dark blue. Maroon and blue are common colors, orange is rare. (3) Salamina (1939), designed by Rockwell Kent, a print and paint design in bright colors. (4) Fantasia (1940), designed by Walt Disney, floral prints (some with nymphs) in colors of blue, brown or maroon; some are plain, some have been hand tinted.

Also popular are the hand-painted designs of Gale Turnbull and the tropical designs of Don Blanding.

Note

There are no clear records as to which pieces were made in Disney's Fantasia; known pieces are marked with a /D.

Pricing

Prices are for the solid colors. Double these base prices for the Blanding and Turnbull decorations. Disney patterns are 5 times (5x) the base for plates (including chop) and 2–3x for other items. Moby Dick

Salamina: 12 ″ chop plate, hand-tinted decal decoration. Designed by Rockwell Kent. *(Photo courtesy of Jack Chipman)*

is 6x for plates and 2–3x for other items. Our America: plates, 7x; other items, 2–3x. Salamina: plates, 15x; other items, 2–4x.

Bowl, 36s, 1 pt, 5 ″	*$8*
Butter, ¼ lb	*$20*
Casserole, 8 ″	*$25*
Chop plate, 12 ″	*$12*
Chop plate, 14 ″/D	*$15*
Chop plate, 17 ″/D	*$22*
Coffee pot, AD	*$35*
Coffee pot	*$25*
Creamer, AD	*$8*
Creamer/D	*$7*
Cup/D	*$6*
Cup, AD	*$10*
Cup, jumbo	*$12*
Dish, 5½ ″	*$4*
Dish, 6 ″	*$8*
Egg cup, single	*$8*
Jam jar	*$30*
Muffin cover/D	*$20*

Mug, 8 oz	$12
Pickle, rd, lug, 6″	$12
Pitcher, disk	$20
Plate, 6½″/D	$2
Plate, 7½″	$4
Plate, 8½″/D	$5
Plate, 9½″	$6
Plate, 10½″/D	$7
Sauce boat	$10
Saucer/D	$2
Saucer, AD	$3
Saucer, jumbo	$4
Shaker/D	$4
Soup, coupe, 7½″	$8
Sugar, AD	$10
Sugar/D	$8
Teapot, 6 cup/D	$20
Tumbler	$12
Tureenette, 7″	$25
Vegetable, rd, 8″	$10
Vegetable, rd, 9″	$10

WALLACE CHINA
COMPANY, LTD.

Huntington Park, California

The company was formed prior to 1930 for the production of vitrified hotel ware. It was purchased by Shenango in 1959 and closed in 1964. Westward Ho is the most popularly collected line.

Marks

This is the mark commonly found on Westward Ho.

Westward Ho (1945)

This line was designed by Till Goodan. The M. C. Wentz Company, giftware wholesalers, bought two of Goodan's western paintings to be used as background at a Los Angeles gift show. They generated so much interest that the artist was approached to create this line of ''barbecue'' ware. Wallace, a hotel ware manufacturer, was chosen to produce the line.

There are three patterns: Pioneer Trails (covered wagon borders with center designs depicting early history of the West), Rodeo (ranch

389

brand borders with center designs depicting rodeo events), and Boots and Saddle (ranch brand borders with boots and saddle design in the center). All are done in dark brown and rust on a tan background. Rodeo had additional color filled in by hand. A three-piece child's set, called a Little Buckaroo Chuck Set, was added in 1949.

Ashtray	*$10–$15*
Child's bowl	*$10–$20*
Child's mug	*$15–$20*
Child's plate	*$15–$25*
Chop plate, 13″	*$75*
Creamer	*$15–$20*
Creamer, small	*$10–$15*
Cup, 7¼ oz	*$15*
Cup, jumbo, 11¾ oz	*$25*
Cup, stack, 7 oz	*$15*
Custard	*$10*
Dish, fruit, 4⅞″	*$12*
Jug, water, 72 oz	*$50*
Mug, ftd	*$35*
Plate, 5⅝″	*$10*

Westward-Ho ashtray.

Plate, 7″	*$12–$15*
Plate, 9″	*$15–$18*
Plate, 10¾″	*$25*
Platter, oval, 15½″	*$50*
Salad, ind, 5¾″	*$15–$20*
Salad bowl, 13″	*$100–$150*
Saucer	*$5–$6*
Saucer, jumbo	*$10*
Saucer, stack	*$5–$6*
Shaker, small	*$10*
Shaker, large	*$15*
Sugar	*$20*
Sugar, small, open	*$15–$20*
Vegetable, rd, 8″	*$25–$50*
Vegetable, rd, 9⅛″	*$35–$50*
Vegetable, oval, 12″	*$45*

THE WATT
POTTERY COMPANY

Crooksville, Ohio

The Watt Pottery Company was founded in 1922 for the production of stoneware, mainly jars and jugs. In 1935, they began production of kitchenware with hand-painted underglaze decorations. A fire destroyed the plant in 1965 and it was not rebuilt.

Watt made a wide variety of kitchenware and a little dinnerware. Its hand-painted underglaze ware is the most collectible, especially with advertising on it.

Marks

Shape numbers were impressed on most pieces. "Watt Ware" or "Watt Oven Ware" impressed in a circle will also be found. Impressed "Watt" in script is an early mark.

> As there aren't many company records available, the same item can have a different name depending on who you are talking with. One person's cookie jar is another's bean pot or canister. This is why we've included shape numbers, when known. Names in capital letters are confirmed as the correct name for these pieces.

Hand-Painted Kitchenware/Dinnerware

The drip jar was sold separately and as a range set with the hourglass shakers. Two sizes of tumblers are known but are rare.

Pricing

Price range is for Red Apple. Add 25% for Pennsylvania Dutch Tulip, Red and Blue Tulip, and Rooster. Other patterns are about 10% less. Advertising pieces are worth 25% over their base price. The exception to this is the dinnerware which is seen in Rio (Wild) Rose. Other patterns on these pieces are rare.

Some bowls came with lids; shape number is the same for both. Add $10–$20 for lids.

BAKE DISH, OBLONG, 1 qt (85)	*$50–$60*
BAKER, 6¼″ (60)	*$15–$20*
BAKER/CASSEROLE, 1 qt, 7¼″ (66)	*$25–$30*
BAKER/CASSEROLE, 1½ qt, 8″ (67)	*$45–$60*
BAKER, 6″ (94)	*$20–$25*
BAKER, 7¼″ (95)	*$25–$30*
BAKER/CASSEROLE, 8½″ (96)	*$40–$50*
Bean server, ind, 4½″ (75)	*$15–$20*
Bowl, 8″ (54)	*$20–$25*
Bowl, berry, 5½″ (4)	*$12–$15*
Bowl, deep, 1 pt (61)	*$20–$25*
BOWL, DEEP, 2 pt (63)	*$30–$35*
BOWL, DEEP, 4 pt (64)	*$35–$40*
BOWL, DEEP, 6 pt (65)	*$40–$50*
Bowl, low, banded, 5″ (05)	*$18–$20*
Bowl, low, banded, 6″ (06)	*$20–$25*
Bowl, low, banded, 7½″ (07)	*$25–$30*

(The #'s 4 to 9 series of mixing bowls came in three styles: impressed horizontal lines with a smooth band at top, plain with a lip, and lipped with one impressed band beneath it. Prices are the same for all three.)

BOWL, MIXING, 4″ (4)	*$30–$40*
BOWL, MIXING, 5″ (5)	*$20–$25*
BOWL, MIXING, 6″ (6)	*$20–$25*
BOWL, MIXING, 7″ (7)	*$30–$35*
BOWL, MIXING, 8″ (8)	*$35–$45*
BOWL, MIXING, 9″ (9)	*$40–$50*
Bowl, popcorn, ind, 6″ (52)	*$20–$25*
Bowl, ribbed, 4¾″ (602)	*$25–$30*

Bowl, ribbed, 5¾″ (603)	*$35–$40*
Bowl, ribbed, 6¾″ (604)	*$45–$50*
Bowl, ribbed, 7¾″ (600)	*$50–$55*
Bowl, ribbed, 8¾″ (601)	*$55–$60*
Bowl, salad, ind, 5½″ (74)	*$20–$25*
BOWL, SALAD, 9½″ (73)	*$60–$75*
BOWL, SALAD, 10½″ (58)	*$75–$85*
BOWL, SALAD, 11″ (106)	*$90–$100*
Bowl, salad/spaghetti, 11½″ (55)	*$50–$60*
Bowl, spaghetti, ind/flat soup, 8″ (44)	*$20–$30*
BOWL, SPAGHETTI, 11″ (24)	*$60–$65*
BOWL, SPAGHETTI, 13″ (39)	*$75–$80*
Canister, small, 5″ (82)	*$65–$80*
Canister, large, 6″ (81)	*$65–$80*
Casserole, 7″ (inner lip)	*$45–$60*
Casserole, 8″ (inner lip)	*$45–$60*
CASSEROLE, 2 qt, 8″ (110)	*$70–$80*
Casserole, 9½″ (flat lid) (73)	*$50–$65*
CASSEROLE, OVAL, 1½ qt (86)	*$60–$70*
CASSEROLE, SQUARE, 2½ qt (84)	*$80–$90*
Casserole, dome cover	*$50–$60*
CASSEROLE, LUG HANDLE, 12 oz (18)	*$40–$50*
Casserole, French (18)	*$50–$65*
Casserole, ribbed, ind (05)	*$35–$40*
Cookie jar, barrel (21)	*$90–$125*
Cookie jar, cone lid (91)	*$110–$125*
Cookie jar, tall, ear handles, 3½ qt (503)	*$100–$135*
COOKIE JAR, 7″ (72)	*$100–$150*
COOKIE JAR, 8½″ (80)	*$125–$175*
COOKIE JAR, ear handles, 2 qt (76)	*$65–$75*
Cookie jar/bean pot, ear handles, 1 gal (502)	*$75–$85*
CRUET W/CHINA-TIPPED CORK (126)	*$45–$55*
Cup, small	*$50–$65*
Cup, large	*$50–$65*
Drip jar (01)	*$50–$65*
ICE BUCKET, 2½ qt (59)	*$150–$200*

Starflower mug. (*Photo courtesy of Dave Pritchard*)

MUG, barrel, 16 oz (501)	*$90–$135*
Mug, coffee (121)	*$85–$125*
Pie baker, 9″ (33)	*$60–$75*
PITCHER/CREAMER, ½ pt (62)	*$35–$40*
PITCHER, 1 pt (15)	*$38–$45*
PITCHER, 2 pt (16)	*$40–$50*
PITCHER, 5 pt, w/ & w/o ice lip (17)	*$90–$100*
PITCHER, 5 pt, sq w/ice lip (69)	*$90–$125*
Pitcher, ribbed	*$25–$30*
Pitcher, slender, w/lid (115)	*$85–$100*
PIZZA PLATE, 14½″ (105)	*$100–$125*
Plate, 6½″	*$18–$20*
Plate, 8½″	*$20–$25*
Plate, 9¾″	*$40–$50*
Plate, 12″	*$50+*
Saucer, small	*$20–$30*
Saucer, large	*$20–$30*
Shaker, cylinder	*$50–$60*
SHAKER, hourglass (117/118)	*$65–$85*

SUGAR, open (98)	*$50–$75*
SUGAR, covered (98)	*$100–$125*
Teapot, 1½ qt (112)	*$250–$350*

Miscellany

Cat/dog dish, turquoise or yellow, 5″	*$20–$25*
Cat/dog dish, turquoise or yellow, 6″	*$25–$30*
Cat/dog dish, turquoise or yellow, 7″	*$30–$35*
Iced tea keg w/faucet (400)	*$350–$400*

WILLETS
MANUFACTURING
COMPANY

Trenton, New Jersey

Founded in 1879, Willets produced white ware and sanitary ware. They also produced Belleek, which is the most prized by collectors. Belleek was produced from approximately 1885 to 1910. The company closed a couple of years after this.

Marks

Mark 1   Mark 2

Mark 1 This is generally considered the earlier of the two marks and is usually found in red. The theory is that Willets decorated all of its ware when it first started making Belleek. That is why this mark is usually seen in one color and the artwork is almost always factory produced.

Mark 2 This is generally considered the later mark. It is the same as mark 1 except the word "BELLEEK" is added. The theory is that when Willets started producing undecorated white ware for sale to outside decorators, the mark was changed. Mark 2 is commonly found in the following colors:

a) Red: Almost always used for factory-decorated items.

b) Brown: Most common color and usually found on professionally decorated and factory-decorated items. Brown is occasionally found on amateur-decorated ware. The theory is that this color mark was used for the better factory-decorated items, and for undecorated white ware sold to outside decorating firms that bought in large quantities.

c) Green: Usually found on amateur-decorated items and some professionally decorated ware. The theory is that this color was used for undecorated white ware products sold in small quantities to amateur artists or professionals who ran small decorating studios.

d) Blue: Used on items decorated at the factory in the monochrome Delft style that was popular around the turn of the century. The word "DELFT" is added to the mark.

e) Raised Mark: Mark was impressed into a wad of clay and attached to the ware. This was reserved for items that could not be stamped because they were too delicate or had no room. Baskets made with thin strands of woven porcelain were often marked this way.

Note

Sometimes "EGG SHELL" was added to the mark of Belleek items that had exceptionally thin bodies.

Belleek

Basket, 3 ½ " high × 5 " wide. Round body with ruffled rim and twig handle. Undecorated, mark 2 in green mark.   *$55–$70*

Basket, 4 " high × 7 " wide. Thin strands of woven porcelain make up the body (called spaghetti work). Braided handle with applied flowers and leaves on the rim and handle. Basket is supported on four tiny feet. Flowers and leaves are painted pink, blue, and green. Factory decorated, raised mark 2. Some damage to the flowers.   *$500–$650*

Bouquet holder, 4 " high. Upside down, cone-shaped center with a ruffled rim inside a round bowl with a ruffled rim. Three twigs attach the side of the cone to the rim of the bowl. Highlighted in pink with gold sponge work. Factory decorated, mark 2 in red.   *$125–$150*

Bowl, 4½" high × 8" wide. Open rose bowl, high shouldered with steeply tapered sides. Silver resist Art Nouveau designs. Artist signed, amateur decorated, mark 2 in brown. *$75–$100*

Bowl, 4½" high × 8" wide. Open rose bowl, high shouldered with steeply tapered sides. Hand-painted roses on a varicolored background. Artist signed, amateur decorated, mark 2 in green. *$90–$125*

Bowl, 4" high × 9" wide. Round shape with ruffled rim. Hand-painted portrait of a colonial lady in a cameo surrounded by gold paste designs and pink flowers. Artist signed, professional decoration, mark 2 in brown. *$250–$325*

Bowl, 4½" high × 9" wide. Round shape open bowl with high shoulders and two dragon-shaped handles. Hand-painted pine cones and needles. Professionally decorated, mark 2 in brown. *$175–$250*

Bowl, 4½" high × 9" wide. Round convex body with ruffled rim and two handles. Hand-painted floral swags on white background. Gilded and pink highlights. Very feminine. Artist signed and dated 1901, professionally decorated, mark 2 in brown. *$150–$175*

Chalice, 11½" high. Tulip-shaped body on long pedestal base. Hand-painted monk smoking a cigar in full color. Artist signed, professionally decorated, mark 2 in brown. *$350–$400*

Charger, 15" in diameter. Hand-painted monochrome gray irises. Professionally decorated, mark 2 in brown. *$275–$350*

Chocolate pot, 9½" high. Pear-shaped body with scalloped rim and curved handle and spout. Molded designs on both body and lid handles. Gilding and gold sponge work. Mark 2 in brown. *$125–$175*

Coffee pot, 7½" high. Ovoid body with long curved handle and spout. Hand-painted birds and flowers. Gilding on handle, spout and lid finial. Professional decoration, mark 2 in brown. *$150–$175*

Coffee pot, 8" high. Bulbous, high-waisted body with square pedestal base, long curved handle and spout. Electrodeposit, sterling silver overlay in twisted Art Nouveau floral designs. Solid silver overlay on handle, spout end, and lid finial. Professionally decorated, mark 2 in brown. *$175–$275*

Creamer, 3½" high. Round body with embossed designs that make the creamer look like it is sitting tilted in a woven basket. Hand-painted yellow rose buds, gold paste vines and leaves. Gilded designs on handle, yellow lustre glaze on "basket." Factory decorated, mark 1 in red. *$125–$175*

Creamer, 4″ high. Bulbous body on a pedestal base with a "C"-shaped handle. Hand-painted tiny roses in a cameo surrounded by gold paste designs. Factory decorated, mark 2 in red.   *$125–$175*

Creamer, 4½″ high. Tapered cylindrical body with dragon handle. "PRINCETON" written on the side in gold letters. Handle is gilded. Mark 2 in brown.   *$65–$95*

Creamer/sugar set, creamer is 3½″ high, sugar is 5″ wide. Creamer has a cylindrical body with molded ribs, ruffled rim, and an ear-shaped handle with molded spirals. Sugar is round with a ruffled rim. Enameled pink flowers with gold paste vines and leaves. Factory decorated, mark 2 in red.   *$175–$225*

Creamer/sugar set, creamer is 4½″ high, sugar is 5″ wide. Creamer and covered sugar have low-waisted ribbed bodies with dragon handles. Gold paste floral designs on a matte finish. Factory decorated, mark 2 in red.   *$150–$200*

Cup and saucer, demitasse, cup is 2″ high, saucer is 4″ wide. Undecorated porcelain cup sits in a sterling silver holder with handle and decorative filigree work. Porcelain saucer is also undecorated. Mark 2 in green.   *$30–$50*

Cup and saucer, cup is 2½″ high, saucer is 5″ wide. Molded ribs and embossed floral designs. Undecorated, mark 2 in green.

          $35–$50

Cup and saucer, cup is 2½″ high, saucer is 5″ wide. Egg shell thin body with molded Irish Tridacna body. Tiny hand-painted flowers and gold fleur-de-lis. Factory decorated, mark 2 in red.   *$80–$100*

Cup and saucer, cup is 2¾″ high, saucer is 5¾″ wide. Indented body on cup, scalloped rim on cup and saucer. Enameled tiny yellow flowers, gold paste, and gilded designs. Factory decorated, mark 2 in red.   *$90–$110*

Cup and saucer, bouillon, cup is 2¾″ high, saucer is 6¼″ wide. Round body with ruffled rim. Gold paste florals on an enameled blue background. Factory decorated, mark 2 in red.   *$75–$125*

Ewer, 12″ high. Bulbous body with long, straight neck, slanted rim, and twig handle. Hand-painted red flowers with gold paste vines and leaves. Matte finish. Factory decorated, mark 1 in red.   *$400–$500*

Humidor, 7″ high. Cylinder shaped with molded pipe on top of lid. Hand-painted portrait of a Cavalier smoking a pipe. Excellent artwork. Artist signed, professionally decorated, mark 2 in brown.

          $450–$525

Jardiniere, 7½" high. Half-ovoid shape with deeply scalloped, folded and ruffled rim. Three small feet molded in a scroll shape. Gold paste florals on a matte finish with gold sponge work on rim and base. Factory decorated, mark 2 in red. $200–$250

Jardiniere, 10" high. Elaborately shaped, wide body on pedestal base with ruffled rim. Two scroll-shaped handles. Hand-painted roses, gilding on handle. Amateur decoration, mark 2 in green. $200–$275

Loving cup, 8" high. Concave body with scalloped rim, footed base, and three "C"-shaped handles molded in vine shapes. Hand-painted red and pink flowers on two sides. "CONGRATULATIONS" in gold letters on third. Gilding on rim, handles, and base. Professionally decorated, mark 2 in brown. $125–$175

Mug, 5½" high. Slightly convex body with angular handle. Hand-painted monochrome brown elk portrait. Professional decoration, mark 2 in brown. Slight scratches. $100–$150

Mug, 5½" high. Tapered body with dragon handle. Hand-painted ears of corn on an orange to brown background. Gilded handle. Artist signed, professional decoration, mark 2 in brown. $125–$175

Mug, 5½" high. Slightly convex body with angular handle. Hand-painted monochrome brown "Delft"-style scene of a windmill by a lake. Professional decoration, mark 2 in brown. $150–$200

Mug, tapered body with dragon handle. Hand-painted Saint Bernard portrait on a varicolored background of orange, brown, and green. Signed by George Houghton, factory artist, dated 1903, mark 2 in brown. Note: Houghton was known for his portraits of animals and women. $400–$500

Picture frame, approximately 8" × 10". Rectangular with tiny hand-painted red flowers. Factory decorated, mark 2 in red. Note: Picture frames are rare. $250–$300

Pitcher, 6" high. Cylindrical body with embossed bamboo stalks. Angular handle is molded in the shape of twisted bamboo stalks. Gold sponge work on body, gilding on handle. Factory decorated, mark 2 in red. $75–$125

Pitcher, 6½" high. Low waisted, ribbed body with dragon handle and embossed mask-shaped spout. Gold paste florals on a matte finish. Factory decorated, mark 2 in red. $185–$215

Pitcher, 7¾" high. Molded nautilus shell shape on a small footed base with molded coral-shaped handle. Highlighted in pink and gold. Factory decorated, mark 1 in red. Rare item. $900–$1100

Pitcher, 9¾" high. Low waisted with scalloped rim and scroll-shaped handle. Embossed designs on body highlighted in gold spray. Hand-painted gold and enameled line and cross designs. Factory decorated, mark 2 in red. $250–$300

Pitcher, 13" high. Cylindrical body with twig handle. Hand-painted red and pink flowers and gold paste stems and leaves. Factory decorated, mark 2 in red. $450–$525

Plate, 9" diameter. Scalloped rim with embossed dots. Hand-painted, stylized floral decorations. Professionally decorated, mark 2 in green. $125–$165

Plate, 11" diameter. Ruffled rim. Two hand-painted pink flowers with gold paste vines and leaves. Factory decorated, mark 2 in red. $195–$225

Salts, set of 6, 1½" wide. Round with ruffled rim. Undecorated, mark 2 in green. $50–$70

Salt, 2" wide. Heart-shaped with a ruffled rim. Tiny hand-painted pink flowers. Factory decorated, mark 2 in red. $20–$25

Swan, 5" long. Open bowl shaped like a swan. Purple and green luster glaze. Artist signed, professional decoration, mark 2 in brown. $100–$150

Tankard, 11½" high. Cylindrical body with embossed designs on the handle and footed base. Hand-painted scene of monks in a group talking surrounded by green and brown floral designs. Nice beige background. Professionally decorated, mark 2 in brown. $300–$350

Tankard, 15" high. Tapered body. Hand-painted monochrome brown monk drinking from a flask. Amateur decorated, mark 2 in brown. $325–$375

Tankard, 15" high. Tapered body with applied dragon handle. Hand-painted mongrel dog portrait with a leather collar on a varicolored background of brown, green, and orange. Signed by George Houghton, factory artist, dated 1903, mark 2 in brown. $700–$900

Tankard, 17" high. Cylindrical body with embossed designs on handle and base. Hand-painted Indian portrait. Artist signed, amateur decoration, mark 2 in green. $300–$350

Tankard/Mug (6) set, tankard is 15" high, mugs are 5½" high. Tapered bodies with dragon handles. Hand-painted berries and blossoms. Heavily gold-tooled rims. Each mug has a different fruit. Gilded handles. Professionally decorated, mark 2 in brown. $750–$950

Teapot, 4½" high. Spherical body with molded ribs, ear-shaped handle and scalloped rim and spout handle. Hand-painted blue flower and green leaves on a salmon-colored background. Gilding on handle, spout, and lid finial. Professionally decorated, mark 2 in brown.

$125–$175

Tray, 6″ long. Oval, bowl-shaped body with rim folded over in three places to make the shape triangular. Rustic handle on the side. Undecorated, mark 2 in green. $65–$85

Vase, 6″ high. Spherical body with small neck and ruffled rim. Large hand-painted yellow roses and leaves. Artist signed, professionally decorated, mark 2 in brown. $175–$250

Vase, 8″ high. Slightly ovoid body with high waist, small flared neck, and ruffled rim. Hand-painted red carnations on a green background. Professionally decorated, mark 2 in brown. $175–$225

Left: Vase, 13½″ high. Hand-painted yellow dandelions on a green background. Professional decoration. Mark 2 in brown. *Right:* Tankard, 15″ high. Hand-painted brown and white dog signed by George Houghton. Factory artist. Mark 2 in brown. *(Photo courtesy of Richard Lewis).*

Vase, 10″ high. Wide cylindrical body with slightly indented neck. Hand-painted scene from the silent movie "The Sheik". Rudolf Valentino is embracing Agnes Ayres in front of a desert background. Artist signed, professionally decorated, mark 2 in brown. Unusual piece of Americana. *$375–$475*

Vase, 11½″ high. High waisted with no neck. Hand-painted black birds on branches. Unusual cartoon quality to the artwork. Professionally decorated, mark 2 in brown. *$250–$300*

Vase, 12″ high. Cylinder-shaped body with small indented neck. Hand-painted purple irises. Amateur decoration, but well done, mark 2 in green. *$225–$275*

Vase, 13″ high. Ovoid body on pedestal base with flared neck, embossed designs on scroll-shaped handles and base. Undecorated, mark 2 in green. *$100–$125*

Vase, 13½″ high. Cylinder shaped with scalloped rim and stepped, footed base. Hand-painted yellow dandelions on a deep green background. Professionally decorated, mark 2 in brown. *$250–$300*

Vase, 15″ high. Ovoid body with small, flared neck. Hand-painted red flowers and green leaves on a light green background. Amateur decoration, mark 2 in green. *$250–$300*

Vase, 17″ high. Cylindrical body with small, indented neck. Hand-painted robins on a branch done in a very oriental manner. Background varies from blue at the top to gray at the bottom. Artist signed, professionally decorated, mark 2 in brown. *$400–$600*

Vase, 17″ high. Ovoid body with short tapered neck. Hand-painted scene of hunting dogs chasing through the woods. Very detailed. Signed by Heidrich, factory artist, mark 2 in brown. *$1000–$1500*

Vase, 18″ high. Bulbous, high-shouldered body on a pedestal base with trumpet-flared neck and elaborate handles. Hand-painted scene of a woman seated on a rock. Gilding on handles, base, and neck. Signed by Nosek, factory artist, mark 2 in brown. *$1000–$1500*

Vase, 20½″ high. Tall, high-shouldered with angular handles, tapered neck, and pedestal base. Hand-painted chrysanthemums on a varicolored background. Professionally decorated, mark 2 in brown. *$550–$675*

Vase, 24″ high. Ovoid body with curved handles and flared neck. Hand-painted red and yellow roses. Signed by Walter Marsh (Ceramic Art Company artist who operated his own china decorating business). Professional decoration, mark 2 in green. Some glaze misses, other kiln defects. *$450–$575*

PART III

APPENDIXES

APPENDIX 1:
COOKIE JARS

The following represents a listing of collectible cookie jars that did not fit into other chapters but should not be left out of this book.

California Originals

Big Bird	*$35–$45*
Christmas Tree	*$85–$95*
Donald Duck on Pumpkin	*$150–$175*
Eeyore	*$125–$150*
Ernie	*$45–$55*
Mickey Mouse on Drum	*$150–$175*
Oscar the Grouch	*$45–$55*
Superman	*$150–$175*
Tigger	*$125–$150*
Winnie the Pooh, both styles	*$60–$65*
Wonder Woman	*$150–$175*

Special Jars

The manufacturer's name, when known, has been put in parentheses.

Barefoot Boy (Gem Forming)	*$250–$275*
Cowboy (Lane)	*$175–$225*

Dennis the Menace	*$300+*
Granny w/Embroidery Hoop	*$200–$250*
Hopalong Cassidy, tall	*$300+*
Hopalong Cassidy, short	*$225–$250*
Howard Johnson	*$300+*
Little Boy in Cowboy Boot	*$300+*
Mammy (Gilner)	*$300+*
Mother Goose (Gilner)	*$125–$150*
Popeye (Vandor)	*$175–$225*
Red Riding Hood (Gem Forming)	*$200–$250*
Southern Belle	*$150–$175*
Tattle Tale	*$150–$225*
W. C. Fields, lifelike colors	*$300+*

ND = price is not determined; item too rare to price.
+ = worth at least sum indicated, but could be higher.

APPENDIX 2:
RAILROAD CHINA

There are hundreds of patterns in the world of collectible railroad china. We have chosen a sampling from low-, medium-, and high-priced lines to give you some taste of what is happening.

California Poppy (AT&SF)

This line was made by Syracuse China, as well as a European firm.

Pricing

Unbackstamped prices are in parentheses after prices for pieces with a backstamp.

Butter chip	$35 ($20)
Chocolate pot	$95 ($75)
Cup	$35 ($25)
Ice cream dish	$50 ($35)
Mustard	($35)
Plate, bread	$35 ($25)
Plate, dinner	$60 ($45)
Plate, lunch	$45 ($35)
Saucer	$35 ($25)
Soup bowl	$45 ($35)
Sugar	($35)

Centenary (B & O)

This line was originally produced for B & O's centennial in 1927.

Pricing

The most collectible of the Centenary are the Scammell pieces. Sterling is next down in value, and the recent Shenango pieces are the lowest in price.

	Scammell	Sterling	Shenango
AD cup/saucer	$75	$45	$35
Butter chip	$55	$40	$10
Cup/saucer	$65	$45	$25
Plate, dinner			
Diesel border	$60	$40	$25
Steam border	$85	$60	$35
Plate, lunch	$50		

Eagle (MOPAC)

Cup/saucer	$65
Plate, bread	$45
Plate, dinner	$75
Plate, lunch	$65
Platter, large	$65

Glory of the West (GN)

This line was made by Syracuse in their Shadowtone process.

Celery tray	$45
Cup/saucer	$75
Plate, bread	$45
Plate, dinner	$100
Platter, small	$45

Hiawatha (CMS & P)

This line was made by Syracuse China.

Bouillon cup	*$145*
Platter, medium	*$175*

Historical (Union Pacific) (Also called Overland)

This line was made by Syracuse China.

Celery tray	*$185*
Cup/saucer	*$210*
Plate, bread	*$105*
Plate, dinner	*$275*
Plate, lunch	*$200*
Platter, medium	*$175*

Keystone (PRR) (Brown)

Keystone was made by Mayer China.

Celery tray	*$50*
Creamer, small	*$45*
Creamer, large	*$55*
Soup bowl	*$45*

Mercury (NYC)

The line was made by both Shenango and Syracuse. Gray and brown versions.

Celery tray	*$30*
Plate, lunch	*$45*

Mimbreno (AT & SF)

This line was made by Syracuse China.

AD cup/saucer	*$150*
Butter chip	*$75*
Cup/saucer	*$85*
Gravy	*$75*
Ice cream dish	*$50*
Plate, bread	*$55*
Plate, dinner	*$85*
Plate, lunch	*$65*

Monad (NP)

Monad was made by Shenango.

Plate, bread	*$25*
Plate, lunch	*$30*

Pullman Indian Tree (Full Indian Tree)

This line was made by both Shenango and Syracuse.

Butter chip	*$75*
Creamer, small	
w/handle	*$50*
no handle	*$30*
Cup/saucer	*$125*
Plate, bread	*$45*
Plate, dinner	*$85*
Plate, lunch	*$65*
Platter, medium	*$95*
Soup bowl	*$65*

Purple Laurel (backstamped)

This line was made by Buffalo, Scammell, Shenango, and Sterling.

Bouillon cup	*$30*
Butter chip	*$25*
Compote	*$65*
Creamer, small	*$25*
Cup/saucer	*$45*
Gravy	*$35*
Ice cream dish	*$35*
Plate, bread	*$25*
Plate, dinner	*$40*
Plate, lunch	*$30*
Platter, small	*$25*
Platter, medium	*$35*
Soup bowl	*$35*

Traveler (CMS & P)

Traveler was made by Syracuse China in their Shadowtone process. First price is for pieces with backstamp, price in parentheses is for pieces without backstamp.

AD cup/saucer	*$55 ($35)*
Bouillon cup	*$25 ($20)*
Butter chip	*($25)*
Plate cover	*($30)*
Soup bowl	*$35 ($25)*

Service Plates

French Quarter (IC)	*$850*
George Washington (C & O)	*$500*
Mission (SP)	*$1000*
Old Bay Anniversary (SAL)	*$300*
Panama Limited (IC)	*$1200*
Shreveport (T & P)	*$875*
State Capitals (MOPAC)	*$350*
State Flowers (MOPAC)	*$200*
Turquoise Room (ATSF)	*$700*

TRAVELER'S DIRECTORY

There are three kinds of places you can visit to enhance your collecting experience. Whether you are traveling or lucky enough to live nearby, check them out. (1) Factory. Seeing pottery being made will broaden your understanding of the processes involved. (2) Factory outlet. It's always useful to see what new production is being done, especially where questions of reissues and reproductions are concerned. And they are wonderful places to pick up souvenirs and gifts for friends. (3) Museum. No book, however good, can be an adequate substitute for actually seeing the pottery. You also get a sense of the scope of a pottery's output from seeing good collections. And who knows, you may find something new to collect.

Hours and days are subject to change. Always call ahead before making definite plans. Also, if you are visiting a museum, check to make sure that what you want to see is on display. Factory tours are free. For group tours, write and see what special arrangements need to be made.

CALIFORNIA

Oakland

The Oakland Museum, 1000 Oak Street, 94607. 415/273-3005. Open Wed–Sun. Art Department has 400-piece collection, 50–60 items on display at one time, Arts & Crafts and Studio Potters featured. No commercial pottery. History Department, 415/273-3842, has separate display of commercial pottery.

COLORADO

Colorado Springs

Van Briggle Pottery, 600 So. 21st Street, 80901. 303/633-7729. Factory tour/gift shop. Extensive collection of early pieces, copies of originals. Closed Sunday.

ILLINOIS

Dundee

Haeger Potteries, 7 Maiden Lane, 60118. 312/426-3441. Plant tour: 5 days. Outlet shop (in plant): 7 days. Includes museum display of Haeger pieces.

NEW YORK

Syracuse

Everson Museum of Art, 401 Harrison Street, 13202. 315/474-6064. A collection of 3500 pieces on permanent display in the Ceramics Gallery; approximately 1300-1500 pieces are American, ranging from early redware and stoneware to the present. No commercial pieces, emphasis is on design. Strong collection of Robineau.

OHIO

Cincinnati

Cincinnati Art Museum, Eden Park. 513/721-5204. Excellent collection of Rookwood.

Cleveland *(See Rocky River, OH)*

Cleveland Museum of Art, University Circle. 216/421–7340. A small but select collection of American pieces, including Tucker, Bennett, American Faience, Rookwood, Weller, Ohr, and twentieth-century Cleveland studio potters.

Western Reserve Historical Society, 10825 East Boulevard, 44106. 216/721–5722. Ohio art pottery including Rookwood, Roseville, Weller, Owens and Ohr, as well as Cleveland School potters including Winter, Gregory, and Schreckengost. Some pottery displayed in period domestic settings.

Columbus

Ohio Historical Society, Interstate 71 and 17th Avenue. 614/466–4663. The Ceramics Gallery has an overview of Ohio pottery, with changing exhibits of over 100 pieces.

Crooksville

Ohio Ceramic Center, 614/697–7021.

East Liverpool *(See Newell, WV)*

Hall China Company, 2356 Elizabeth Avenue. 216/345–9045. Mon–Fri, 9 AM–1 PM. There is a fascinating self-guided plant tour. Little has changed in the way Hall makes its china and you see clearly the care, skill, and patience that gives Hall its famous quality.

Hall Closet. 216/345–4543. Just outside the Hall factory. Mon–Sat, 9 AM–5 PM. Hall's retail shop where seconds are sold. Most of what is available here is from current production runs. There's something new almost every day. You'll get a good idea of the colors Hall is presently producing.

Museum of Ceramics, 25 Fifth Avenue. 216/345–0098. March–October, Tue–Sat, 10 AM–6 PM. A warm, friendly museum that will awe you with the beauty and range of the ware made in the East Liverpool area from the 1850s to the 1930s. A highlight is the excellent Lotus Ware collection, much of which is on permanent display.

Norwich

National Road Museum, 8850 East Pike, 43767. 614/872–3143. Closed Dec–Feb. Over 250 pieces of Roseville and Weller on permanent display.

Rocky River (Just west of Cleveland)

Cowan Pottery Museum, Rocky River Public Library, 1600 Hampton Road, 44116. 216/333–7610. Seven days; closed Sundays during the summer. From 800 to 1,000 pieces make this the largest public collection of Cowan in the country, understandable as his studio was in Rocky River. The collection has everything from production art wares to rare pieces such as Schreckengost's punch bowl and Gregory's King and Queen decanters. As well as group tours, there are group programs, either on site or at your location.

Roseville

The Robinson-Ransbottom Pottery Company, Ransbottom Road, 43777. Factory tour/outlet store (614/697–7735), 5 days. Store closed Jan–Feb.

Zanesville

Zanesville Art Center, 614/452–0741.

OKLAHOMA

Sapulpa

Frankoma Potteries, 2400 Frankoma Road, 74006. 918/224–5511. Plant tour: 6 days. Outlet shop: 7 days.

TENNESSEE

Erwin

Unicoi Heritage Museum, Erwin-Johnson City Highway, Routes 19 and 23. 615/743–9449. Tuesday through Sunday, May to October. Two rooms with exhibits that change regularly.

WEST VIRGINIA

Newell (Across the river from East Liverpool, Ohio)

Homer Laughlin China Company, 304/387–1300. Plant tours, outlet shop and museum.

COLLECTORS CLUBS/ NEWSLETTERS

Almost all clubs publish newsletters, and subscribing to a newsletter is like being in a club. I suggest sending a self-addressed stamped envelope for information or a dollar for a sample newsletter.

Abingdon Pottery Collectors, Mrs. Elaine Westover, RR 1, Abingdon, IL 61410

American Ceramic Arts Society, 1775 Broadway, New York, NY 10019

Blue Ridge Club, Phyllis Ledford, Rte 3, Box 161, Erwin, TN 37650

Blue Ridge Newsletter, Norma Lilly, 144 Highland Drive, Rte 5, Box 62, Blountville, TN 37617

Blue Willow Report, Connie Rogers, 1733 Chase Street, Cincinnati, OH 45223

Hall China Connection, P.O. Box 401, Pollock Pines, CA 95726

Hot Tea, Tina Carter, 882 South Mollison, El Cajon, CA 92020

National Autumn Leaf Collector's Society, Shirley Easley, 120 West Dowell Road, McHenry, IL 60050

Novelty Salt & Pepper Shakers Club, Rd 2, Box 2131, Stroudsburg, PA 18360

Our McCoy Matters, Jean Bushnell, 317 S. Carolina Avenue, Pasadena, CA 21122

Pottery Lover's Newsletter, Ray Thomas, 5155 Manchester Drive, Zanesville, OH 43701

Purinton Newsletter, Bob Hoover, Rd 4, Box 94, Blairsville, PA 15717

Red Wing Collectors Society, Rte 3, Box 146, Monticello, MN 55362

Table Toppers, 1340 West Irvington Park Road, Chicago, IL 60613. Ceramic, glass, and metal

Tea Leaf Club International, Julie Rich, 9720 Whiskey Run, Laurel, MD 20707

Tile Heritage Foundation, P.O. Box 1850, Healdsburg, CA 95448. For preservation, research, and restoration of ceramic surfaces. A non-profit corporation

Vernon Views, P.O. Box 945, Scottsdale, AZ 85252

GLOSSARY

There have been many discussions about the definitions of pottery, porcelain, earthenware, and china. This section will give you simple definitions of the most commonly used terms, including pottery and porcelain, so that you will understand references made in this book. Many glossaries assume a certain level of knowledge; I assume nothing and have tried to define every term that could be new and especially useful to the novice collector.

For those who wish to understand the process of manufacture, it is laid out starting with the entry "Clay."

AD After Dinner. See Demitasse.

Applied Decoration Any decoration that is applied, such as painting and gilding, as opposed to a decoration that is in the mold. See Sprig.

Art Pottery Ornamental ware either hand-decorated by an artist or glazed with a special controlled effect. In the strictest sense, pottery made and decorated by hand. See also Production Ware.

Art Ware See Production Ware.

Baker Industry terminology for the open, oval dish usually called a vegetable dish.

Banding Similar to lining but the gold, silver, or color applied is wider than a line.

Batter Jug See Batter Set.

Batter Set (Also Waffle Set) Consists of a batter jug, syrup jug, and undertray. This came into use at the time the electric waffle maker was invented, which allowed waffles to be made at the table instead of the stove.

421

Belleek China Delicate, pale-cream colored, highly translucent porcelain with iridescent glaze. Sometimes called "egg-shell china" because of its extreme thinness. First developed in Ireland.

Bennington Ware See Rockingham.

Bisque Firing This is the first firing. The greenware is subjected to high heat which removes the remaining moisture and hardens the body. For the next step, see Bisque ware.

Bisque Ware (Also Biscuit Ware) Any clay ware that has been hardened through a first firing. Bisque ware can be left undecorated (see Parian for one example). For the next step, see Glaze, Overglaze, and Underglaze.

Body This term is usually used when referring to the color and composition of the clay. Keep in mind that the color of a piece of ware can be in the body or on it. See Engobe and Glaze.

Bone China A form of porcelain that contains bone ash, made from calcined cattle bones, for added translucency and whiteness.

Bouillon Cup and Saucer A two-handled cup, similar to a teacup, used for serving clear soups. It is not as low as a Cream Soup.

Breakfast Set Service for one consisting of a demitasse coffee pot, sugar and creamer, a regular size cup and saucer, covered muffin, egg cup, cereal dish, and breakfast plate. Service for two was also made with two cups, saucers, egg cups, dishes, and plates.

Casting Slip is poured into plaster molds. The plaster draws moisture out of the clay so the ware can be handled when it is unmolded. For next step, see Greenware.

Casual China True porcelain dinnerware that is thicker, heavier, and more durable than fine china, but not translucent. Generally intended to be less formal than a traditional set of porcelain.

Ceramics In its original and true meaning, ceramics means the art of making any article of clay. Americans use the word to cover all of the silicate industries where the burning process is essential in manufacture.

China Another name for porcelain, so used because true porcelain was first made in China. Today, china has become a generic term for almost anything that is used for dinnerware. See Porcelain.

Chocolate Pot Taller, slimmer, often more elegant version of a coffee pot.

Chop Plate Large round or square serving plate, usually 12 inches or more in diameter.

Clay The manufacturing process starts with clay. There are different kinds of clay, and other minerals are added to impart desired qualities to the finished product. Clay and these other materials are mixed with water to make Slip. (See Casting.) Then impurities are removed, the water is pressed out, the clay is dried, and the air is expelled. Now the clay is ready to be shaped. For next step, see Forming.

Compote (Also, incorrectly, Comport) A dish on a stem, in various sizes, for serving candy, nuts or fruit.

Coupe A dinnerware shape that does not have a rim. Generally refers to flatware.

Coupe Soup A shallow, flat round bowl without handles or rim, seven or eight inches in diameter.

Crackle (Also Craquelle) A glaze that intentionally resembles Crazing. Dedham Pottery (q.v.) is a good example.

Crazing Minute cracks in the glaze which are caused by the uneven contraction of glaze and body. The body and glaze are formulated so that contraction should occur at an even rate. Crazed pieces are discarded at the factory. However, exposure to heat and/or moisture can cause crazing at a later time.

Cream Soup and Saucer A two-handled low bowl used for serving bisques and cream soups. Often comes with an underplate that is slightly larger than the tea saucer.

Crockery Earthenware.

Decal (Also Decalcomania) (1) A transfer decoration which is printed on special emulsion-coated paper and then coated with plastic film. When ready to use, the plastic is peeled off with the decoration adhering to it and applied to the ware. In firing, the plastic burns away and the printed decoration "melts" into the glaze. This is the last step. The word is used in both the singular and plural. (2) Paper decals were available for sale during the 1930s. One could moisten the back and affix it to any object, from shower doors to cribs to kitchen items. You will find pieces of ware with these decals. Some collectors remove them, as they were not applied by the manufacturer; other collectors leave them, as they reflect the period when the ware was made. They do not increase the value of a piece.

Decorating Kiln See Glost Kiln.

Decoration See Glaze, Overglaze, and Underglaze.

Decorator Usually refers to the person who applies lines, bands, decals, or decorative highlights.

Demitasse A small-size cup and saucer, sometimes with matching cream, sugar, and pot, for after dinner coffee. These items were also used as children's dishes and as parts of Breakfast Sets.

Dipping That process of covering a bisque body with a glaze by immersion in the liquid, either by hand or machine.

Dish In modern usage, dish is often a synonym for plate. Traditionally, it refers to an open container, shallow and concave, for holding or serving food.

Drip Jar A covered container, intended to be kept on or near the stove, for storing bacon drippings and other cooking fat for further use. Sometimes found marked with the word "Drips" or, rarely, "Lard." See Range Set.

Dutch Casserole Round, straight-sided casserole with hollow lug handles for easy portability.

Earthenware Opaque ware, somewhat porous, with a clear, transparent glaze. Coarse earthenware is not fired to as hard a state as fine earthenware. When earthenware is made of refined clays and fired at a high temperature to a hard state but is still somewhat porous, it is referred to as fine earthenware in England and semi-vitreous ware in the United States.

Egg Cup Single egg cup: small, like a custard cup, no handle, for use with one or two eggs. Double egg cup: an hourglass-shaped double cup of two sizes for use with one or two eggs.

Embossed Ware A raised or molded decoration produced either in the mold or formed separately and applied before the first firing. See Sprig.

Engobe A white or colored slip used as an intermediate layer between the body of an article and the glaze. Sometimes a white engobe is used over colored clays so that the ware appears to be made of white clay.

Epergne A decorative centerpiece often consisting of several elements, usually small vases, grouped together.

Faststand Gravy Boat A gravy boat, often with two spouts and no handle, that is attached to a plate.

Firing Process of heat treatment of ceramic products for the purpose of securing resistance and permanency of product. Also called burning. See Bisque Firing, Glost Firing, and Decoration Firing.

Flatware Tableware, such as plates and platters. See Hollowware.

Forming The making of a piece of clay into an object, no matter what process is used. See Casting, Jiggering, and Throwing. For the next step, see Greenware.

French Casserole A round casserole with a stick handle. Large French casseroles may have a lug handle opposite the stick handle for easier handling.

Frog A flat-bottomed, perforated object, usually round or oval, made to hold stems in a flower arrangement. Frogs can have a figural component. Used primarily with bowls.

Gadroon An in-the-mold decoration, usually found on the edge or rim of an item, that resembles a braided rope. Also called Gadroon Edge.

Gilding The application of precious metals such as gold and platinum (which resembles silver).

Glaze A mixture of mineral substances, either transparent or colored, which will melt and harden on the surface of the clay body during the glost-firing process. It is used as a covering for ceramic wares in order to (1) make a porous body nonporous, (2) secure greater permanency, and (3) beautify an object. Literally a glass. This can be the next-to-last step in the manufacturing process (see Glost Firing), or an overglaze decoration can be applied. See Decals, Overglaze.

Glost Firing Firing that matures the glaze which after cooling produces a hard, glass-like surface. This firing is not as hot as the bisque firing nor as long.

Glost Kiln Oven for firing glazed pieces. Decal-decorated pieces can also be fired here.

Gravy or Sauce Boat A low, oval bowl with handle and spout.

Greenware After the piece has been formed, it is allowed to dry further. At this stage it can be handled, but care must be taken. For next step, see Bisque Firing. (For an exception to this process, see Once Fired.)

Grill Plates A dinner-size plate divided into three or more compartments.

Hand Painting Can refer to work ranging from the artist who painted Indian Head Rookwood vases to the artisans who decorated ware per a sample set in front of them. A clear glaze is usually applied over this work.

Hollowware Tableware serving pieces such as bowls, casseroles, pitchers, creamers, and sugars. See Flatware.

Hotelware See Restaurant Ware.

Ironstone See White Granite.

Jiggering Process used for making plates and other fairly flat items. The clay is placed on a form that represents the top of the piece, pressed down and spun. A template representing the outline of the underside of the piece is placed against the clay and finishes the shaping. See Greenware.

Jug Industry term for a pitcher. There were many kinds. Refrigerator jugs were usually flat sided and designed to take up as little space as possible in the refrigerator. The popular Ball jug was first introduced by Hall China in 1938.

Jumbo Cup and Saucer A specialty item. Over-sized coffee cup, sometimes with the word "Mom/Mother" or "Dad/Father" on it.

Kiln An oven-like structure for the firing of greenware, glazes, and decorations. These are not fired together, as each requires different firing temperatures.

Kitchenware Items that are used in the kitchen (canisters, batter and range sets), refrigerator (water jugs, leftovers) or oven (casseroles, bean pots).

Lead Glaze A shiny glaze containing lead oxide.

Liner (1) See Underplate. (2) A person who applies a line to a piece of ware.

Lining (1) A decorative process. A thin line of gold, silver or color is applied to the ware by hand or machine. Can be found around a rim, foot, spout, lid, and knob among other places. (2) The interior color of a piece of hollowware. If a bowl is blue on the outside and ivory on the inside you can say, "It is a blue bowl lined with ivory."

Lug Handle A tab-like handle. Sometimes they come with a cutout. This is called "pierced."

Lug Soup (Also Onion Soup or Puree Bowl) Slightly larger than a cream soup, but handles are lug instead of open.

Matte Glaze A flat, non-gloss finish, sometimes rough.

Nappy Round, uncovered vegetable or salad dish usually eight or nine inches in diameter.

Once Fired Some ware is produced by glazing greenware and firing only once.

Open Stock Dinnerware that can be bought by the individual piece, as opposed to being available only in sets.

Overglaze When decorations are applied to the ware after the glost firing, they are known as overglaze decorations. A wide range of colors may be used because the heat in the decorating kiln need not be as high to "harden the colors," i.e., to fuse them onto the glaze. The colors are apt to be brighter and sharper. You can identify overglaze decorations by running your finger over the ware from the background to the decoration. If you feel a change in texture, it is overglaze. See Decals and Print and Paint.

Parian Unglazed porcelain (bisque ware) intended to resemble marble.

Party Plate A luncheon-size plate with a cup ring near the rim. Used to hold a teacup and tea sandwiches, cookies, or cake.

Pate-sur-Pate (French) The successive application of semi-fluid clay to build up a design in slight relief. First employed in China during the eighteenth century.

Pickle Dish Small, nine inch platter used for pickles, condiments, or as an underplate for the gravy.

Pitcher See Jug.

Platter Oval serving tray varying from approximately 8 to 20 inches in length.

Porcelain A clear, translucent ware with a body which is non-porous, non-absorbent, or "vitrified." To be a true porcelain, a piece of ware should show the shadow of your hand when held before light. If artificial color has been introduced into the body, the translucency is reduced. When a piece of porcelain is struck, there is a clear, bell-like tone.

Pottery (1) (Also called Earthenware) Opaque, non-vitrified ware. (See Porcelain) (2) The factory where ware is made, regardless of whether it is pottery or porcelain.

Premium A piece of china given away as part of a promotion. Promotions took many different forms; you could get a dish when you bought a box of soap, gasoline, furniture, and more. You could buy dishes with coupons from local route salesmen. And of course there was dish night at the movies.

Print and Paint (Also Print and Fill) The outline of a design is printed on bisque ware or glazed ware, filled in with color by hand, and then fired. A clear glaze is then applied. This is the last step.

Production Ware (Also Art Ware) Art pottery that has been decorated by an artisan rather than an artist. Also refers to non-art pottery.

Ramekin A small, flat-bottomed dish with fairly vertical sides and a very narrow rim, usually accompanied by a plate, used for serving individual portions of food.

Range Set A three-piece set, consisting of a Drip Jar and two Range Shakers, usually kept on the stove (range). Some stoves were specifically designed to accommodate these pieces.

Range Shaker A large shaker, intended for cooking use as opposed to table use. See Range Set.

Redware Earthenware made from a clay with a high amount of ferrous oxide. This gives the body its red color. Usually has a lead glaze.

Refrigerator Jug See Jug.

Restaurant Ware (Also Hotel Ware, Institutional Ware) The thick, vitrified china dinnerware made to stand up to heavy use.

Rim (Also Shoulder) The lip of a plate or bowl. It can be narrow or wide, plain or embossed, depending on the design.

Rockingham Yellowware with a brown glaze that is usually mottled but can be almost solid. Sometimes called Bennington ware because a goodly amount of Rockingham was made in the potteries of Bennington, Vermont. Rockingham was also produced in large quantities at potteries in East Liverpool, Ohio, as well as at other potteries. Rock, as it is casually referred to, was in continuous production into the twentieth century and was later revived by some companies in a style that has little relation to the original—a creamy foam with brown undertones edging a brown glaze.

Salt Glaze Salt is thrown into the kiln where it vaporizes and combines with the silica in the body of the ware, producing a shiny glaze.

Seconds Ware with imperfections from the manufacturing process. Depending upon the extent of the imperfections, they could be sent either to a reclaim department, an outlet shop for sale, or to an outside decorator.

Semi-porcelain Resembling porcelain but having little or no translucency and more porosity. It is made from more refined raw materials but is not vitrified. This is a trade name or designation that is a misnomer. Being semi-porcelain is like being semi-pregnant.

Semi-vitreous (Also Semi-vitrified) An alternate term for semi-porcelain.

Service or Cover Plate A plate an inch or so larger than a dinner plate, used at formal events to hold the container for the first course. Can be ornately decorated.

Sgrafitto A decoration achieved by scratching through a surface of slip or glaze to the body beneath, which is often a different color. Sometimes a sgrafitto design was filled in with color.

Slip A liquid clay. It can be used in manufacture (see Casting) and in decoration (see Engobe and Slip Trailing). It can also be applied with a brush.

Slip Decoration See Slip Trailing.

Slip Trailing Slip is applied to the greenware through a tube or nozzle, much like icing is applied to a cake.

Specialty Ware A term used by dinnerware manufacturers that applied to other lines they made: card plates, children's sets, jardinieres, jumbo cups, spittoons, tea sets, and much more.

Sponge Ware Color is applied with a sponge or rag in a random or precise pattern.

Sprig A molded piece of clay applied to a piece of greenware with slip.

Squeeze-bag Technique See Slip Trailing.

Stoneware This ware is made from clays which have some impurities in them so that they burn to a dark color. Will stand a relatively high temperature and burn to a dense hard body, as hard and non-porous as china, but lacking the light color, delicacy, and translucency. Usually covered with a salt or lead glaze.

Syrup Jug/Pitcher See Batter Set.

Tankard A tall drinking cup with a handle.

Terra Cotta From the Italian meaning "cooked earth." A hard, semi-fired, absorbent clay used for both decorative and construction products. Colors can range from grayish to dark reddish-orange, light to medium reddish-brown, or strong brown to brownish or deep orange.

Throwing Forming of a piece of ware by hand, on a potter's wheel. See Greenware.

Toilet Ware Toilet sets were used before the advent of indoor plumbing though they were made well into the twentieth century. They consisted of some or all of the following: a brush vase (toothbrush holder), chamber pot (bedroom vessel for body wastes), combinet (lidded pail, combination chamber pot and slop jar), covered soap dish or soap slab, ewer and basin (also called pitcher and bowl), jarette (jar with lid and two handles), mouth ewer, mug and slop jar (large pail used to receive waste water from wash basin and contents of chamber pot). Most dinnerware manufacturers also made toilet ware.

Transfer Printing A design is etched onto a copper or steel plate, which prints it onto a piece of film which is then applied to the body in the bisque stage. A sponge is used to remove the paper, leaving behind a colored image. The colors are mixed with oil before being applied. The ware is usually then fired in a low temperature kiln to burn off the oil and harden the color before the glaze is applied. The range of colors is limited since many colors change or fade out completely if subjected to great heat.

Translucent A good deal of light can pass through the article. This is possible when firing has been intense enough to cause vitrification. (See Vitrified).

Twin Tea Two slender, rectangular pots which sit side-by-side on a tray. One pot, with a long spout, is for tea; the other, with a short spout, is for hot water, used to dilute the tea.

Underglaze If designs and colors are put on the bisque before it is glazed, the decoration is known as underglaze. After this process, a clear glaze is applied and the ware is fired a third time. (See Hand Painting, Print and Paint, Transfer Printing.)

Underplate (Also called Undertray or Liner) The following items took an underplate: gravy boat (the plate does double duty as a pickle plate), batter sets, cream soups (actually a saucer that is slightly larger than a tea saucer), casseroles, and tureens.

Utility Ware Usually used in reference to stoneware (can mean earthenware as well). Refers to bowls, crocks, churns, jugs, and toilet items.

Verge That part of a plate or bowl where the rim and well meet.

Vitrified Glass-like. Non-porous ware which has been fired at a higher temperature than earthenware and contains silica, which makes a body non-absorbent.

Waffle Set See Batter Set.

Wall Pocket Flat-backed vase with hole for hanging on a wall. Can be used without flowers as a decorative object.

Ware The product of a pottery. It can describe the product at any stage of manufacture (greenware, bisque ware, decorated ware), or the output of a pottery as a whole ("The ware produced at

Lenox was exceptionally fine.'') It is used both in the singular and plural.

Well The major surface of a plate or bowl that is surrounded by the rim.

White Granite (Also White Ironstone, Pearl China, Pearl White, Pearl Granite, Porcelain Granite, Graniteware, Flintware, and Opaque China) Commercial names intended to inspire confidence in the strength of the ware, which was harder and stronger than earthenware. Ground stone was used in the body. Color varies from creamy white to bluish or grayish-white.

White Ware Pottery or porcelain with a white body, so called to distinguish it from redware and yellowware. See White Granite.

Yellowware Body color varies in hue from ecru to mustard. Made from a naturally occurring clay. See Rockingham.

BIBLIOGRAPHY

A complete bibliography in the field of pottery and porcelain would require a large volume of its own. The books here are either related to the potteries covered in the book or are of general interest to pottery collectors and worth reading even though they fall outside the purview of this book. Some were used in preparing this book. If a book is not listed, I may not know of it, or more likely, I don't feel it is worth recommending. I have listed some out-of-print books because they are worth looking for.

The books listed on specific potteries are those I recommend. Some are excellent, some leave something to be desired. However, if you intend to buy or sell by mail, most dealers and collectors use these books as references.

Where possible, I have listed price and ordering information. "W/ prices" means that prices are printed in the book. "W/price guide" means a separate booklet. "Photos throughout" means black-and-white photos.

Coming Attractions

Books in the works that could not be listed below: (1) A book on Teco to be published in conjunction with an exhibit at the Erie Art Museum (see Dale, Sharon for address). (2) A book on George Ohr to be published in conjunction with an exhibit at the American Craft Museum. (3) Two books on California pottery by Jack Chipman (see below). The first, *California Pottery,* is due in September 1990, from Chronicle Books, San Francisco. (4) *Collecting Railroad Cups and Saucers* by Richard Luckin (see below). This should be available around the end of 1989. (5) *A Pennsbury Pottery Book* by Lucille Henzke, with 400 color photos. Due late Fall 1989 or early Spring 1990.

BOOKS

Barber, William Atlee, *The Pottery and Porcelain of the United States/ Marks of American Potters.* The first and still one of the most important histories of American pottery and porcelain. (Out of Print)

Bess, Phyllis and Tom, *Frankoma Treasures.* Phyllis and Tom Bess, 14535 East 13th Street, Tulsa, OK 74108. $15.95 + $1.50 P&H. W/Price Guide. Color sections; photos throughout.

Bray, Hazel V., *The Potter's Art in California: 1885 to 1955.* Oakland Museum Store, 1000 Oak Street, Oakland, CA 94607. $9.95 + $2.75 P&H (CA residents add .65 tax). No prices. Color section; photos throughout. Art potters and studio potters. Catalog of the museum exhibition.

Buxton, Virginia Hillway, *Roseville Pottery, For Love . . . or Money.* Tymbre Hill Publishing Company. W/price indicator. Color throughout. Catalog reprints. (Out of Print)

Chipman, Jack and Judy Stangler, *The Complete Collector's Guide to Bauer Pottery.* Jack Chipman, P.O. Box 1429, Redondo Beach, CA 90278. $14.95 + $1.00 P&H. Color section; photos throughout, catalog reprints. Thorough and well researched.

————, *Bauer Pottery Price Guide and Supplement.* Jack Chipman, P.O. Box 1429, Redondo Beach, CA 90278. $5.95 + .50 P&H.

Clark, Garth and Margie Hughto, *A Century of Ceramics in the United States: 1878–1978.* Abbeville Press, 488 Madison Avenue, New York, NY 10022. $75.00 + $2.00 P&H. Color section; photos throughout. A good twentieth-century historical overview. This is a revised and updated edition of *A Century of Ceramics in the United States: 1878–1978,* which is now out of print.

Dale, Sharon, *Frederick Hurten Rhead: An English Potter in America.* Erie Art Museum, 411 State Street, Erie, PA 16501. $25.00 + $2.00 P&H. Color section; photos throughout. No prices.

Derwich, Jenny B. and Dr. Mary Latos, *Dictionary Guide to American Pottery and Porcelain (19th & 20th Century).* Jenstan, P.O. Box 674, Franklin, MI 48025. $30.00 (includes P&H). No photos, prices. Encyclopedic listing of hundreds of potteries.

Dole, Pat, *Purinton Pottery.* Pat Dole, P.O. Box 4782, Birmingham, AL 35206. $9.95 + $1.00 postage. W/prices. Color section; photos throughout.

Dubiel, Jay and Bruce Johnson, *Dedham Pottery Catalog: 1938.* Dedham Folio, P.O. Box 826, Halifax, VA 24558. $9.95 + $1.00 P&H. Photos throughout. No prices. A reprint of the only known catalog with a preface by Marilee Meyer. Essential.

Duke, Harvey, *Hall China, A Guide for Collectors.* ELO Books, P.O. Box 627, Brooklyn, NY 11202. $14.95 + $1.50 P&H. W/Price Guide. Color throughout.

———, *Hall 2.* ELO Books, P.O. Box 627, Brooklyn, NY 11202. $14.95 + $1.50 P&H. W/Price Guide. Color section; photos throughout. With its companion, the best reviewed books on Hall China.

Eidelberg, Martin, *Eva Zeisel: Designer for Industry.* Catalog from the traveling exhibit. University of Chicago Press, 11030 So. Langley Avenue, Chicago, IL 60628. $24.95 + $1.50 P&H. No prices. Color and black-and-white throughout. Catalog of the museum exhibit.

Evans, Paul, *Art Pottery of the United States.* Feingold & Lewis Publishing, 1088 Madison Avenue, New York, NY 10028. $45.00 + $2.00 P&H. No prices. Color section; photos throughout. The classic updated.

Frelinghuysen, Alice Cooney, *American Porcelain: 1770–1920.* Metropolitan Museum of Art, Fifth Avenue at 82nd Street, New York, NY 10028. $40.00. Color and black and white. Catalog of the exhibit: A wealth of information.

Garmon, Lee and Doris Frizzell, *Collecting Royal Haeger.* Jo-D Books, 81 Willard Terrace, Stamford, CT 06903. $19.95 + $2.00 P&H. W/prices. Color section, photos throughout; catalog reprints.

Gaston, Mary Frank, *American Belleek.* Mary Frank Gaston, P.O. Box 32, Bryan, TX 77806. $19.95 + $1.00 P&H. W/prices. Color throughout.

Gates, William C., Jr., *The City of Hills and Kilns: Life and Work in East Liverpool, Ohio.* The East Liverpool Historical Society, East Liverpool, OH 43920. Fascinating history of a pottery town. (Out of Print)

———, *The East Liverpool Pottery District.* East Liverpool Museum of Ceramics, 400 East Fifth Street, East Liverpool, OH 43920. $20.00 + $1.00 P&H. Histories of the potteries and over 2,000 marks with chronological information for this important pottery center.

Hall, Burdell and Doris, *Morton's Potteries: 99 Years.* B and B Antiques, 210 West Sassafras Drive, Morton, IL 61550. $10.00 + $1.50 P&H. Price guide $2.50 postpaid. Color section; photos throughout. W/price guide.

Hennessey, William J., *Russel Wright: American Designer.* MIT Press, 55 Hayward Street, Cambridge, MA 02142. $15.00 + $2.50 P&H. No prices. Color section; photos throughout. Catalog of the museum exhibit.

Henzke, Lucille, *American Art Pottery.* Thomas Nelson Inc., New York, NY. Color section, photos throughout; catalog reprints. No prices. The first important study. (Out of Print)

——, *Art Pottery of America.* Schiffer Publishing, Box E, Exton, PA 19341. $45.00 + $2.00 P&H. No prices. Color section, photos throughout: catalog reprints. Both books are much more than just pretty pictures.

Huxford, Sharon and Bob, *Fiesta.* W/prices. Color throughout.

——, *McCoy Pottery.* W/prices. Color throughout.

——, *Roseville Pottery, First Series.*

——, *Roseville Pottery, Second Series.* W/price guide. Color throughout, also black-and-white photos and catalog reprints.

——, *Weller Pottery.* W/price guide. Color throughout; catalog reprints. Each of the above titles is $19.95 + $1.00 P&H. Jo-D Books, 81 Willard Terrace, Stamford, CT 06903.

Kovel, Ralph and Terry, *The Kovels' Collector's Guide to American Art Pottery.* Crown Publishers, Inc., One Park Avenue, New York, NY 10016. $13.95 + $3.00 P&H. No prices. Color section, photos throughout. Thorough overview.

Laumbach, Sabra Olson, *Harrington Figurines.* Ferguson Communications, P.O. Box 146, Hillsdale, MI 49242. $19.95 + $1.50 P&H. W/prices. Color throughout.

Lehner, Lois, *Lehner's Encyclopedia of U. S. Marks on Pottery, Porcelain and Clay.* Jo-D Books, 81 Willard Terrace, Stamford, CT 06903. $19.95 + $1.00. Covers over 1800 potteries and 8000 marks. Truly encyclopedic.

Luckin, Richard, *Dining on Rails.* RK Publishing. No prices. Photos throughout. (Out of Print)

——, *Teapot Treasury (and related items).* RK Publishing, 621 Cascade Court, Golden, CO 80403. $24.95 postpaid. No prices. Lots of photos throughout.

McDonald, Ann Gilbert, *All About Weller: A History and Collector's Guide.* Antique Publications, P.O. Box 553, Marietta, OH 45750. $24.95 + $2.50 P&H. W/price guide. 296 black and white and 25 color plates. Catalog reprints. Paper cover.

Nelson, Maxine Feek, *Versatile Vernon Kilns, Book II.* Maxine Feek Nelson, 873 Marigold Court, Carlsbad, CA 92008. $9.95 + $1.00 P&H. W/prices. Color throughout. Great depth of information.

Nelson, Scott, *A Collector's Guide to Van Briggle Pottery.* Scott Nelson, P.O. Box 5327, Rockville, MD 20851. $30.00 for book, $3.00 for price guide. $2.00 P&H. Color section; photos throughout. Meticulous research.

Newbound, Betty, *Blue Ridge Dinnerware.* Jo-D Books, 81 Willard Terrace, Stamford, CT 06903. $14.95 + $1.00 P&H. W/prices. Color throughout. Good for identification.

Nichols, Harold, *McCoy Cookie Jars.* Nichols Publishing, P.O. Box 1125, Ames, IA 50010. $15.95 postpaid. W/prices. Color throughout.

Perry, Barbara, Ed., *American Ceramics: The Collection of Everson Museum of Art.* Rizzoli International, $75.00/hardcover, $35.00/paper.

Roberts, Doris, *Hull Pottery.* Jo-D Books, 81 Willard Terrace, Stamford, CT 06903. $19.95 + $1.00 P&H. W/prices. Color and black-and-white throughout. Catalog reprints.

Schneider, Robert, *Coors Rosebud Pottery.* Robert Schneider, 1507 Western Studio 104, Seattle, WA 98101. $12.95 + $1.00 P&H. W/prices. Color throughout. Catalog reprints.

Spargo, John, *Early American Pottery and China.* Charles E. Tuttle Company, P.O. Box 410, 28 So. Main Street, Rutland, VT 05701. $12.50 + $2.00 P&H.

Supnick, Mark, *Collecting Hull Pottery's "Little Red Riding Hood."* Mark Supnick, 8524 NW 2nd Street, Coral Springs, FL 33071. $10.95 + $1.00 P&H. W/prices. Color throughout.

———, *Collecting Shawnee Pottery.* Mark Supnick, 8524 NW 2nd Street, Coral Springs, FL 33071. $10.95 + $1.00 P&H. W/prices. Color throughout.

Viehl, Lyndon C., *The Clay Giants: The Stoneware of Red Wing, Goodhue County, Minnesota.* Wallace-Homestead Book Company, P.O. Box 5164, FDR Station, Dept. 31, New York, NY

10150. $18.95. Separate price guide is $2.50. P&H is $2.00/1st book, .50 each additional book. No color; copious photos throughout.

Watt, William Iliff, *Watt Pottery Collectibles*. Watt Pottery Collectibles, Box 5, Roseville, OH 43777. $6.95 (includes P&H). No prices; photos throughout.

Westfall, Ermagene, *Cookie Jars*. Ermagene Westfall, RR 11, Box 222, Richmond, MO 64085. $9.95 + $1.00 P&H. W/prices. Color throughout.

PERIODICALS

Also see Clubs/Newsletters.

Arts and Crafts Quarterly, Station E, P.O. Box 3592, Trenton, NJ 08629. Devoted to the Arts and Crafts movement, with regular articles about Art Pottery. Back issues are $6.00. Send SASE for current subscription rates.

For the following newspapers, a good idea would be to send a dollar for a sample issue and current subscription rates.

The Antique Trader, P.O. Box 1050, Dubuque, IA 52001.

The Daze, 12135 No. State Road, Otisville, MI 48463.

The New Glaze, P.O. Box 4782, Birmingham, AL 35206.

INDEX

Turnbull, Gale, 383
Tuscany. *See* Tokay

Ultra
  Leigh Potters, Inc., 237–238
  Vernon Potteries, Ltd./Vernon Kilns,
    386–388
Universal Potteries, Inc.
  Ballerina, 369–370
  kitchenware, 371–373
  marks, 369
  Mt. Vernon, 373–374
  Upico, 374–376
Upico, Universal Potteries, Inc., 374–
  376
Utility Trays, Ballerina platters, 369–
  370
Utility Ware, Knowles China Company,
  Edwin M., 230–231

Van Briggle Pottery
  listing of items, 377–379
  marks, 377
Vases
  Haeger Potteries, 129–131
  Hull Pottery Company, A. E., 214,
    216
  Shawnee Pottery Company, 322–
    323
Vernon Potteries, Ltd./Vernon Kilns
  Bits series, 380–381
  Disney figurines, 381–382
  marks, 380
  Montecito, 382–386
  state/city plates, 386
  Ultra, 386–388
Victory, Salem China Company, 312–
  313
Virginia, Harker Pottery Company,
  159–160
Virginia Rose, 10
  Homer Laughlin China Company,
    181–182
Vistosa, Taylor, Smith & Taylor
  Company, 367–368
Vogue
  Mt. Clemens Pottery Company, 269
  Taylor, Smith & Taylor Company, 368

Wagon Wheels dinnerware, 100
Wallace China Company, Ltd.
  Little Buckaroo Chuck Set, 390
  marks, 389
  Westward Ho, 389–391
Wall pockets, Shawnee Pottery
  Company, 323
Ward, Florence, 85

Water Lily, Hull Pottery Company,
  A. E., 205–206
Watt Pottery Company
  hand-painted kitchenware/dinnerware,
    392–396
  marks, 392
Weller, 7
Wells, Homer Laughlin China
  Company, 182–183
Westchester, Canonsburg Pottery
  Company, 57–58
Westward Ho, Wallace China Company,
  Ltd., 389–391
Wheaton Glass Company, 337
White Clover, Harker Pottery Company,
  160–161
Wildflower, Hull Pottery Company,
  A. E., 206–207
Willets Manufacturing Company
  Belleek, 397–404
  marks, 397–398
Windsor, Royal China Company, 308–
  309
Woodfield, Steubenville Pottery
  Company, 359–360
Woodland
  Hull Pottery Company, A. E., 207–210
  Morton Pottery Company, 267
World's Fair
  Cronin China Company, 75
  Homer Laughlin China Company,
    184–188
  Paden City Pottery Company, 279
Wright, Russel, shapes designed by
  American Modern, 357–359
  Casual China, 217–219
  Esquire, 230
  Highlight, 278
  for Sterling China Company, 351–
    353
W. S. George Pottery Company. *See*
  George Pottery Company, W. S.

Yellowstone, Homer Laughlin China
  Company, 183–184
Yorktown, Knowles China Company,
  Edwin M., 231–233

Zeisel, Eva, shapes designed by
  Town and Country, 295–296
Zephyr
  Cronin China Company, 73–75
  French-Saxon China Company, 103–
    105
  Harker Pottery Company, 161–162
Zephyrs, Robinson-Ransbottom Pottery
  Company, 304–305

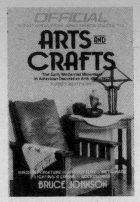

THE ONLY BOOK OF ITS KIND!

From Gustav Stickley to Frank Lloyd Wright, from Rookwood to Tiffany, this is the *only* guide to offer a *complete* look into the Arts and Crafts movement.

☆ Features detailed information on the craftsmen who produced furniture, pottery, and accessories of the Arts and Crafts movement...how to distinguish between them...important *shopmarks*...current values...fully illustrated.

☆ Written by *the* nationally acclaimed expert in the field—*Bruce Johnson*—author of the syndicated column "Knock On Wood" and *The Weekend Refinisher.*